MW00680485

The Journey

A Trip Through the Bible

By Don Elliott

The Journey: A Trip Through The Bible

© 2007 by Don Elliott

All rights reserved. No part of this work may be reproduced or transmitted in any form or by any means electronic or mechanical, including photocopying, recording, or by any information storage or retrieval system, except for brief quotations in reviews, without permission in writing from the publisher.

PLC Publications books, monographs and other resources are available at special discounts in bulk purchases for educational and ministry use. For more details, contact:

136 Tremont Park Drive
Lenoir, North Carolina 28645

Call us at 1-800-368-0110
Or Visit PLC Publications on the Web at www.layman.org

All Scripture quotations, unless otherwise indicated, are taken from the HOLY BIBLE, NEW INTERNATIONAL VERSION®. NEW INTERNATIONAL VERSION®. Copyright ©1973, 1978, 1984 by International Bible Society. Used by permission of Zondervan. All rights reserved.

Cover Design: HeuleGordon, Inc.; Grand Rapids, Michigan
Book Design: Paula R. Kincaid

Printed in the United States of America

Dedicated to Lynn, my wife and friend,
who complements me in every way.

The Journey

A Trip Through the Bible

Table of Contents

Introduction

Let's go on a journey together.

The components of a journey (trip, excursion, voyage, jaunt) are familiar to us all. We have a desire to get away from the routine of daily living and see new and exciting places. We think through the cost of money and time because taking off on a trip is never easy or cheap. We plan the details because there is something about the unknown that always scares us, so we try to project ourselves into the daily, even hourly, component of the excursion to answer eventual questions like, "What are we doing Tuesday morning?"

Then, with those going on the trip with us, we share the hopes and wishes for a bon voyage. The joy of the journey is multiplied as others share in the same vision of going to another land and culture. We complete our packing , and we are off on our adventure.

The journey of this book has some of the same components, even though we may not leave our hometown.

The desire for this journey through the Bible is to break out of a daily routine of not living for God as we ought and not knowing that Scripture is where we get to know God and ourselves. Basically, it is a desire for God:

As the deer pants for streams of water, so my soul pants for you, O God (Psalm 42:1).

The cost of this journey is time and effort. The precious commodity of time might be dearer to some of us than money. However, there is another cost for this trip through the Word of God. It demands discipline. It calls for focus. It is work.

Do your best to present yourself to God as one approved, a workman who does not need to be ashamed and who correctly handles the word of truth (II Timothy 2:15).

The plan for this journey is a systematic, book-by-book jaunt through the entire Bible. Over 52 weeks, Genesis through Revelation will be covered by means of teaching, reading, memorizing, praying, applying and sharing the unique contribution of every section of Scripture. Assignments will be given every week encouraging a daily focus on each portion of the Bible. This makes *The Journey* a year-long excursion into meditating upon the Word of God.

Oh, how I love your law! I meditate on it all day long (Psalm 119:97).

This journey is worth sharing. It is not meant to be done alone or experienced alone. It is not designed to be a one-time expedition that is just to be endured and forgotten. The truths taught and the lessons learned, therefore, are meant to go beyond the individual student and the isolated classroom. There is a dynamic to the study of Scripture that transforms the individual so that others also might be transformed. The experience of the Early Church is supposed to be ours:

They devoted themselves to the apostles' teaching and to the fellowship, to the breaking of bread and to prayer. ... And the Lord added to their number daily those who were being saved (Acts 2:42, 47).

The joy of this journey will provide the ultimate assessment of its value. Knowledge of Biblical facts is not the goal here. Being able to simply quote the Bible or tell someone that we have read the whole Bible is not what we are going for. The pure exercising of a discipline, even though that is commendable, is not the target. It is to experience the joy of knowing God and living for Him.

The etymology of the word "journey" is interesting. It comes from the French word *journee*, which means "a day's work or travel." The combination of the length of a day and the expression of work as the original definition of a journey helps us to see how we are to proceed on this journey through the Bible. It will not be accomplished in one day, but will call for an almost daily effort. It will take a year to complete the journey, and it will call for a special effort and focus. Truly, a journey of a thousand miles starts, and continues, with one step.

Basically, *The Journey* is a Bible survey. There are some particular convictions that will govern the study of the books of the Bible and the lessons drawn from them. These convictions are drawn from the Reformed tradition, where Biblical truth, theological integrity and practical living converge into a life lived with joy for the glory of God. Each conviction is important to our understanding of the nature of the Word of God, its impact on our lives, and how the Biblical world and our personal worlds are connected by the work of the Holy Spirit. Along with Scripture, the Westminster Confession is quoted to accentuate the Biblical and theological roots of each conviction.

Convictions for the Journey

1. THE BIBLE IS THE WORD OF GOD WRITTEN.

Deuteronomy 8:3b – "… man does not live on bread alone but on every word that comes from the mouth of the LORD."

Isaiah 40:8 – "The grass withers and the flowers fall, but the word of our God stands forever."

II Timothy 3:16 – "All Scripture is God-breathed. …"

II Peter 1:20, 21 – "Above all, you must understand that no prophecy of Scripture came about by the prophet's own interpretation. For prophecy never had its origin in the will of man, but men spoke from God as they were carried along by the Holy Spirit."

Westminster Confession of Faith, chapter 1, paragraph 2:
"Under the name of Holy Scripture, or the Word of God written, are now contained all the books of the Old and New Testaments. … All which are given by inspiration of God to be the rule of faith and life."

2. JESUS CHRIST IS THE WORD OF GOD LIVING.

John 1:1-5; 14 – "In the beginning was the Word, and the Word was with God, and the Word was God. He was with God in the beginning. Through Him all things were made; without Him nothing was made that has been made. In Him was life, and that life was the light of men. The light shines in the darkness, but the darkness has not understood it. … The Word became flesh and made His dwelling among us. We have seen His glory, the glory of the One and Only, who came from the Father, full of grace and truth."

Matthew 5:17, 18 – "Do not think that I have come to abolish the Law or the Prophets; I have not come to abolish them but to fulfill them. I tell you the truth, until heaven and earth disappear, not the smallest letter, not the least stroke of a pen, will by any means disappear from the Law until everything is accomplished."

Westminster Confession of Faith, chapter 1, paragraph 7:
"All things in Scripture are not alike plain in themselves, nor alike clear unto all; yet those things which are necessary to be known, believed, and observed, for salvation, are so clearly propounded and opened in some place of Scripture or other, that not only the learned, but the unlearned, in a due use of the ordinary means, may attain unto a sufficient understanding of them."

3. STUDYING THE BIBLE BRINGS BLESSINGS.

Isaiah 55:11 – "… so is my word that goes out from my mouth: It will not return to me empty, but will accomplish what I desire and achieve the purpose for which I sent it."

II Timothy 3:16, 17 – "All Scripture is God-breathed and is useful for teaching, rebuking, correcting and training in righteousness, so that the man of God may be thoroughly equipped for every good work."

Revelation 1:3 – "Blessed is the one who reads the words of this prophecy, and blessed are those who hear it and take to heart what is written in it, because the time is near."

Westminster Confession of Faith, chapter 1, paragraph 6:
"The whole counsel of God, concerning all things necessary for His own glory, man's salvation, faith, and life, is either expressly set down in Scripture, or by good and necessary consequence may be deduced from Scripture. …"

4. THE STUDY OF THE BIBLE CAN BE SPIRITUALLY BENEFICIAL ONLY BY THE WORK OF THE HOLY SPIRIT.

John 16:13, 14 – "But when He, the Spirit of truth, comes, He will guide you into all truth. He will not speak on His own; He will speak only what He hears, and He will tell you what is yet to come. He will bring glory to me by taking from what is mine and making it known to you."

John 17:17 – "Sanctify them by the truth; your Word is truth."

Hebrews 4:12 – "For the Word of God is living and active. Sharper than any double-edged sword, it penetrates even to dividing soul and spirit, joints and marrow; it judges the thoughts and attitudes of the heart."

Westminster Confession of Faith, chapter 1, paragraphs 5 and 6:
"… our full persuasion and assurance of the infallible truth and divine authority thereof, is from the inward work of the Holy Spirit, bearing witness by and with the Word in our hearts."

"… we acknowledge the inward illumination of the Spirit of God to be necessary for the saving understanding of such things as are revealed in the Word. …"

WEEKLY ASSIGNMENTS FOR THE JOURNEY

The Journey will be most effective and enjoyed when the weekly assignments are done. The assignments are designed to have the student delve into the book or books being studied *before* the teaching begins. The assignments encourage the student to:

Read … the entire book for the next week or at least read seven chapters (one a day) to get a taste of the book.

Memorize … two or three verses so that the unique truths from the book being studied will be deeply meditated upon.

Pray … that being informed by the content of the next book, your prayer life will be deepened.

Apply … think about the particular truths from the next book by applying them to your daily life. Identify what you need to believe about God, repent of as sin and obey as a commandment.

Share ... go beyond your own experience of the next book to share its truths within your family or with an unchurched friend.

STUDY QUESTIONS FOR SMALL GROUPS

If the time allows, the teaching period should be followed by the class being divided into small groups for a 15-20 minute period so that students can interact after they have done their work and heard the teaching. Questions used in the small groups could be the questions suggested in the "Apply" section of the assignments:

In the light of _____ (the particular book being studied and taught):

- What do you need to believe about God?

- What do you need to repent of as sin?

- What do you need to obey as a command?

The Old Testament

Chapter One: Genesis

Assignment

Read ...

Genesis, Chapters 1-50, or selected chapters from Genesis (one a day for a week) as follows:

Chapters 1-3	–	Creation.
Chapters 6-8	–	Noah and the flood.
Chapter 12	–	The call of Abraham.
Chapter 22	–	The testing of Abraham/Isaac.
Chapter 32	–	Jacob.
Chapter 37	–	Joseph.
Chapter 50	–	Egypt.

Memorize ...

Genesis 1:1 – "In the beginning God created the heavens and the earth;"

   and/or

Genesis 15:6 – "Abraham believed the LORD, and He credited it to him as righteousness."

   and/or

Genesis 50:20a – "You intended to harm me, but God intended it for good. …"

Pray ...

Giving thanks to God as the Maker of heaven and earth.

Asking for the mercy of God in the light of the wickedness of the world.

Seeking the Lord's direction for your life.

Confessing the schemes and sins of your life.

Resting in the good providence of God in the light of hurts and hardship.

APPLY ...

In the light of Genesis, what are you to:

>   BELIEVE about God?

>   REPENT of as sin?

>   OBEY as a command from God?

SHARE ...

According to what you have learned from Genesis:

-   Spend some time sharing one insight from Genesis with a family member or friend. What was that insight and how did the conversation go?

-   Ask the Lord to give you an opportunity to talk with an unchurched person about one truth from Genesis regarding God. Describe that contact and how you thought it went.

Genesis: Where It All Began

INTRODUCTION

Years ago, Alex Haley went on an adventure and wrote a book that touched all of America. He did a study of his ancestry that took him back into the various characters of his bloodline – all the way back to Africa – and their experience in slavery. It became a TV mini-series that, even today, still ranks as one of the Top 10 most-watched shows of all time.

Roots touched that desire in all of us to know where we began, from where and whom we came. Instinctively, we all know that our beginnings had nothing to do with us.

Genesis is *Roots* for the Christian. Everything starts there. It is the "Book of Beginnings," and from it we know more about our God and ourselves.

TITLE

"Genesis" was the title given to this book in 250 B.C. in the Greek translation of the Hebrew Old Testament which is known as the Septuagint. The word *gennas* occurs 10 times in the book and forms an outline for Genesis. *Gennas* means origin, source, beginning, generation, birth.

Whenever the word *gennas* occurs in Genesis, it is translated as "the book of generations" (King James Version) or "the account of" (New International Version). Usually, it is followed with a genealogy:

Genesis 2:4   – Creation.

Genesis 5:1   – Adam's line.

Genesis 6:9   – Noah's line.

Genesis 10:1   – Noah's sons (Shem, Ham, Japheth).

Genesis 11:10 – Shem.

Genesis 11:27 – Terah (father of Abraham).

Genesis 25:12 – Ishmael (Abraham's son by Hagar).

Genesis 25:19 – Isaac (Abraham's son by Sarah).

Genesis 36:1   – Esau (Jacob's twin brother).

Genesis 37:2   – Jacob.

Genesis describes the beginning of everything – the Earth, all plant and animal life, mankind as male and female, the Sabbath, marriage, sin, sacrifices, salvation, the family, civilization, government, nations and Israel.

Genesis describes the beginning of everything … except God.

THEME VERSE

In the beginning God created the heavens and the earth.
Genesis 1:1

Genesis is the first book of the Pentateuch, which means "five books." The Pentateuch also is called the Torah, the Law, or the Five Books of Moses, and it includes Genesis, Exodus, Leviticus, Numbers and Deuteronomy.

GENERAL OUTLINE

Genesis 1-11	**Genesis 12- 50**
Beginning of human race	Beginning of the Hebrew race
Primeval history	Patriarchal history
Four great events	Four great people
Over 2,000 years	300 years

I. GENESIS 1 – 11 (FOUR GREAT EVENTS)

1. THE CREATION (1, 2)

God's sovereignty and might are demonstrated as His initiative of creation. No reason is given except that it is His good pleasure and will to create. God did not create because He was lonely or bored. He created in such a way that He would get all the glory, even though He created creatures with "free will" and great potential.

Two things we must never forget about creation:

* The creation of mankind.

So God created man in His own image, in the image of God He created him; male and female He created them. (Genesis 1:27)

The "image of God" is foundational for us to see the dignity of all human beings, even when that image is marred by sin.

* The creation of all things.

God saw all that He had made, and it was very good. (Genesis 1:31)

We don't think about everything being "very good" when we look at the world today, but let's not forget that this was how everything was first created and it is God's redemptive goal for all things. God is always good and is always working for our good.

2. THE FALL (3 – 5)

Yet, the creation did not stay "good." Genesis 3 opens with a base note:

Now the serpent was more crafty than any of the wild animals the LORD God had made. He said to the woman, "Did God really say, 'You must not eat from any tree in the garden?'"

There is great mystery here. From where did the evil come? Why did Adam and Eve sin? These questions are important, but they are not the point of Genesis 3. Adam and Eve disobeyed the Lord and the good creation did not stay good. Sin entered into the scene and a "fall" occurred with specific curses issued by God.

The Fall must not be forgotten today. In our struggle with evil and sin in the world, in the Church, in our families and in our lives, we must always remember this condition as a reality that only God can redeem and change. It will not be eradicated until Christ comes again and heaven is our home.

In the context of the Fall, the first statement of the Gospel is proclaimed:

"And I will put enmity between you and the woman, and between your offspring and hers; He will crush your head, and you will strike His heel" (Genesis 3:15).

3. The Flood (6 – 9)

The sin of mankind grew as mankind multiplied and spread throughout the earth. The impact of sin got to a fever pitch in Genesis 6:5:

The LORD saw how great man's wickedness on the earth had become, and that every inclination of the thoughts of his heart was only evil all the time.

God's judgment of this wickedness is dramatically demonstrated in the flood. In the midst of this great judgment is great grace:

But Noah found favor in the eyes of the LORD (Genesis 6:8).

The story of Noah and the Ark is a part of our childhood memories, and the fanciful images of an elderly Noah loading up pairs of animals onto this enormous boat are popular even today.

But the story of the flood shows the sin in man's heart, the wrath of God toward sin, the demonstration of grace in the midst of judgment and the continued covenant of God for His people. God is still committed to what He has created, even though sin has dramatically changed the landscape.

4. The Tower of Babel (10, 11)

The Tower of Babel is the story of emerging nations and the humanistic effort at unity that seeks for something bigger than man, but does not seek the Lord God.

Babel literally means "gateway to a god." The Hebrew word for "Babel" sounds like a word that means "confusion," and it is used later on for Babylon.

This Tower of Babel endeavor begins with unity and success, but it ends with scattering and confusion. Once again, the sin of mankind is judged by God.

II. GENESIS 12 – 15 (FOUR GREAT PEOPLE)

1. Abraham (12 – 24)

Genesis 12 is a pivotal chapter in Scripture. Even though God has judged the nations at Babel, He now takes a step that will lead to the blessing of all nations.

God calls one man to be the father of one nation from which will come the one Savior of the world:

I will make you into a great nation and I will bless you ... and all peoples on earth will be blessed through you (Genesis 12:2a, 3b).

God establishes a covenant with Abraham and his descendants that is marked by the sign of circumcision (Genesis 17). There, God changes his name from Abram ("exalted father") to Abraham ("father of many"), showing the Lord's intent to use the descendants of Abraham to reach the whole world.

Abraham's life is filled with stories that are significant:

- His nephew Lot.

- His wife Sarah.

- Melchizedek – Genesis 14:18-20 (cp. Hebrews 7).

- Sarah's handmaid Hagar.

- Abraham's son through Hagar, Ishmael.

- Sodom and Gomorrah.

- Angelic visitations.

- Abraham's son of promise through Sarah, Isaac.

Abraham will be a name that reverberates throughout Scripture, even to the time of Jesus and the epistles of Paul.

2. Isaac (25, 26)

Isaac, the son of promise to Abraham and Sarah, was given to them in their old age when they thought they could never have any children.

The most dramatic episode is told about Isaac as a boy when the Lord tested Abraham to sacrifice Isaac on Mount Moriah (Genesis 22). Like Genesis 3:15, this is another foreshadowing of a substitute who would be sacrificed in the place of sinners.

3. Jacob (27 – 36)

Jacob comes to us in Genesis as one of the most notorious patriarchs because of his life of scheming and deception. In Jacob, we find a kindred spirit who often is selfish and manipulative, yet he longs for God and His blessing.

The stories about Jacob's relationships still ring in our ears:

- Jacob and his twin brother, Esau.

- Jacob scheming with his mother Rebekah to deceive his father and receive Esau's blessing.

- Jacob being deceived by his uncle Laban.

- Jacob's love for Rachel, although he had children by three other women.

- Jacob's 12 sons, who would become the heads of the 12 tribes of Israel.

- Jacob's relationship with his God is dramatically shown in his vision of the ladder to heaven and in his wrestling with God (Genesis 32), when his name was changed to Israel ("he struggles with God").

4. Joseph (37 – 50)

Joseph dominates the last 14 chapters of Genesis, which show the providence of God to take care of this family with 12 sons that eventually would become the nation of Israel.

Joseph was mistreated by his brothers and sold into slavery because, evidenced by the coat of many colors, they saw him as their father's favorite. Joseph did not help matters because his dreams portrayed him as bigger and brighter than the rest of the brothers.

Joseph was sold into slavery and ended up in Egypt. In a remarkable story of rags to riches, Joseph rose from prison to the palace, from slavery to the throne.

The providential care of Joseph is a lesson for all time. The Lord watched over Joseph through trials and temptations and brought him to a position of power and influence. The Lord led to the provisioning of Egypt through years of famine. But the greater plan of the Lord is shown in the prosperity of Joseph's whole family, as Genesis ends with Jacob and all the sons coming to Egypt to live in peace.

A tender moment in Genesis 50 is when Joseph's identity is revealed to his brothers, who had sold him into slavery. Imagine the shock of seeing the brother they thought they had disposed of as now equal to the Pharaoh in Egypt. They knew they deserved death for their evil deed, but Joseph knew that the Lord's hand had been in it all. Genesis 50:19-21:

But Joseph said to them, "Don't be afraid. Am I in the place of God? You intended to harm me, but God intended it for good to accomplish what is now being done, the saving of many lives.

So then, don't be afraid. I will provide for you and your children." And he reassured them and spoke kindly to them.

Genesis begins with the good creation of God and ends in the good providence of God. It is true: God is good … all the time.

Lessons From Genesis

1. All things are created by God. The first reason to praise God is creation. God deserves praise even if He never did any act of father-like providence or Savior-like redemption because He made us. As the child's catechism reminds us:
    Q. Who made you?
    A. God.
    Q. What else did God make?
    A. God made all things.
    Q. Why did God make you and all things?
    A. For His own glory.

2. All things are controlled by God. Even though sin enters into the good creation and humankind falls, the hands of God never are tied. Nothing surprises Him, not even the serpent in the garden. What He creates by grace, He seeks to save by grace. In the increase of wickedness and evil, God still interjects Himself into the affairs of men to covenant, call and convert. What the evil of man might intend, the goodness of God can mend.

NOTES

CHAPTER TWO: EXODUS

Assignment

READ ...

Exodus, Chapters 1-40, or selected chapters from Exodus (one a day for a week) as follows:

Exodus 1   –   Setting for Exodus.

Exodus 3   –   Moses and the burning bush.

Exodus 12   –   Passover.

Exodus 14   –   Crossing the Red Sea.

Exodus 20   –   The Ten Commandments.

Exodus 32   –   The golden calf.

Exodus 33   –   Moses and the glory of the Lord.

MEMORIZE ...

Exodus 3:14 – "God said to Moses, 'I AM WHO I AM;'"

and/or

Exodus 20:2 – "I am the LORD your God, who brought you out of Egypt, out of the land of slavery;"

and/or

Exodus 33:19 – "And the LORD said, 'I will cause all my goodness to pass in front of you, and I will proclaim my name, the LORD, in your presence. I will have mercy on whom I will have mercy, and I will have compassion on whom I will have compassion.'"

and/or

Exodus 34:6 – "And He (God) passed in front of Moses, proclaiming, 'The Lord, the Lord, the compassionate and gracious God, slow to anger, abounding in love and faithfulness. ...'"

PRAY ...

Giving glory to God for His bringing us out of slavery to freedom.

Thanking the Lord for His laws that show us our need for a Savior and our duty in life.

Asking to see the Lord's goodness and glory.

That your place of worship would be filled with the glory of God.

APPLY ...

In the light of Exodus, what are you to:

> BELIEVE about God?
>
> REPENT of as sin?
>
> OBEY as a command from God?

SHARE ...

According to what you have learned from Exodus:

- Have a conversation in your family or with a friend about the Ten Commandments. Get their thoughts on the current issue in this country regarding the public display of the Ten Commandments.

- Ask an unchurched friend what he knows about Moses. Don't do this to try to embarrass him. Do it to identify a contact point through which to share something that you learned from Exodus about this man who was called a friend of God.

Exodus:
A Story of Freedom

INTRODUCTION

Freedom has been a pulsating theme throughout history. It is a unique heritage of ours in the United States. As Americans, we love to sing:

My country, 'tis of thee,
Sweet land of liberty,
Of thee I sing;
Land where my fathers died,
Land of the pilgrim's pride,
From every mountain side
Let freedom ring.

But freedom, liberty and independence are not American inventions. They burn in every soul made by God that is in bondage to sin.

Exodus is a book of freedom, deliverance and redemption. The freedom of Exodus is based in the Divine nature and the gracious work of our God to deliver His people – whether it be Israel then or the Church today – from sin and bondage.

TITLE

"Exodus" is a Greek title that means "departure, going out, leaving." It depicts Israel's departure from slavery in Egypt and her journey to freedom as the nation of God's people.

CONTEXT

Exodus follows Genesis chronologically, with one clarification: There is a 350-year period of silence between the two books. What happened during those 350 years is important in order to understand the context of Exodus.

This period was a time of generations passing and Israel growing:

Now Joseph and all his brothers and all that generation died, but the Israelites were fruitful and multiplied greatly and became exceedingly numerous, so that the land was filled with them"
(1:6, 7).

But this period also marked the passing of generations of the kings of Egypt:

Then a new king, who did not know about Joseph, came to power in Egypt" (1:8).

The scene was set for slavery.

THEME VERSE

I am the LORD your God, who brought you out of Egypt, out of the land of slavery.
Exodus 20:1

I. BONDAGE (1, 2)

The Hebrews were so numerous that now they were perceived to be a military threat. Since the new pharaoh did not know Joseph, the favored status of the Hebrews changed to the unfavored status of slaves.

The pharaoh was so afraid that he put together a plan of partial extermination of the Hebrews that called for killing Hebrew baby boys. Then the focus in the story is put on one family and the birth of one boy. By God's providence, he was saved, placed in pharaoh's court and even nursed by his own mother. Pharaoh's daughter named him Moses (2:10), which means "to draw out," remembering that Moses was drawn out of the water.

Moses' first 40 years were spent as an Egyptian, with all of the education, opportunities and wealth available in Pharaoh's court. Somehow he learned he was a Hebrew and, in an attempt to deliver his people by his own strength, he murdered an Egyptian.

Moses' next 40 years were spent as a shepherd in Midian. Imagine his thoughts as he looked back on his life in Egypt and the great opportunity he had to help Israel, yet here he was in the desert. Moses, at 80, probably was a broken man who didn't think he had much of a future.

II. DELIVERANCE (3 – 12)

Then God appears in a remarkable way. He speaks to Moses through the burning bush and calls him to be the deliverer of Israel. God reveals Himself with a new name, Yahweh – I AM WHO I AM – a very mystical name, but one that is always used as the covenant name for God in His relationship with His people Israel.

Moses' response to this call of God was disbelief. He did not think he could do what God called him to do, but the Lord persisted in the call and sent him to Pharaoh with a simple message: "Let my people go."

Pharaoh did not eagerly respond. He increased the labor of the Hebrews and demanded more production. The people were discouraged, and Moses was unsure. God again showed up in an even more remarkable way.

God caused 10 plagues to strike Egypt. In succession, blood, frogs, gnats, flies, livestock disease, boils, hail, locusts, darkness and the death of the firstborn occur to demonstrate to Pharaoh that God meant business when it came to the freedom of His people.

Accompanying the tenth plague was the initiation of the Passover Feast (12). In this perpetual commemorative meal, God established a means for the people of Israel to remember His deliverance. The meal featured the blood of a lamb and unleavened bread to eat. The Passover is significant for us today because it is the Old Testament forerunner of the sacrament of Communion.

III. JOURNEY (13 – 18)

Pharaoh eventually let Israel go. According to Exodus 12:37, there were about 600,000 men. Add to this number the women and children, and the total could have been approximately two million people.

God guided them with a cloud by day and fire by night, but there was a problem: Pharaoh changed his mind and with his army pursued Israel into the desert with the intent of bringing them back.

At the Red Sea (14), we have the most dramatic act of God's deliverance in the Old Testament. With the Egyptian army approaching on one side and the Red Sea on the other, Israel appeared doomed. But Moses declared:

Do not be afraid. Stand firm and you will see the deliverance the LORD will bring you today
(14:13).

The waves parted … Israel passed through the sea on dry ground … and the Egyptians were destroyed. As Israel continued its journey, it was not long before the people began to grumble and complain:

If only we had died by the LORD's hand in Egypt! There we sat around pots of meat and ate all the food we wanted, but you have brought us out into this desert to starve this entire assembly to death (16:3).

To feed the people, the Lord provided daily bread – manna, meaning "What is this?" – and water.

IV. LAW (19 – 40)

Israel, as the freed people of God, was faced with a whole new existence. The rest of Exodus and the book of Leviticus show the distinctions of their being the people of God who have been freed, delivered and saved.

The Israelites were distinctive because they were a people commanded by God. Moses received the law directly from God on Mount Sinai. It contained laws which were civil, ceremonial, dietary and moral in nature. The Ten Commandments in Exodus 20 provide the foundation of the moral law for the rest of Scripture.

As God's covenant people, Israel was also distinctive because her people were judged by God. While Moses was on the mountain, the people rebelled. They came to Aaron, Moses' brother, and demanded, "Come, make us gods who will go before us. As for this fellow Moses who brought us up out of Egypt, we don't know what has happened to him" (32:1). Aaron made a "golden calf" and the people began to dance.

Moses returned and was filled with anger because of the rebellion of the people. The judgment of God is dramatic, although Moses interceded for the people. Many died in the judgment, but many were saved. The children of Israel were now ready for their trek toward the land "flowing with milk and honey."

The Lord then revealed Himself to Moses in an extraordinary way. In Exodus 34:6, the Lord declared His character:

The LORD, the LORD, the compassionate and gracious God, slow to anger, abounding in love and faithfulness, maintaining love to thousands and forgiving wickedness, rebellion and sin.

This is the first occurrence of an Old Testament refrain of God's gracious and loving nature, which also is found in Numbers 14:18; Nehemiah 9:17; Psalms 86:15, 103:8 and 145:8; Joel 2:13; and Jonah 4:2.

By the end of Exodus, Israel becomes the distinctive people of God privileged to worship Him. Instructions from the Lord are given to build the tabernacle. This was to be the place where the Lord would choose to reside and the people could come to worship. They would become a people among whom the Lord dwelt:

Then the cloud covered the Tent of Meeting, and the glory of the LORD filled the tabernacle (40:34).

Exodus begins with Israel in bondage in Egypt but, after the Lord delivers the people and gives them His law, they become a people among whom the Lord actually resides.

Lessons From Exodus

1. God never forsakes His people. Generations may pass and conditions may change, but the Lord remains true to His promises and commitments to His people.

2. God always delivers His people. It may seem late. It will by means be unexpected, but it clearly will always be God. The Lord is the one who brings His people out of bondage into a new life.

3. God consistently commands His people. The people of God are delivered for a new life characterized by obedience, faith and worship. God's gift of freedom for His people leads to the fullness of a holy life.

NOTES

CHAPTER THREE: LEVITICUS

Assignment

READ ...

Leviticus, Chapters 1-27, or selected chapters from Leviticus (one a day for a week) as follows:

Leviticus 1	–	The burnt offering.
Leviticus 8	–	The ordination of Aaron as priest.
Leviticus 10	–	The death of Nadab and Abihu.
Leviticus 11	–	The holiness code.
Leviticus 16	–	The Day of Atonement.
Leviticus 18	–	Unlawful sexual relations.
Leviticus 19	–	Various laws and encouragements to love your neighbor.

MEMORIZE ...

Leviticus 11:45 – "I am the LORD, who brought you up out of Egypt to be your God; therefore be holy, because I am holy;"

and/or

Leviticus 17:11 – "For the life of a creature is in the blood, and I have given it to you to make atonement for yourselves on the altar; it is the blood that makes atonement for one's life;"

and/or

Leviticus 19:18 – "Do not seek revenge or bear a grudge against one of your people, but love your neighbor as yourself. I am the LORD."

PRAY ...

Thanking the Lord that He has made a provision for the cleansing of our sins, even if it is the way of sacrifice.

Confessing your sin and recognizing the seriousness of sin that calls for the shedding of innocent blood.

Confessing any impurity in your life and asking the Holy Spirit to make you more holy (sanctification).

APPLY ...

In the light of Leviticus, what are you to:

> BELIEVE about God?
>
> REPENT of as sin?
>
> OBEY as a command from God?

SHARE ...

According to what you have learned from Leviticus:

- Have a conversation in your family or with a friend about the whole matter of laws. Leviticus is filled with all kinds of laws regarding punishment for crimes and regulations for clean living. Talk about what happens when laws go too far in our spiritual lives, as well as when laws are not honored enough.

- Ask an unchurched friend about what he or she thinks "holiness" means. Share with him the Biblical teaching on holiness, which is the call of God for His people to be set apart for His special purposes.

Leviticus:
Handbook for Holiness

INTRODUCTION

Holiness is not what we normally think it is. We can think of a "holiness church" and equate holiness with silly and bizarre behavior, but we cannot dismiss the Biblical call to holiness so easily.

Something or someone that is "holy" has been "set apart" for a special purpose and reason. If we are "holy," we are not our own. We belong to God, and we are to live like it. We don't, however, always do that.

The concept of "holiness" occurs 87 times in Leviticus – more than any other book in the Bible.

Leviticus is not the easiest book to read. It is like the *Book of Order* for Presbyterians. It has procedures, policies, rituals, guidelines and directions for the priests – the Levites – and, in particular, the high priest – Aaron and the sons of Aaron.

There are not many stories in Leviticus … only laws, case studies and regulations. Frankly, it is boring, but Scripture was not given to entertain. It was given to teach how to be right with God, and Leviticus does help with this. Leviticus can be understood as a challenge for anyone who believes in plenary inspiration – that "all" of Scripture is inspired and profitable for training in righteousness.

TITLE

"Leviticus" means "pertaining to the Levites." The Levites were the priestly tribe that had the responsibility of caring for the tabernacle, offering the sacrifices and providing for the feasts.

The phrase, "The Lord said to Moses," occurs countless times in Leviticus, showing that a special revelation is taking place as the Lord instructs Moses concerning who will lead in the execution of the rules and regulations of Leviticus.

THEME VERSE

I am the Lord your God; consecrate yourselves and be holy, because I am holy.
Leviticus 11:44

Exodus and Leviticus need to be seen as complementary books. Exodus gives the story of salvation, and Leviticus gives the process of sanctification. Exodus is all about getting to Mount Sinai, and Leviticus is all about living at Mount Sinai. Exodus provides the direction for building the tabernacle, and Leviticus provides the direction of using the tabernacle. In theological terms, Exodus teaches justification – how we are to get right with God; and Leviticus teaches sanctification – how to stay right with God.

I. WAY TO GOD (1 – 17)

FIVE OFFERINGS (1 – 7)

The basic offerings to be observed are described in the first pages of Leviticus. They form the variety of ways in which the Israelites were to come to God as sinners. Three of them are voluntary and two are compulsory. The burnt offering (1) was offered morning and evening for all of Israel, but was personal – a voluntary offering to show devotion to the Lord. The burnt offering consumed the whole sacrifice: body, tail, hoofs, etc.

The meal (grain) offering (2) was observed by bringing grain – the only bloodless offering – but it was offered with the burnt offering.

The peace (fellowship) offering (3) was an offering that symbolized peace with God and inward peace. The Hebrew word for peace – *shalom* – means "wholeness." This *shalom* was seen as the ultimate state of spiritual bliss available in this life, and it came by way of one personally participating in the ceremony by eating part of the offering. The priest would also eat part of it. The peace offering was the main offering during feasts, because visiting pilgrims could eat it and be provided nourishment as well. I Kings 8:63-65 tells of the dedication of the temple, when Solomon offered 20,000 cattle and 120,000 sheep and goats as peace offerings over 14 days.

The sin offering (4) was a compulsory offering when someone sinned unintentionally. It was offered when the sinner admitted a wrong but added, "I didn't know," or "I didn't mean to."

The guilt (trespass) offering (5) was a compulsory offering when someone sinned intentionally. A restitution for the wrong committed would accompany the guilt offering.

Additional details on all the offerings are given in Leviticus 6 and 7 to provide more practical information about the actual offering of the sacrifices.

Priesthood Regulations (8 – 10)

Of equal importance to the nature of the offerings is the one who offers the offerings: the priest. The Lord told Moses that Aaron and his sons were to be consecrated for this service, and their ordination, vestments and behavior were to match the holiness (act of being set apart) of the offerings.

From the very beginning, however, there was a problem. Aaron's sons, Nadab and Abihu, offered "unauthorized fire before the Lord," and immediate judgment came upon them. Then the Lord spoke:

> *"Among those who approach me I will show myself holy; in the sight of all the people I will be honored" (10:3).*

Yet Aaron remained silent.

Laws of Cleanness (11– 15)

The holiness of the people, or their being set apart for God, was not only to be observed by the offering of sacrifices or the performance of priests, it also was to be demonstrated in everyday life. Purity laws were to have an influence on what the people ate (11), purification after childbirth (12), the treatment of infectious skin diseases (13, 14), and bodily discharges (15). The distinction of the people of God did not just affect their souls and the forgiveness of their sins, but also their bodies. They were to be holy in every aspect of their existence.

Day of Atonement (Yom Kippur) (16, 17)

The Day of Atonement was to be the highlight of the year for Israel. Aaron was to cast lots over two goats: one to be sacrificed and the other to be released into the desert as the "scapegoat," representing the taking away of their sins to be remembered no more.

The connection of blood and atonement are made clear in Leviticus 17:

> *For the life of a creature is in the blood, and I have given it to you to make atonement for yourselves on the altar; it is the blood that makes atonement for one's life. (17:11)*

This is a crucial old covenant truth that is fulfilled in the shedding of the blood of Christ for the Atonement of the sins of the whole world.

II. WALK WITH GOD (18 – 27)

The first half of Leviticus (1 – 17) teaches that "God is holy and we are not." Therefore, the emphasis on the sacrifices to be made and the priests who were to make them was most important. The second half of Leviticus (18 – 27) teaches that "God is holy and so are we to be holy." After being forgiven, there is to be a resolve to live as one forgiven. Holiness is to become the way one lives day-by-day.

This holiness code begins with the moral law, especially sexual ethics. Immoral sexual relations are forbidden (18), and the Ten Commandments are expanded to be the basis for all moral behavior (19). The civic matter of capital punishment for the breaking of the moral law (20) emphasizes in Israel the seriousness of disobeying the Lord.

The Lord already had directly punished Nadab and Abihu for their unacceptable sacrifice, but the high standards for the priesthood had to continue to be observed and honored (21, 22).

Israel was to observe some holy times during the year to highlight the work of God on their behalf. The feasts of Passover, First Fruits, Pentecost, Trumpets, Tabernacles and the Day of Atonement (23) were to mark the passing of a year with special ritual and meaning. Special years also were to be observed. The Sabbath Year and the Year of Jubilee (25) were to bring rest and equity to the land.

At the heart of holiness for Israel, however, was their covenant relationship with the Lord. Leviticus 26, which can be compared with Deuteronomy 28, gives the covenant promises that were both blessings and curses. There would be blessings for obedience and curses for disobedience. Israel was to be holy in their covenant relationship with their God or they would be judged. These covenant promises, especially regarding curses, put into spiritual context all of the history of Israel, especially since Israel would later be unfaithful to this covenant.

Leviticus should be studied with the New Testament book of Hebrews. Hebrews gives the new covenant perspective that upholds Christ as the superior priest who offers Himself as the superior sacrifice. Read Hebrews 9:6-14.

Lessons from Leviticus

1. God is holy. The standard for holiness is in the person of God. It is not found in a religion or a law or a called people. It is found in the nature of who God is and in the work of what God does.

2. We are unholy. When we compare ourselves with God, there is no contest. He is holy and we are not. In the brilliance of His glory and majesty we pale in significance. Our sinfulness is discovered not in comparison with one another, but in the light of God's nature.

3. We are to become holy because God is holy. There is to be no compromise or settlement. Because God is holy and we are not, someone has to change – and it is not God. We have been set apart for God, so we are in need of being cleansed in order to be God's.

4. We can only become holy by sacrifice. We cannot, however, become holy by our own effort or goodness. It takes a God-provision that pleases Him and changes us. That provision is the shedding of innocent blood in our stead. A substitutionary sacrifice is necessary for our cleansing.

NOTES

CHAPTER FOUR: NUMBERS

Assignment

READ ...

Numbers, Chapters 1-36, or selected chapters from Numbers (one a day for a week) as follows:

Numbers 1	–	Command to number the people.
Numbers 6	–	The Nazarite vow and the priestly blessing.
Numbers 1	–	The people complaining.
Numbers 13, 14	–	Exploring Canaan.
Numbers 17	–	Budding of Aaron's rod.
Numbers 20	–	Moses' sin and punishment.
Numbers 21	–	Bronze snake.

MEMORIZE ...

Numbers 6:24-26 – "The LORD bless you and keep you; the LORD make His face shine upon you and be gracious to you; the LORD turn His face toward you and give you peace."

and/or

Numbers 14:18 – "The LORD is slow to anger, abounding in love and forgiving sin and rebellion. Yet He does not leave the guilty unpunished. ..."

PRAY ...

Thanking the Lord that you are numbered among His people. You are known by name.

Asking for the strength to follow God's will and to accept His discipline.

Confessing where you have rebelled and complained against the Lord.

Asking for the blessing of the Lord upon your life and your family, your church and your nation.

APPLY ...

In the light of Numbers, what are you to:

> BELIEVE about God?
>
> REPENT of as sin?
>
> OBEY as a command from God?

SHARE ...

According to what you have learned from Numbers:

- Talk with your family or a friend about how the people of God (the Church) can be rebellious against, complaining about and dissatisfied with the things of God. Then talk about how the Lord responds to our shortcomings.

- Share with a friend who is not active in a church the truth that the Lord is compassionate, slow to anger and abounding in love – even in the face of our sin.

Numbers:
A Pilgrimage With God

INTRODUCTION

A pilgrimage is one of the best descriptions of the Christian life. The Christian life is a pilgrimage … a journey … a movement from one point to another.

A pilgrimage is filled with pleasure and pain, good and bad times, sweet and bitter experiences, joy and sorrow, plenty and want.

Christians are always "on the road." There is no such thing as instant maturity, a downhill slide or a final destination in this life.

The greatest Christian classic in history, the book that is second only to the Bible in the number of copies printed, is John Bunyan's *The Pilgrim's Progress*. It has remained in demand because it describes the Christian life as a pilgrimage. We are all "on the road." We are all pilgrims.

Numbers gives us the pilgrimage of the nation of Israel between the time of its deliverance from slavery in Egypt to its arrival on the edge of the Promised Land – and it is not a pretty picture. The book of Numbers does not end with "and they all lived happily ever after."

We need to get real about the Christian life – our pilgrimage with God. Often, we are a stubborn and complaining people. We want our way and not God's way most of the time. We struggle with unbelief, rebellion, greed, lust and pride. And if we give in to those sins, God will discipline us. We are His children, and a good Father always disciplines His children. This is the message of Numbers.

TITLE

"Numbers" refers to the "numbering" of the people or the taking of a census to count the people of Israel. There are two censuses in Numbers, one in chapter 1 and the other in chapter 26; one taken at the start of their wandering in the wilderness and one taken at the end of 40 years of wandering in the wilderness.

Two "numbers" stand out in Numbers:

Numbers 1:46   –   603,550.

Numbers 26:51   –   601,730.

There are about 40 years between these two censuses, and you would expect the second to be larger than the first, but it's not. The second number is smaller because that is the story of Numbers. The people of God struggle with Him and often grumble against Him, and the Lord disciplines them. Numbers can be seen as a book that majors in discipline – a discipline carried out by God.

The Hebrew name for Numbers is *wayedabber*, which means, "And the LORD spoke." Most Hebrew names for books in the Old Testament are the first words of the book. But this Hebrew title – "And the LORD spoke" – is significant to the message of Numbers. The phrases "The LORD spoke to Moses" and "Moses spoke to Israel" are stated in one way or another 150 times in Numbers. We don't normally think of Moses as a prophet, but he is portrayed in Numbers as one of the great prophets of God.

THEME VERSES

The LORD replied, "I have forgiven them, as you asked. Nevertheless, as surely as I live and as surely as the glory of the LORD fills the whole earth, not one of the men who saw my glory and the miraculous signs I performed in Egypt and in the desert but who disobeyed me and tested me ten times – not one of them will ever see the land I promised on oath to their forefathers. ... In this desert your bodies will fall – every one of you twenty years old or more who was counted in the census and who has grumbled against me. Not one of you will enter the land I swore with uplifted hand to make your home, except Caleb son of Jephunneh and Joshua son of Nun."
Numbers 14:20-23, 29, 30

I. THE OLD GENERATION (1 – 14) (2 MONTHS; SINAI TO KADESH)

In Numbers, chapter 1, the Lord commands a census to be taken counting all the men over 20 years of age, excluding the Levites. The count was by tribes, and the total was 603,550 (1:46). Usually, the purpose for a census in the Bible is to prepare an army for war (read Numbers 1:3). Here, the Lord was preparing them for the battles ahead.

Their preparation for the pilgrimage continued in the early chapters of Numbers, as they were organized in their camping formation around the tabernacle and in their marching formation. Their preparation also was spiritual in calling for purity (5), uplifting special vows (Nazarite vow in Numbers 6), the dedication of the tabernacle (7), the ordination of the Levites (8), and in the celebration of the Passover (9).

In the middle of this preparation was the priestly blessing that Aaron and his sons were to declare over Israel (6:24-26):

The Lord bless you and keep you; the Lord make His face to shine upon you and be gracious to you; the Lord lift up His countenance upon you and give you peace.

The pilgrimage of Israel supernaturally was guided by the Lord using the cloud. The cloud was the visible symbol of the Lord's presence – and it was no ordinary cloud. It appeared and settled above the tabernacle, and it also could have the appearance of fire.

Whenever the cloud lifted from above the tent, the Israelites set out; wherever the cloud settled, the Israelites encamped (9:17).

This is the way the Christian pilgrimage should be: ordered by God, obeying God and worshiping God; then we are blessed by God and guided by Him. But the people of God are not always faithful.

The Israelites move out in the order given by God, under the guidance of the cloud and under the leadership of Moses, but after just three days the people complain. "Now the people complained about their hardships in the hearing of the LORD ..." (11:1). Basically, they had gotten tired of the manna and wanted other food. We all know that we had better be careful what we ask for, because sometimes we will get it. God gave them meat. Quail came in droves, and then, as they ate, the anger of the Lord struck them with a plague and many of them died.

The rebellion was not limited to the people wanting other food. It reached even to the leadership, where Moses' own family turned against him. Miriam, Moses' sister, and Aaron, Moses' brother, had gotten jealous of Moses' position. In the midst of this family struggle, we have a parenthetical statement about Moses that is very insightful: "Now Moses was a very humble (meek) man, more humble than anyone else on the face of the earth" (12:3). Moses was not the problem here. So, again, we see the anger of the Lord, this time against

Moses' family. Moses did what he often did – he interceded and cried for the Lord to be merciful, and He was.

Numbers 13 and 14 give us one of the classic stories of Scripture. It is the story of the 12 spies. The Lord commanded that spies be sent into the land to check it out, but they returned with a split decision. Ten said there were giants in the land and Israel had no chance against them. Two (Joshua and Caleb) said there were giants in the land, but the Lord would be with them. The people sided with the majority report, and the Lord's anger was kindled. Moses interceded once again for God's mercy, and it was given, but not without a judgment:

> The LORD replied, "I have forgiven them, as you asked. Nevertheless, as surely as I live and as surely as the glory of the LORD fills the whole earth, not one of the men who saw my glory and the miraculous signs I performed in Egypt and in the desert but who disobeyed me and tested me ten times – not one of them will ever see the land I promised on oath to their forefathers. ... In this desert your bodies will fall – every one of you twenty years old or more who was counted in the census and who has grumbled against me. Not one of you will enter the land I swore with uplifted hand to make your home, except Caleb, son of Jephunneh, and Joshua, son of Nun."
> Numbers 14:20-23, 29-30

After the Lord's pronouncement of judgment, the people acknowledged their sin of not trusting the Lord and set out on their own to attack the giants. Their resolve, however, was only presumption, and they were defeated by the Canaanites.

II. THE PILGRIMAGE (15 – 20) (38 YEARS – WILDERNESS)

Forty years of wandering in the wilderness begins.

The first thing the Lord called Israel to do was to get back to the basics of worshiping Him. Chapters 15-19 reinstitute some of the laws of Exodus and Leviticus on offering sacrifices, observing the Sabbath and the duties of the Priests and Levites. Even as Israel was being disciplined in the wilderness, they were not to forget worship.

But there was more rebellion from the Israelites. A Levite named Korah, who was joined by 250 other Israelite leaders, turned against Moses and Aaron. Numbers 16 gives the details of the sudden and dramatic judgment of God against this group. In the midst of this judgment the centrality of Moses' leadership of Israel was affirmed.

The Lord's choice of Moses was concretely demonstrated in Numbers 17 with the budding of Aaron's rod. The Lord told Moses to get a rod from each of the 12 tribes and place them in front of the Ark. It was Aaron's rod that "not only sprouted, but had budded, blossomed and produced almonds" (17:8). Aaron's rod became part of the contents of the Ark (along with manna and the stone tablets of the Ten Commandments) so that Israel never would forget that Moses and Aaron were the leaders of God's choosing.

Moses' sin that kept him out of the Promised Land is depicted in Numbers 20. It is an intriguing passage that does not seem to be blatantly evil, especially in the context of the rest of Numbers, where the sin of the people is so obvious and persistent. The truth, however, is that Moses – even though he was the Lord's choice to lead Israel – was not immune to disobeying the Lord.

The passage seems to depict the sin as Moses hitting the rock with the staff to bring forth water rather than speaking to it. Sin, however, is hardly ever an observable action. Murder is always more than simply taking someone's life. Adultery is always more than simply sex outside of marriage. Lying is always more than not telling the truth. Sin always goes deeper.

The Lord told Moses and Aaron:

> Because you did not trust in me enough to honor me as holy in the sight of the Israelites, you will not bring the community into the land I give them (20:12).

III. THE NEW GENERATION (21 – 36) (NINE MONTHS; JOURNEY TO MOAB)

It is now toward the end of the 40 years of wandering. Many have fallen in the wilderness. Every family has lost a father and a mother, a grandfather and a grandmother. The generation left has only known the desert existence. Those under 20 at the start of the desert experience are now around 60 years of age. They are the new leaders and those who will have the "land flowing with milk and honey" as their destiny.

This new generation was granted a victory over an enemy, but they also grew impatient with Moses' leadership and spoke against Moses and the Lord. So, the Lord sent a judgment of venomous snakes. In the midst of this judgment, God provides a unique deliverance: The Lord said to Moses: "Make a snake and put it up on a pole; anyone who is bitten can look at it and live." So, Moses made a bronze snake and put it up on a pole. Then, when anyone was bitten by a snake and looked at the bronze snake, he or she lived (21:8, 9).

This would be an incidental occurrence except for John 3:14, where Jesus said, "Just as Moses lifted up the snake in the desert, so the Son of Man must be lifted up, that everyone who believes in Him may have eternal life."

The story in Numbers 22-25 is a convoluted episode of a pagan prophet named Balaam and Balak, the king of Moab. Balak wanted Balaam to curse Israel, but the Lord would not allow him to curse, only to bless Israel. The Lord communicated with Balaam in a way guaranteed to get his attention – his donkey. The Angel of the Lord speaks through Balaam's donkey and Balaam becomes convinced of the Lord's truth. Balaam, though, also gives advice to Israel that leads her people into idolatry. There is a lot of mystery and confusion in this section of Numbers, but it shows that the distinction between a true prophet and a false prophet is often not clear. What is clear is that in the rest of Scripture, Balaam is a symbol of false prophets and false teaching. Check out Joshua 13:22, 24:9, 10; Nehemiah 13:1-3; Micah 6:5; II Peter 2:15; Jude 11; and Revelation 2:14.

The second census is taken in Numbers 26 and describes the new generation that had been hardened by the desert experience.

Chapters 27-36 give various events and regulations that show this new generation getting ready to go into the Promised Land.

Numbers is a realistic, yet tragic, picture of the people of God. We possess the grace, law and covenant of our God, yet we choose to go our own way time and time again. Numbers basically tells us that while we are unfaithful, God remains faithful, even in the midst of His discipline.

Lessons From Numbers

1. God's deliverance demands obedience. The people of Israel had been delivered out of slavery (the message of Exodus), but that was not the end of the story. They entered into a new stage of their walk with God and immediately were confronted with a test.

2. Our disobedience demands discipline. God so loves His children that He cannot leave them in their disobedience. He will do anything to correct them and make them holy. Discipline is exercised throughout Numbers as an expression of the love of God for Israel. "Endure hardship as discipline; God is treating you as sons" (Hebrews 12:7).

NOTES

CHAPTER FIVE: DEUTERONOMY

Assignment

READ ...

Deuteronomy, Chapters 1-34, or selected chapters from Deuteronomy (one a day for a week) as follows:

Deuteronomy 4	–	God's love for His people.
Deuteronomy 5	–	The Ten Commandments.
Deuteronomy 6	–	The *Shema*.
Deuteronomy 10	–	Fear God.
Deuteronomy 18	–	A Prophet like Moses.
Deuteronomy 28	–	Blessings and curses.
Deuteronomy 34	–	Death of Moses.

MEMORIZE ...

Deuteronomy 6:4, 5 – "Hear, O Israel: The LORD our God, the LORD is one. Love the LORD your God with all your heart and with all your soul and with all your strength;"

and/or

Deuteronomy 8:3b – "... man does not live on bread alone but on every word that comes from the mouth of the LORD;"

and/or

Deuteronomy 10:12, 13 – "And now, O Israel, what does the LORD your God ask of you but to fear the LORD your God, to walk in all His ways, to love Him, to serve the LORD your God with all your heart and with all your soul, and to observe the LORD's commands and decrees that I am giving you today for your own good?"

Pray ...

Thanking the Lord that He is your God and He is committed to you.

Committing yourself to love the Lord with your whole heart, soul and strength.

Desiring a healthy fear of the Lord in your life.

Confessing that your life with the Lord has not been as wholehearted as it should be.

Apply ...

In the light of Deuteronomy, what are you to:

> BELIEVE about God?
>
> REPENT of as sin?
>
> OBEY as a command from God?

Share ...

According to what you have learned from Deuteronomy:

- Read Deuteronomy 6:4-9 and talk within your family about how you can pass on the truths of the faith to your children. If you do not have children at home, discuss with a family member or friend about the need to live out the faith before your children and all children.

- Be bold and tell someone you know who is not active in a church that you love the Lord. Share with him about how you show your love for God.

Deuteronomy:
A Book of Remembrance

INTRODUCTION

We have all been through transitional periods, which are times of leaving one place and entering into a new one. These transitions can be moving from one home to another, changing jobs, going to college, getting married, experiencing the death of a loved one, retirement or a new spiritual commitment.

Israel's transitional period entailed 40 years of wandering in the wilderness to enter the Promised Land.

A transitional time is a time for special instruction. It is a time to think twice about what has happened and what is ahead; to remember again what is important and what is trivial; to refocus on what is true, best and good. It is a time to go back to the basics.

The message of Deuteronomy is to remember truths in order to face a challenging transitional time. It is Moses helping Israel face this transitional period through which they would cease being a nomadic people and become residents in a new homeland. Deuteronomy is a book that goes back to the basics of what it means to be the people of God who are about to step out in the new adventure of occupying what the Lord will provide.

TITLE

"Deuteronomy" means "second law." It is a retelling of the law for a second time. The first time was 40 years earlier when the Lord first gave the law to Moses on Mount Sinai, which is recorded in Exodus and Leviticus. This second time is after the years of wandering, while Israel is on the verge of entering the Promised Land. The generation that heard the law the first time died in the desert. This new generation needs to hear the law a second time from the lips of Moses to be trained to be the people of God.

Deuteronomy is a remembrance, a recapitulation, a repeating and a return to the basics. It is a book of remembrance of who Israel's God was, who Israel's people were, where they had come from and where they were going.

THEME VERSE

Hear, O Israel: The LORD our God, the LORD is one. Love the LORD your God
with all your heart and with all your soul and with all your strength.
Deuteronomy 6:4, 5

This is called the *Shema* – Hebrew for "hear" – and it became the one verse known by Jews above all other verses of the law. It calls the people of God to focus on the Lord and their duty to love the Lord with all that is within them.

BACKGROUND

The nation of Israel was east of Jordon in the land of Moab. The people were preparing for the conquest of the land, and Moses was teaching them the law once again so that they might be faithful.

The Law in Exodus and Leviticus was primarily for the priests and the Levites. The Law in Deuteronomy was for all the people.

Because of the pressing preparations of Israel to go into the Promised Land, several words dominate Deuteronomy: "remember" occurs 20 times; "hear" 50 times; "do," "keep," "observe" and "obey" 177 times; and "love" 21 times.

Deuteronomy seems to have been a favorite book of Jesus because He quoted more from Deuteronomy than any other book in the Old Testament – even Psalms. An example of the Lord's use of Deuteronomy is when He fought the temptations of Satan in Matthew 4 and Luke 4. "Man shall not live by bread alone, but by every word that comes from the mouth of God" (8:3).

I. REMEMBER GOD'S FAITHFULNESS IN THE PAST – 'LOOKING BACK' (1 – 4)

In Deuteronomy 1-4, Israel is warned about the danger of a bad memory. Moses reminded her people of the past (the story of Numbers) when they sent spies into the land, rebelled against the Lord and did not go in, and so, the wanderings in the desert occurred. Yet, even in this time of punishment, the Lord was faithful in delivering them from their enemies and being with them.

When we look at the past, do we see only our failures, or do we see God's faithfulness? This is a special feature of Deuteronomy. As Moses looks back, he doesn't see just what happened, he sees *why* everything happened, and Moses always saw God at work. It was the Lord who loved, chose and delivered Israel. It was the Lord who provided for the people in the desert and gave them victory over their enemies. It was the Lord who had promised a land filled with milk and honey and that He would bring them to that land. Moses only saw what God had done.

II. REMEMBER GOD'S LOVE IN THE PRESENT – 'LOOKING UP' (5 – 26)

Remembering the Lord's faithfulness in the past caused Moses to see the Lord's love in the present. "Looking back" leads to Moses "looking up," and as Moses looked up, he remembered God's holiness, and that led him to loving obedience.

The main motivations for obedience are given in Deuteronomy 5 and 6.

Deuteronomy 5: The Ten Commandments (also found in Exodus 20). God is holy, so we are to be holy.

Deuteronomy 6: the *Shema*. God loves us, so we are to love God.

Moses is described in Deuteronomy 18:15 as "a prophet like Moses." Usually, Moses isn't thought of as a prophet, but he might be the model prophet, because he received so much directly from God and passed it on to the people. This hope for "a prophet like Moses" anticipates a line of prophets to follow – and one very special Prophet in the future, the Messiah (John 1:21, 25, 26).

The rest of this section, through chapter 26, is a recapitulation of the law with its admonitions for offerings, instructions to priests and regulations to be observed.

III. REMEMBER GOD'S PROMISES FOR THE FUTURE – 'LOOKING FORWARD' (27 – 34)

Looking back gives the perspective of God's faithfulness in the past. Looking up provides the truth that God is holy and loving, and obedience and faith are the orders of the day. Looking forward directs us to the promises of God in the covenant, so as to provide hope in uncertain times.

A covenant, as the child's catechism puts it, is "an agreement between two or more persons." It is an agreement initiated by God. This covenant, or agreement, is one where the Lord is always faithful. He can do no other. He would not be God if He were anything less than faithful to His promises. The people of God are called to be faithful to their promises to God, but they are not always faithful. The covenant, therefore, has "blessings and curses" to show what will occur with obedience and what will happen with disobedience.

Deuteronomy 28 is a remarkable chapter that describes the conditions of the covenant, with blessings for obedience and curses for disobedience. In the light of the covenant and all the opportunities lying ahead for the nation of Israel, Moses challenged them to make a choice:

> *Now choose life, so that you and your children may live and that you may love the Lord your*
> *God, listen to His voice, and hold fast to Him. For the Lord is your life, and He will give you*
> *many years in the land He swore to give to your fathers, Abraham, Isaac and Jacob.*
> *Deuteronomy 30:19, 20*

Then the last events in the life of Moses are given in rapid-fire fashion:

- Chapter 32 – Moses' song of praise. Moses is faithful in his understanding that the Lord deserved all the praise for His deliverance of Israel. Moses never placed himself in the place of the Lord.

- Chapter 33 – Moses' blessings on Israel. Moses occupied a place of leadership that Israel needed and would miss. Even though Moses had been preparing Israel for the day when they would go into the Promised Land under Joshua's leadership, Moses knew that his blessing on them was important.

- Chapter 34 – Moses' death and burial. Moses' death is shrouded in mystery, but his care at the end is not in doubt. God took care of him in a personal and powerful way. Moses' end was like that of Elijah, so Moses would be remembered and revered for generations to come.

Lessons From Deuteronomy

1. God's faithfulness in the past is sure, so we need to trust. Our faith is not in a God who is apathetic or inactive. Our God has been moving and working in all of history and in all our lives. We are to trust in the One who is always faithful.

2. God's love in the present is sure, so we need to obey. Our call now is to obey the God who loves us. We respond to God's love by loving Him in obedience. Being confident of His care gives us the courage and strength to say "Yes" to Him.

3. God's promises for the future are sure, so we need to hope. In order to face an uncertain future, especially with the experience of a painful present, we need to know that our God is in control. We are confident because of His covenant.

Notes

Chapter Six: Joshua

Assignment

READ ...

Joshua, Chapters 1-44, or selected chapters from Joshua (one a day for a week) as follows:

Joshua 1 – The Lord calls Joshua to follow Moses.

Joshua 3 – Crossing the Jordan River.

Joshua 6 – The fall of Jericho.

Joshua 7 – The sin of Achan.

Joshua 10 – The Sun stands still.

Joshua 23 – Joshua's farewell address.

Joshua 24 – The covenant renewed.

MEMORIZE ...

Joshua 1:9 – "Have I not commanded you? Be strong and courageous. Do not be terrified; do not be discouraged, for the Lord your God will be with you wherever you go;"

and/or

Joshua 23:10 – "One of you routs a thousand, because the Lord your God fights for you, just as He promised."

and/or

Joshua 24:14, 15 – "Now fear the Lord and serve Him with all faithfulness. ... But if serving the Lord seems undesirable to you, then choose for yourselves this day whom you will serve. ... But as for me and my household, we will serve the Lord."

PRAY ...

Confessing to the Lord the greatest fear in your life right now, then asking for His strength and courage to face that fear.

Thanking the Lord for all the victories He has given you in your life, whether in body, finances, relationships, family, church, etc.

Searching your own life to see if there is any sin that is a pitfall for your good or the witness of the Church.

Recommitting yourself and your family to the Lord. Recognize that your serving the Lord is the greatest commitment of your life.

APPLY ...

In the light of Joshua, what are you to:

BELIEVE about God?

REPENT of as sin?

OBEY as a command from God?

SHARE ...

According to what you have learned from Joshua:

- Read Joshua 24:14, 15 and talk within your family about what it means for your house to serve the Lord. What would be some of the unique distinctives for your family if you served the Lord together?

- Joshua is told in 1:9, "Do not be afraid," and then he challenges Israel in 24:14 to "fear the LORD." Take a risk and ask someone who is not very religious to help you understand this.

Joshua:
Fulfillment of a Promise

INTRODUCTION

Anybody can make a promise. Only God can make a promise and also fulfill that promise. God is always faithful to His promises, and the nation of Israel was on the verge of finding out about the fulfillment of a promise.

The children of Israel had been delivered out of slavery in Egypt (Exodus) and were called to be holy, just as the Lord is holy (Leviticus). They rebelled against the Lord and were judged by wandering in the wilderness for 40 years (Numbers). They arrived at the borders of the Promised Land and were instructed again by Moses to be the covenant people of God (Deuteronomy).

But now Moses is dead, and the Promised Land had to be taken.

The new generation of Israelites was about to receive new leadership in Joshua. The people also were about to witness the fulfillment of the promise of God. This promise had started with Abraham, was lost in Egypt for 350 years, but now was about to become reality.

TITLE

In Numbers 13:8 and 16, Joshua's name was Hoshea, meaning "salvation," but it was changed by Moses to Joshua, meaning "Yahweh is salvation." Joshua's name in Hebrew meant the very same as the name of Jesus in Greek: "The Lord is salvation."

THEME VERSE

Be strong and courageous, because you will lead these people to inherit
the land I swore to their forefathers to give them.
Joshua 1:6

These were the words from the Lord to Joshua after Moses died. Joshua now had the leadership of Israel on his shoulders. He had seen Moses in that role time and time again, but Moses was gone. Joshua needed to know that just as the Lord had been with Moses, He now would be with him.

Moses had a unique relationship with Joshua. A mentoring relationship had developed, and Joshua had been prepared to take Moses' place. Here are some passages revealing the preparation of Joshua to lead Israel:

- Exodus 17:8-13 – Before Mount Sinai and the receiving of the Law, Joshua was a military leader, and Moses was the national leader.

- Exodus 24:12 – While Moses was on Mount Sinai receiving the Law from the Lord, Joshua was his servant, serving like an apprentice.

- Exodus 33:11 – Joshua was close to Moses, who was close to God.

- Numbers 13:8 – Joshua was one of the 12 spies to report about going into the Promised Land.

- Numbers 14:30 – Joshua and Caleb were the only two of the 12 spies who wanted to go ahead and conquer the land, even though it was inhabited by giants.

- Numbers 27:18-23 – Joshua received a commissioning from Moses.

- Deuteronomy 1:38; 3:28 – Moses had the task of encouraging and strengthening Joshua.

- Deuteronomy 31:1-8 – Moses gave a charge to Joshua before all Israel.

- Deuteronomy 34 – Moses died.

- Joshua 1:1-9 – Joshua is encouraged directly by God. Before this, no word from the Lord came directly to Joshua, only through Moses. But now Moses was dead.

Joshua was one of the few men of the Bible about whom there is no recorded sin. That doesn't mean he didn't sin, but that he was an exceptional leader.

I. CONQUEST (1 – 12)

Mobilization (1, 2): Israel is mobilized for the conquest of the Promised Land. The leadership was satisfied with Joshua being called by the Lord and was encouraged with those words that are so inspiring:

Be strong and courageous. Do not be terrified, do not be discouraged, for the Lord your God will be with you wherever you go.

Not only was the leadership established and encouraged, but also a strategy was employed. Once again, spies were sent out, but this time only two. They receive unexpected help from the harlot Rahab in Jericho. Notice, in Matthew 1:5, the genealogy of Jesus, Rahab is in the line of the Messiah. She was the great-grandmother of David.

The report of the spies was very different from the report of those at Kadesh Barnea. Joshua 2:24:

The Lord has surely given the whole land into our hands, all the people are melting in fear because of us.

Forward March! (3 – 5): With a new leader and a new strategy, Israel is ready to march forward and take the land.

The crossing of the Jordan River in chapters 3 and 4 gives a repeat miracle like the crossing of the Red Sea, as the people cross the Jordan River on dry ground. A memorial is set up so that the people would never forget what the Lord had done.

Two activities in chapter 5 show the nation of Israel's dependence on the Lord:

- The men were to be circumcised, because the new generation that had been raised in the desert had not been circumcised.

- Passover was observed.

The people of the covenant observed two "sacraments" connected with the call and command of God. We understand circumcision to be the Old Testament shadow of baptism and Passover to be the same for Communion.

Then, an episode occurs that demonstrates this whole thing is not just about Joshua and Israel. It has to do with God. The commander of the army of the Lord appears. Who is this? Is it a theophany (an appearance of the Lord) or is it angelic (a messenger from the Lord)? It is more than likely a theophany, because it parallels the burning bush experience, with the same command given to Joshua as it had been to Moses:

Take off your sandals, for the place where you are standing is holy.

Fall of Jericho (6): Joshua probably had his own plan about how to take Jericho, but the Lord also had one, and it was shocking. March around the city seven times and, the seventh time, blow the trumpets.

As the plan of God is executed by Joshua and Israel, they experience the victory from the Lord (6:20) – "the wall collapsed" (New International Version) or "the wall fell flat" (King James Version). What power and might! What is a wall to God? Nothing is impossible for God.

The Central Campaign (7, 8): Something surprising occurred. In their attack on Ai, they are overconfident and are defeated. Joshua struggles with the Lord over the defeat.

And Joshua said, "Ah, Sovereign Lord, why did you ever bring this people across the Jordan to deliver us into the hands of the Amorites to destroy us? If only we had been content to stay on the other side of the Jordan!" (7:7).

But the Lord reveals that there is a problem. There had been a sin in Israel. They discovered that a man named Achan had sinned by keeping some of the booty of Jericho for himself and his family. After Achan is judged for this sin, Israel attacks Ai again (8) and this time there is victory.

The Gibeonite Deception (9): A con job is played on Joshua and Israel by one of the Canaanite tribes. Pretending that they had traveled a long distance, they said they had heard of the favor of God on Israel, so they came to offer themselves as servants. Chapter 9:14 gives an insight into what went wrong here: "The men of Israel sampled their provisions but did not inquire of the Lord." They made a treaty with them, even though they had been deceived. When the truth came out, Joshua remained faithful to his promise to them even though it had been coerced, and the Gibeonites were made servants to Israel.

The Southern Campaign (10): A battle breaks out against a coalition of five Amorite kings coming together to combat Israel's advance. In this struggle, there is demonstration of the Lord's power and might that is unique and awe-inspiring.

The sun stopped in the middle of the sky and delayed going down about a full day. There has never been a day like it before or since – a day when the Lord listened to a man. Surely the Lord was fighting for Israel! (9:13b, 14).

The Northern Campaign (11): The victories from the Lord continue. A summary of the conquest is succinctly given in 11:23 – "So Joshua took the entire land, just as the Lord had directed Moses, and He gave it as an inheritance to Israel according to their tribal divisions. Then the land had rest from war." Chapter 12 gives a list of all the defeated kings of Canaan.

II. SETTLEMENT (13-24)

The conquered land is settled among the 12 tribes of Israel. There is so much detail in Chapters 13-22 that the overall view is lost: The Lord fulfilled His promise to Israel. The Israelites now possessed the Promised Land. They were in possession of the promise.

Notice that Caleb gets his inheritance. His words (14:10-12) tell it all:

Now then, just as the Lord promised, He has kept me alive for forty-five years since the time He said this to Moses, while Israel moved about in the desert. So here I am today, eighty-five years old! I am still as strong today as the day Moses sent me out; I'm just as vigorous to go out to battle now as I was then. Now give me this hill country that the Lord promised me that day.

Joshua's Farewell in Chapters 23 and 24 is inspirational. In Chapter 23, he gives his farewell to all the leaders of Israel, sounding a lot like Moses in Deuteronomy, as he tells Israel things like:

Page 42   The Journey

It was the Lord your God who fought for you (23:3).

Be very strong; be careful to obey all that is written in the Book of the Law of Moses (23:6).

Hold fast to the Lord your God, as you have until now (23:8).

So be very careful to love the Lord your God (23:11).

If you violate the covenant of the Lord your God, which He commanded you, and go and serve other gods and bow down to them, the Lord's anger will burn against you, and you will quickly perish from the good land He has given you (23:16).

Joshua then gathers all of Israel together at Shechem (24) and delivers as inspirational a message as there is in all of Scripture. The highlight comes in verses 14 and 15:

Now fear the Lord and serve Him with all faithfulness. Throw away the gods your forefathers worshiped beyond the River and in Egypt, and serve the Lord. But if serving the Lord seems undesirable to you, then choose for yourselves this day whom you will serve, whether the gods your forefathers served beyond the River, or the gods of the Amorites, in whose land you are living. But as for me and my household, we will serve the Lord.

Joshua dramatically declares the Lord's fulfillment of His promise of bringing Israel to a land flowing with milk and honey. What happened along the way, however, was that as leader, Joshua, who started out in the shadow of Moses needing encouragement ("Be strong and courageous"), ended up making his own mark and encouraging the people ("But as for me and my household, we will serve the Lord").

Lessons From Joshua

1. God calls leaders who need His strength and encouragement. Whenever God calls a person to lead His people, that person is never equipped on his own. He is in need of God's grace to lead. God gave it to Moses, and He gave it to Joshua. Leaders are not called by God because they are adequate and talented. They are called to lead, dependent upon God's grace.

2. God fulfills His promises to His people. God had promised Israel a land flowing with milk and honey – the Promised Land. It took 40 years of wandering in the wilderness, but God kept His promise: He brought Israel into Canaan.

Notes

Chapter Seven: Judges and Ruth

Assignment

Read ...

Judges, Chapters 1-21, and Ruth Chapters 1-4 or selected chapters from Judges and Ruth (one a day for a week) as follows:

Judges 2	–	The covenant pattern in Judges.
Judges 4	–	The story of Deborah.
Judges 6, 7	–	The story of Gideon.
Judges 13	–	The birth of Samson.
Judges 16	–	Samson and Delilah.
Ruth 1	–	Naomi and Ruth.
Ruth 4	–	Ruth marries Boaz

Memorize ...

Judges 21:25 – "In those days there was no king in Israel: every man did that which was right in his own eyes" (King James Version).

and/or

Ruth 1:16 – "Where you go I will go, and where you stay I will stay. Your people will be my people and your God my God."

Pray ...

Thanking the Lord for the many ways in which He has delivered you from your own foolishness and sins.

Thanking the Lord for the one particular person He has used in your life to help you during a very difficult time.

Offering yourself to the Lord to help in the lives of others who might be in great distress or trouble.

Thanking the Lord for those special relationships that nourish and strengthen you.

Recommitting yourself to your husband or wife, recognizing that it was the Lord who brought you together and who desires to bless you in your marriage.

APPLY ...

In the light of Judges and Ruth, what are you to:

> BELIEVE about God?

> REPENT of as sin?

> OBEY as a command from God?

SHARE ...

According to what you have learned from Judges and Ruth:

- In the light of the love story in Ruth, talk with your spouse about how you met and who the instrumental people were that the Lord used to bring you together. If you are not now married, talk to someone you consider a friend about how much he or she means to you.

- The people in the society during the time of Judges were described as "doing what was right in their own eyes." Ask someone who may not be active in a church what he thinks of that description and if he sees some parallels within America today.

Judges:
Recycled Misery

INTRODUCTION

Historians have calculated that the world's great civilizations have lasted an average of 200 years. Most of them started with bondage, experienced liberty, enjoyed abundance and prosperity, and then went through a downward spiral through selfishness and weakness to another time of bondage.

The old saying, "History always repeats itself," is not always right, but there is definitely a repeating cycle in Judges – and it is not a pleasant cycle.

Judges tells the stories of recycled misery for Israel.

TITLE

Judges is a Hebrew word that also could be translated "ruler," "deliverer" or "savior."

This is not your ordinary judge. This is not the kind of judge who sits in a courtroom with a jury to settle disputes or decide in criminal cases.

The "judge" in the Book of Judges is a person who had two functions:
1. Liberating from oppression.
2. Maintaining justice.

THEME VERSES

They forsook the Lord, the God of their fathers, who had brought them out of Egypt.
They followed and worshiped various gods of the peoples around them.
They provoked the Lord to anger.
Judges 2:12

In those days there was no king in Israel: every man did that which was right in his own eyes.
Judges 21:25 (King James Version)

I. DETERIORATION (1, 2)

Compromise (1): Compare Joshua 1:1 with Judges 1:1. They are both obituaries:
Joshua 1:1 – Moses died and Joshua took over.
Judges 1:1 – Joshua died and there is a question: Who will lead?

The task for all the tribes of Israel after the conquering of the land and the settlement in the land was to finish driving out the Canaanites, which the Lord commanded – but tribe after tribe did not do it. They compromised with the Canaanites who lived in the land and did not drive them out as the Lord had commanded.

Consequences (2:1-5): The angel of the Lord confronted them with the consequences of their compromises with the Canaanites. The Lord will not drive them out and the Canaanites will become "thorns in the sides" of the Israelites.

Cycle (2:6-23): After Joshua and his generation (2:10), another generation grew up that neither knew the Lord nor what He had done for Israel.

The deterioration in Judges did not happen overnight. It took place from one generation to another. Erosion is silent, but sure. Verses 2:11-19 give the cycle shown throughout Judges:

1. Sin.

2. Servitude.

3. Supplication.

4. Salvation.

5. Silence.

And then it starts all over again with sin.

II. DELIVERANCE (3 – 16)

Seven cycles of apostasy are described with the judges God that raised up. Four of the cycles had judges who are not generally known: Othniel (3:7-11); Ehud and Shamgar (3:12-31); Tola and Jair (8:33 – 10:5); and Jephthad (10:6 – 12:15).

Three judges, though, stand out during these cycles of misery. One was a prophetess, Deborah. Deborah is one of those women who steps out in faith and action when men are halting. She stands out as a godly, courageous woman in a time of danger.

Israel had been oppressed by an evil king named Sisera. They cried to the Lord and Deborah was provided. She called for Barak to help, and together they delivered Israel. But Israel did not learn its lesson, and it fell into idolatry again. A 40-year period of rest was followed by another bondage.

Another cycle in Judges gives the impact of Gideon. The oppressors this time were the Midianites, and the times were so terrible that the people hid in caves and in the mountains. The people prayed and Gideon was provided.

Gideon was a man who was not sure when he heard the Lord's call. He wanted signs and assurances. He is best known for "laying out a fleece" as a sign to know God's will (6:36-40). The victory in chapter 7 over the Midianites is legendary. He started with an army of 32,000 that was reduced to 10,000 and then reduced again to 300 – all so the Lord could teach them the lesson that He would bring them victory. The 300 carry out an ingenious plan, and the Midianites are defeated ... all to the glory of God, not Gideon.

The seventh and last cycle of misery given in Judges comes after the common description of their sin: "Israel did evil again in the sight of the LORD" (13:1). This time the judge the Lord provides is a man appointed by God before his birth – even before his conception – and the oppressors were the Philistines.

The story of Samson is one replete with unfulfilled potential and missed opportunities. He is as tainted a man of God as we have in the whole of Scripture, marked by physical strength, an enormous ego and a flaming sexual appetite. Samson stands alone in great victories over the Philistines, almost like a Superman, but all it takes is an unfaithful Lois Lane – Delilah – to betray him. He is weakened, blinded and put into shackles, but the day would come – even when the Philistines were worshiping their god and celebrating their victory over Samson – that Samson prayed, the Lord restored his strength, and he brought down the Philistine temple. The text simply states: "... he killed many more when he died than while he lived."

III. DEPRAVITY (17 – 21) APPENDIX

This is the R-rated section of the Bible – rated R for sex and violence. It is one of the lowest levels of sin found in the Bible and has two identical verses that serve as bookends:

In those days Israel had no king; everyone did what was right in his own eyes (17:6; 21:25).

Religious Apostasy (17 – 18)

This story of a man named Micah (not the prophet Micah) is one of money, idolatry and the corruption of a Levite that led to religious apostasy. Then, this religious apostasy affects the tribe of Dan to the extent that they give up their inheritance to migrate to another area.

The details are confusing and disturbing, but they tell the truth of what happens when people do what is right in their own eyes. True worship, prayer and a Word from the Lord are all absent from this episode.

Moral Depravity (19 – 21)

These chapters tell the story of a Levite and his concubine, which led to a nightmare of sexual abuse, homosexuality, murder, revenge, graphic violence and awful shock. It speaks of the wicked men of Gibeah, who are portrayed as being as wicked as Sodom and Gomorrah, but they aren't remembered that way. The prophet Hosea does remember, however, as he speaks of the "days of Gibeah" in his prophecy (Hosea 9:9; 10:9).

The rest of Israel was called to rise up against Gibeah and the people did, except for the tribe of Benjamin, which sided with Gibeah because it was a Benjaminite town. This also led to the annihilation of the tribe of Benjamin.

These are snapshots of the evil in the land that started with the evil in hearts. The people did what was "right in their own eyes," but the Lord's evaluation was that it was "evil in the sight of the Lord."

Ruth:
A Love Story

Ruth, whose name means "friendship," is the main character of this love story. She dominates this book, but is never mentioned anywhere else in the Bible except in the genealogy of Jesus in Matthew 1:5 as the grandmother of David.

Ruth is like a meteor that flashed across the dark sky – brilliant for a moment, but then gone. She is one of those least-known saints of the Bible who stands out in simple godliness and goodness.

Ruth 1:1 makes it clear that this story takes place during the period of Judges. Judges was a time of immorality and idolatry and anarchy – when there was no king and everyone did what was right in his own eyes.

THEME VERSE

But Ruth replied, "Don't urge me to leave you or to turn back from you. Where you go I will go, and where you stay I will stay. Your people will be my people and your God my God."
Ruth 1:16, 17

I. RIGHT REACTION TO LOSS (1)

The time of the Judges was bad enough with its loss of morality, freedom and true religion. Add to that a famine – a natural disaster that produced an economic loss and tragic deaths in the family, and you have one of the worst situations possible.

In such a terrible time, the focus is placed on one family "from Bethlehem (house of bread) in Judah." Elimelech is the father and Naomi is the mother. They have two sons: Mahlon and Kilion.

The whole family moves to Moab to escape the famine. While there, Elimelech, the head of the family, dies and Naomi is left a widow with two sons. The sons marry Moabite women – Orpah and Ruth – and good Jewish boys just did not marry Moabite women.

Ten years pass. Both sons die, and suddenly this family is without men – a house filled with widows. Things get worse for the women. A famine comes to the land. The famine ends, and Naomi decides to go back home to Judah. She gives her daughters-in-law encouragement to stay in their homeland and find new husbands. Both of them refuse, and Naomi insists. Orpah leaves, but Ruth stays – stating her resolve and commitment in the theme verse (1:16, 17).

But Ruth replied, "Don't urge me to leave you or to turn back from you. Where you go I will go, and where you stay I will stay. Your people will be my people and your God my God."

Naomi and Ruth return to Bethlehem and Naomi expresses her grief and questions to God. Naomi means "pleasant," but she felt anything but pleasant. She is honest and God-centered in her grief. There is no sin in her deep sorrow.

II. RIGHT RESPONSE TO LONELINESS (2)

Ruth was a Gentile in a Jewish world … a foreigner in a strange land.

But Ruth knew that life had to go on. So she became a "gleaner," someone who picked up leftover grain from a harvested field. Gleaning was the closest thing to welfare in Israel. Owners of fields were required by law to leave some of the harvest in the field for the poor to "glean" in order to feed themselves.

Ruth gleans in the field owned by Boaz, who turns out to be a relative of Naomi's. Boaz notices her and wants to know, "Whose young woman is that?" Boaz promises to protect Ruth from his workers. He shows favor to her, especially when he hears her story and sees her faithfulness.

Naomi learns in whose field Ruth had been gleaning. She is surprised and pleased and sees the Lord's hand in it. She calls Boaz not only a relative, but also a "kinsman-redeemer."

A kinsman-redeemer was the closest relative of a widow, and he had greater responsibility to care for the property and wife of the dead relative. One of the responsibilities of the kinsman-redeemer was to marry the widow.

III. RIGHT ATTITUDE TOWARD COURTSHIP (3)

Naomi teaches Ruth about the customs of courtship. The details may seem strange to us, but there are some good and godly principles of courtship:

Available, but careful (3:1-7).

Responsive, but pure (3:8, 9).

Interested, but patient (3:10ff).

The relationship between Boaz and Ruth developed, but they were patient enough to touch every base. The closer relative was a possible barrier.

IV. RIGHT APPROACH TO MARRIAGE (4)

Verses 4:1-12 – Boaz deals with the problem of the closer relative having "rights" to Ruth. He does not scheme. He doesn't fight for her. He just seeks to do what is right. The other kinsman relinquished his "rights" so Boaz could marry Ruth.

They marry and have a son, Obed, who has a son, Jesse, who has a son, David.

The Books of Judges and Ruth give the low and high points in this period of Israel's history. Even when things are at their worst, God calls His people to stand and be faithful.

Lessons From Judges and Ruth

1. When people do what is right in their own eyes, they hurt themselves and others. The message of Judges is this cycle of misery that was experienced because there was no king, and everyone did what they wanted to do. The result was devastating.

2. When people do what is right in God's eyes, they help themselves and others. The message of Ruth is a love story showing that when a woman does what is good, she becomes a blessing to the generations that follow her.

NOTES

CHAPTER EIGHT: I SAMUEL

Assignment

READ ...

I Samuel, Chapters 1-31, or selected chapters from I Samuel (one a day for a week) as follows:

> I Samuel 1   –   The birth of Samuel.
>
> I Samuel 3   –   The call of Samuel.
>
> I Samuel 10   –   Saul anointed as king.
>
> I Samuel 15   –   The Lord rejects Saul as king.
>
> I Samuel 16   –   David anointed as king.
>
> I Samuel 17   –   David and Goliath.
>
> I Samuel 18   –   Saul's jealousy of David.

MEMORIZE ...

I Samuel 16:7 – "The LORD does not look at the things man looks at. Man looks at the outward appearance, but the LORD looks at the heart;"

and/or

I Samuel 17:47 – "All those gathered here will know that it is not by sword or spear that the LORD saves; for the battle is the LORD's, and He will give all of you into our hands."

PRAY ...

Interceding for the president and all of our government officials, realizing that the Lord has established governments.

Asking the Lord to change you from the inside out. Do not settle for appearances only. Pray for a heart like God's.

For your enemies and those who seek to harm you.

For the faith to realize that the struggles you have against wickedness are won not by your own strength or wisdom, but by the Lord. "The battle is the Lord's."

APPLY ...

In the light of I Samuel, what are you to:

>BELIEVE about God?

>REPENT of as sin?

>OBEY as a command from God?

SHARE ...

According to what you have learned from I Samuel:

- God called one woman, Hannah, to have one son, Samuel, who would lead Israel into a new era of the Lord's grace and glory. Realize what the Lord can do with little beginnings. Talk with your family or friends about how He might take you and others who do not yet have much to offer to God's Kingdom and use you for an advancement of the Gospel right where He has placed you.

- Ask someone you know who is turned off by the Church if he or she thinks that those in the Church live for the appearance of being good people. If the way is clear, then share with this person God's perspective of looking on the heart.

I Samuel:
A New Beginning

INTRODUCTION

The dark period of Judges was continuing. A refrain throughout Judges was, "And there was no king in Israel." The people lived by this rule: "Every man did what was right in his own eyes."

There was a need for change in Israel. There was a need for a new beginning. Israel was self-destructing from the inside with corruption, idolatry and immorality. The end of Judges is marked by Israelites destroying Israelites, in particular the tribes of Dan and Benjamin. If something dramatic did not happen, the future of Israel was in doubt. I Samuel is about that new beginning.

The main change that was needed, of course, was to follow the Lord as their King – not to do what was right in their own eyes, but to do what was right in His eyes. Israel, though, was not of the mind to do that.

So God is about to do a new thing in leading Israel. He is going to give them what they wanted – a king. I Samuel presents this new beginning, starting with a woman (Hannah) and a baby (Samuel), and ending it with one king (David) replacing another (Saul).

TITLE

"I and II Samuel" are named for the man, Samuel, who was used by God to establish kingship over Israel. He was the last judge of Israel and he anointed the first two kings, Saul and David. Samuel is God's man for this time.

In the Hebrew Bible, I and II Samuel were one book, not two.

THEME VERSE

> *But the LORD said to Samuel, "Do not consider his appearance or his height,*
> *for I have rejected him. The LORD does not look at the things man looks at.*
> *Man looks at the outward appearance, but the LORD looks at the heart."*
> *I Samuel 16:7*

I. SAMUEL (1 – 8)

Birth and Call of Samuel (1 – 3)

In chapter 1, God does what He often does – He has a new beginning with a birth and a focus on one family. A godly woman, Hannah (which means "grace"), is the object of God's grace as she seeks the Lord's blessing to enable her to have a child. She makes a special vow to God, asking if He would give her a son, and He does. Samuel (which means "heard by God" – you could say "answered prayer") is born and she dramatically dedicates Samuel to the Lord. Hannah's heart is filled with praise, which is shown in a powerful prayer in chapter 2. Samuel grows up in the temple. You would think that would be heavenly, but it was not. Eli, the priest, had sons who were wicked.

> *Now Eli, who was very old, heard about everything his sons were doing to all Israel and how they slept with the women who served at the entrance to the Tent of Meeting (2:22).*

But Eli failed to restrain them (3:13), so God was about to judge Eli and his sons.

In spite of this bad environment, Samuel walks with God, and his call, even as a little boy (3), is powerful and unique.

Defeat and Victory (4 – 7)

The cycle of Judges occurs when Israel sins, is put into slavery by an enemy – this time the Philistines – then cries out to God. Israel makes supplication for deliverance and God provides salvation – a deliverance – by way of another judge. This time it is Samuel, who is raised up by God to lead Israel, and he becomes the last judge before the line of kings begins.

Israel Wants a King (8)

Samuel fell prey to the same problem Eli had – disobedient sons. So the question of who would follow Samuel was answered by Israel with a desire to be like other nations: Israel wanted a king. Samuel is displeased with this request, but he took it to the Lord in prayer and the Lord said, "Let them have a king."

This is an intriguing twist, because it starts with the desire of Israel to be like other nations, and it obviously is an expression of rebellion against the Lord as their King – but the Lord allows it! Sometimes God will give us what we want, even when it is not the best for us.

We need, however, to be careful not to go too far and think that God was like Eli or Samuel in letting rebellious children get what they wanted. He did have a greater plan going on about kingship, the place of David, and the kingly expectations of the Messiah. The truth is that the Lord can even use our foolishness to accomplish His greater purposes.

II. SAUL (9 – 15)

The Selection of Saul (9 – 12)

One of the most enigmatic characters in the whole Bible is then introduced – Saul. If we had looked for a king, we would have been drawn to Saul. He was attractive and humble. Samuel anoints him as king; the Spirit of the Lord comes to him in power; the people accept him as king; he leads Israel in victory over an enemy; and Samuel gives a farewell speech. Everything seems fine.

The Rejection of Saul (13 – 15)

Saul, though, could not stand prosperity. In rapid succession, he commits three fatal mistakes:

- Chapter 13: Saul shows himself to be impatient and impulsive. Under the pressure of a Philistine attack, he disobeys the Lord and is rebuked by Samuel.

- Chapter 14: Saul shows himself to be unwise and overbearing. He makes a rash vow that his son Jonathan breaks out of innocence. Saul would have killed him, except for the intervention of his army.

- Chapter 15: Saul shows himself to be disobedient and arrogant. God commanded Saul to totally destroy the Amalekites, and Saul really thought he had done the job, until Samuel confronted him with his disobedience.
Saul then was rejected by God as the king because he had rejected the Lord.

III. Saul and David (16 – 31)

David in Saul's Court (16 – 19)

The Lord rejects Saul as king and sends Samuel out on a quest to find the next king. This is where we find our theme verse. Samuel, in his search for the next king, was led to the house of Jesse, and the elder sons looked like king material to Samuel, but they were not. The Lord had someone else in mind who would have a heart like His own.

Man looks at the outward appearance, but the Lord looks at the heart (16:7).

David is then anointed as the next king of Israel in a small family ceremony, but his reign does not begin immediately. There is still the matter of Saul.

I Samuel 17 might be one of the best known chapters in the Bible. It is the story of David and Goliath – and in it, David shows his faithfulness, courage and focus on the Lord getting all the honor and glory.

A pattern then begins that dominates I Samuel: Saul's jealousy of David. David begins to prosper and grow in popularity, and Saul becomes insecure and murderous.

David Flees From Saul (20 – 27)

David runs from Saul for 14 years. He has around him a band of mighty men who were discontented with Saul and committed to David, but they lived in caves and moved from place to place. It is during this time of danger and moving around that David wrote many of his Psalms. He was in great need of refuge and strength and a fortress, and David understood that the Lord was those things for him.

During this time, David also had several opportunities to kill Saul, but he refused to do so out of honor for Saul as the king and out of honor for God as the ultimate judge. The imprecatory Psalms (those that call for God to take care of one's enemies) sometimes are disturbing because they sound so bloodthirsty, but they are just the opposite. The "enemy" David was referring to in those Psalms was Saul. David had the opportunity to take matters into his own hands several times, but he refused because he trusted the Lord to take care of his enemies. He didn't have to do it, so it is just the opposite of being bloodthirsty.

Saul's Downfall and Death (28 – 31)

Saul then hits a downhill slide. He is fearful about his war with the Philistines, and he consults a witch, while he continues to hate David. David is successful in his battles against the enemies of Israel, but Saul is not. Saul's life ends in defeat, suicide and disgrace.

Lessons From I Samuel

1. Like Samuel, we can accomplish great things for God when the call of God is upon our lives.

2. Like Saul, we can be great in our own eyes, but if we fall into great sin we will have a great fall.

3. Like David, we can only be great if we have a heart for God.

NOTES

CHAPTER NINE: II SAMUEL

Assignment

READ ...

II Samuel, Chapters 1-24, or selected chapters from II Samuel (one a day for a week) as follows:

II Samuel 2	–	David anointed king.
II Samuel 6	–	The Ark brought to Jerusalem.
II Samuel 7	–	God's covenant with David.
II Samuel 11	–	David and Bathsheba.
II Samuel 12	–	Nathan confronts David.
II Samuel 18	–	Absalom's death.
II Samuel 22	–	David's Psalm of praise.

MEMORIZE ...

II Samuel 12:13 – "Then David said to Nathan, 'I have sinned against the LORD;'"

and/or

II Samuel 22:2, 3 – "The LORD is my rock, my fortress and my deliverer; my God is my rock, in whom I take refuge, my shield and the horn of my salvation. He is my stronghold, my refuge and my savior."

PRAY ...

Thanking the Lord for His call upon your life. Do not take any pleasure in the misfortune of others. Only be thankful for what the Lord has done for you.

For your enemies and those who seek to harm you.

Confessing the sin in your life that is not known by anyone else.

For your children that they might love one another and love the Lord.

Giving God all the glory for what has happened in your life, whether painful or pleasant.

APPLY ...

In the light of II Samuel, what are you to:

> BELIEVE about God?
>
> REPENT of as sin?
>
> OBEY as a command from God?

SHARE ...

According to what you have learned from II Samuel:

- David had all kinds of problems with his children. He even had one son, Absalom, who led a rebellion against his father. Talk with your family about how to handle situations when family members do not get along. How does the Lord want you to handle such situations?

- Talk with someone, whether he or she is in church or not, about something you learned from David. Maybe it was the way he treated those who sought to hurt him, or maybe it was his sexual sin, or maybe it was his struggles as king. But whatever you share, talk about having a heart for God and how that heart can stand any situation.

II Samuel:
The Ups and Downs of a King

INTRODUCTION

Life has its ups and downs. There are times of victory and defeat, joy and sorrow, pleasure and pain, sin and forgiveness. Life is not monotonous. With the ups and the downs, such things as defeat, sorrow, pain and sin do not have the final word, but they do occur, and they do hurt.

II Samuel is the story of David who was very familiar with the ups and downs of life. Even though he was a king, he was supremely a child of God and, as such, he experienced life like any child of God. He won victories for the Lord. He sinned against the Lord. He honored his friends and struggled with his family.

Yet in the ups and downs of his life, David was held by the grace of God.

THEME VERSE

And now, LORD God, keep forever the promise you have made concerning your servant and his house.
Do as you promised, so that your name will be great forever. Then men will say, "The LORD Almighty
is God over Israel!" And the house of your servant David will be established before you.
II Samuel 7:25, 26

II Samuel focuses on David as king of Israel. In the New Testament, there are 59 references to David – more than any other Old Testament character.

Yet, if we had been choosing a king, we probably would not have chosen David because we look on the outward appearance, and the Lord looks at the heart.

I. DAVID'S TRIUMPHS (1 – 10)

The first 10 chapters of II Samuel are as positive as any section of Scripture. They are uplifting and encouraging.

David's Reign Over a Divided Nation (1 – 4)

David begins his reign as king slowly and spiritually. He begins slowly by reigning over Judah, the Southern Kingdom, for seven years. Yes, there is conflict with the other tribes and with the remaining house of Saul, but there is no hurry. Slowly but surely the house of David increases and the house of Saul decreases.

David, though, also begins his reign as king spiritually. David inquires of the Lord about what to do, step by step. He was not always consistent in seeking the Lord's will, but whenever he got off track, he would return to His God.

David's Reign Over a United Nation (5 – 7)

David is made king over all of Israel, and he moves from Hebron to Jerusalem. David brings the Ark of the Covenant to Jerusalem – and Jerusalem would never be the same again. From this point on, Jerusalem is the epicenter of God's people and plan.

David desires to build a temple for the Lord. But the Lord speaks through Nathan, the prophet, that while David's throne would be established forever (the theme verse), the building of the temple would be left to David's offspring. That privilege will be Solomon's.

David's Reign Over an Expanding Nation (8 – 10)

David began to lead Israel from victory to victory. No enemy could stand before David, and the nation of Israel was growing into a powerhouse nation in the region. Chapters 8 and 10 are filled with battles and victories, but right in the middle of all this fighting (9) is a precious story of David's grace and mercy.

He desired to do something compassionate to anyone remaining from Saul's house, and one man is found – Mephibosheth. Mephibosheth is a pitiful cripple in exile, but David brought him to sit at his table so that he might show him respect and honor. This is one of those episodes in David's life when his being a man after God's own heart is evident.

II. David's Transgressions (11, 12)

Notice! The most vulnerable time in life is when we are successful, prosperous, popular and at ease. This was exactly David's station in life – and he sinned against the Lord.

Commitment of Sins (11)

Whenever we think of David and Bathsheba, we probably think only of one sin – adultery. The full account, however, includes a cover-up that led to the murder of Bathsheba's husband, Uriah.

Now, think about that. Adultery and murder committed by the man after God's own heart. It should be a warning about the struggle with sin and temptation in everyone. Remember I John 1:8:

If we claim to be without sin, we deceive ourselves and the truth is not in us.

Confrontation of Sins (12)

The grace of God to David is dramatically shown as the prophet Nathan confronts David with his sin. David demonstrates he is a man after God's own heart because, when he is confronted with his sin, he confesses his sin. No denial. No blame. No excuses. No rebellion. There are consequences for David's sins that are sobering reminders that the effects of some sins can continue even after one is forgiven.

Read Psalm 51. It is a penitential Psalm written by David on the occasion of his confession and repentance because of his sins with Bathsheba.

This marks a transition in the book of II Samuel. The first 10 chapters are triumphant and joyful as David builds the Kingdom of Israel. Then he is foolish and sensual, as he commits the dual sins of adultery and murder. The rest of II Samuel is a downhill slide into difficulty, as David experiences the consequences of sin.

III. David's Troubles (13 – 24)

David's triumphs now turn into tragedies – personal, family and national troubles. They begin to strike like lightning bolts.

Family Troubles (13 – 18)

It starts with family troubles. Chapter 13 tells the sorry tale of Amnon's incestuous rape of Tamar, his half-sister; and Absalom, Tamar's full brother, then kills Amnon. These were all sons and daughters of David.

Then Absalom leads a revolution against his father, and David has to flee Jerusalem. A civil war begins, and Absalom is murdered by David's general, Joab. David grieved over Absalom, his rebellious son, with such depth and pathos that it breaks your heart just to read it:

O my son Absalom! My son, my son Absalom! If only I had died instead of you – O Absalom, my son, my son!

National Troubles (19 – 24)

II Samuel ends with the last years of David's reign being marked by opposition, rebellion, famine and war – not happy times.

Chapters 22-24 give us David's last words and acts that include a Psalm of praise (chapter 22, the same as Psalm 18), a tribute to the "mighty men" who had stood beside him all along and the building of an altar to worship the Lord.

Lessons From II Samuel

David can teach us many things about being a person with a heart for God. Some of those most poignant lessons are:

1. We must leave things in God's hands. Whether it is dealing with an enemy or building a business, we are dependent on Him, and we are not to exclusively take matters into our own hands.

2. We must know that times of prosperity and ease are perilous. When we don't have to depend on God, we usually don't depend on Him. We easily can yield to temptation.

3. We must realize that our sins can affect others – our family and our community. We must know there is no such thing as a "secret sin" (because nothing is hidden from God) or a "victimless sin" (because our sins have consequences for us and others).

NOTES

NOTES

CHAPTER TEN: I KINGS

Assignment

READ ...

I Kings, Chapters 1-22, or selected chapters from I Kings (one a day for a week) as follows:

I Kings 2	–	David's charge to Solomon.
I Kings 3	–	Solomon asks for wisdom.
I Kings 8	–	Dedication of the temple.
I Kings 12	–	Beginning of the Divided Kingdom.
I Kings 18	–	Elijah on Mount Carmel.
I Kings 19	–	The Lord appears to Elijah.
I Kings 22	–	King Ahab and King Jehoshaphat.

MEMORIZE ...

I Kings 8:23 – "O LORD, God of Israel, there is no God like you in heaven above or on earth below – you who keep your covenant of love with your servants who continue wholeheartedly in your way;"

and/or

I Kings 18:39 – "When all the people saw this, they fell prostrate and cried, 'The LORD – He is God! The LORD – He is God!'"

PRAY ...

Asking the Lord to keep us faithful, generation after generation, so His Kingdom might come and His will be done.

Committing yourself to build the Kingdom of God now, like David and Solomon gave themselves to build the temple for God.

For the Lord to send His prophets to us today – men and women who are faithful to the Lord, like Elijah and Elisha.

For wisdom to face the unbelief and immorality of the people of God. Even though God's Kingdom is often divided, ask the Lord to keep your faith and obedience undivided.

APPLY ...

In the light of I Kings, what do you:

> BELIEVE about God?
>
> REPENT of as sin?
>
> OBEY as a command from God?

SHARE ...

According to what you have learned from I Kings:

- David and Solomon were focused on building the temple for the Lord. It was to be for the glory of God, and it was costly, difficult and beautiful. Talk to your family or someone in the Church about how such an effort for the temple compares to the same kind of effort for us today in the Church.

- Share the story of Elijah at Mount Carmel (I Kings 18) with someone who is not in a church. Most people today believe that one religious view is just as valuable as another. This will probably be the opinion of your friend. Challenge him or her to think about the truth that there is one Lord, one God.

I Kings:
From United to Divided

INTRODUCTION

I Kings begins with King David reigning over a united Israel. It ends with Israel fractured into a divided kingdom, with Israel in the north and Judah in the south. In between is the sad story of King Solomon building the temple for the Lord It ends with the tearing down of the Kingdom of the Lord. Solomon shifts from being the wisest man in the world to one of the most foolish. The end result is that Israel is broken apart.

In the midst of the division and degradation of Israel, God reveals Himself to be the God who keeps His covenant with His people and who sends His prophets. This is the story of I Kings.

THEME VERSE

> O LORD, God of Israel, there is no God like you in heaven above or on earth below – you who keep
> your covenant of love with your servants who continue wholeheartedly in your way.
> I Kings 8:23

I. THE UNITED KINGDOM – SOLOMON, THE LAST KING (1 – 12:24)

David is dying, and there is tension in the family over who will be king, but David exercises his influence so that Solomon, his son by Bathsheba, will be the next king of Israel.

Solomon is a young king at 20 years old. He receives a final charge from David before David dies, and Solomon has the weight on his shoulders of ruling the kingdom. It did not take long before Solomon got his first test when the Lord offered, "Ask for whatever you want me to give you." Solomon asked for "a discerning heart" or wisdom, and this pleased the Lord.

Solomon then sets his wisdom and wealth in the direction of building the temple that his father wanted to build. A high point in I Kings occurs in chapter 8, when the temple is dedicated, and Solomon prays a model prayer of dedication. I Kings 8:66 describes the impact on all Israel:

> On the following day (after the dedication) he (Solomon) sent the people away. They blessed the
> king and then went home, joyful and glad in heart for all the good things the LORD had done for
> His servant David and His people Israel.

It was at the dedication of the temple, after Solomon's prayer, that the Lord appeared to Solomon and renewed the covenantal promises of God. As it is recorded in II Chronicles 7:14:

> If my people, who are called by my name, will humble themselves and pray and seek my face

and turn from their wicked ways, then will I hear from heaven and will forgive their sin and will heal their land.

This is the very highest point of Israel's national existence. Her spiritual life is healthy. Prosperity is high. The expanse of the kingdom is far beyond her boundaries, shown by the visit of the Queen of Sheba. Verses 10:23, 24 put it plainly:

King Solomon was greater in riches and wisdom than all the other kings of the earth. The whole world sought audience with Solomon to hear the wisdom God had put in his heart.

It was not, however, to stay this way. I Kings 11 parallels II Samuel 11. In II Samuel 11, we saw David, who was at the peak of his power, have his lapse with Bathsheba. Solomon did the same thing in I Kings 11:

Verse 1: "King Solomon, however, loved many foreign women. ..."

Verse 4: "As Solomon grew old, his wives turned his heart after other gods, and his heart was not fully devoted to the Lord his God, as the heart of David his father had been."

Solomon's adversaries grew, and many of them were within his own kingdom.

II. The Divided Kingdom – The First Phase (12:25 – 16)

What then happened was the ending of 120 years of a united kingdom (40 years with Saul, 40 years with David and 40 years with Solomon) and the beginning of a 300-year period of a divided kingdom.

After Solomon dies, his son, Rehoboam, takes the throne. Jeroboam, who had opposed Solomon at the end of his reign, sets up shrines in other cities, so that the people do not have to go to the temple in Jerusalem, and the pattern of idolatry in the Northern Kingdom (Israel) is established. A refrain often repeated for the evil kings of Israel states that, "He did not turn away from the sins of Jeroboam."

A civil war begins. North against South, Israel against Judah, ten tribes against two tribes, Samaria (city) against Jerusalem (city).

III. The Ministries of Elijah and Elisha (17 – 22)

In the midst of such a terrible time, the Lord shows His mercy and grace by sending His prophets. Most of the prophets we know from the Old Testament, especially the writing prophets (Major Prophets and Minor Prophets), ministered during this time of the divided kingdom.

The ministries of two non-writing prophets, however, stand out in I and II Kings. Elijah and Elisha are powerful men of God sent to the people of God, even in their most evil times.

Elijah is like a bolt of lightning across the sky. His name means "The Lord is my God," and that was his main message. When he confronted the prophets of Baal at Mount Carmel, it was to dramatically show that "the Lord is God." Elijah confronted the most wicked pair – Ahab and Jezebel – during the divided kingdom, and he was not immune to times of despondency, even after great victories. When Elijah was at his lowest point, the Lord made it clear that Elijah was not the only faithful one. "Yet I reserve seven thousand in Israel – all whose knees have not bowed down to Baal and all whose mouths have not kissed him" (19:18). It was immediately after this that Elisha comes onto the scene.

I Kings ends with a focus on King Ahab of Israel and King Jehoshaphat of Judah. King Ahab, along with his queen, Jezebel, led Israel in idolatry and the proliferation of false prophets. In one dramatic episode in chapter 22, King Jehoshaphat asked King Ahab to go to battle with him against Ramoth Gilead. Jehoshaphat had one request: "First seek the counsel of the Lord." Ahab consulted with his prophets of Baal (400 of them) and they all encouraged him to go ahead, because the Lord was with him. But Jehoshaphat was not satisfied. He asked if there was not one prophet of the Lord of which to inquire. Ahab said there was Micaiah, however he "never prophesies anything good about me, but always bad" (22:8).

Micaiah prophesied that Israel would be defeated, and still Ahab entered the battle, but in disguise. He is struck by a random arrow and dies, and the prophecy of Micaiah came true.

Lessons From I Kings

1. There is great blessing in following the Lord. David's life ended filled with blessing and prosperity. The Lord allowed him to live long enough to see his son, Solomon, become king and to make preparations for the building of the temple. Faithfully following the Lord will lead us to embrace the promises of the covenant.

2. There is great responsibility in following the Lord. Solomon was given a great task in building the temple. The construction was costly and the labor was long, but God called Solomon to do it. The Lord provided all that was necessary for Solomon to carry out His call.

3. There is great cost in not following the Lord. With Solomon's unfaithfulness and the divided nation turning after other gods, Israel suffered greatly. Not only was the nation no longer united, idolatry and immorality became a way of life, as they did what was evil in the sight of the Lord.

4. There is great hope in the Lord. Even in the light of Israel's unfaithfulness, the Lord sent the prophets. The Lord of the covenant did not give up on His people, even though they had given up on Him. A word from the Lord was always available, waiting for the people to believe and repent again.

NOTES

Assignment

READ ...

II Kings, Chapters 1-25, or selected chapters from II Kings (one a day for a week) as follows:

II Kings 2   – Elijah passes his mantle to Elisha.

II Kings 4   – The ministry of Elisha.

II Kings 5   – The healing of Naaman.

II Kings 12 – Repairs to the temple by Joash.

II Kings 19 – Jerusalem is delivered while Hezekiah was king.

II Kings 23 – Renewal under Josiah.

II Kings 25 – The fall of Jerusalem.

MEMORIZE ...

II Kings 6:16 – "'Don't be afraid,' the prophet answered. 'Those who are with us are more than those who are with them;'"

and/or

II Kings 19:15, 16 – "And Hezekiah prayed to the LORD: 'O LORD, God of Israel, enthroned between the cherubim, you alone are God over all the kingdoms of the earth. You have made heaven and earth. Give ear. O LORD, and hear; open your eyes, O LORD, and see. ...'"

PRAY ...

Thanking the Lord for spiritual leaders like Elijah and Elisha.

Expecting the God of all miracles to show Himself with power and might like He did during the ministry of Elisha.

Examining your own heart to see if you have done what was evil in the sight of the Lord.

For the renewal of the Church like it occurred during the reign of Joash, Hezekiah and Josiah.

APPLY ...

In the light of II Kings, what do you:

> BELIEVE about God?
>
> REPENT of as sin?
>
> OBEY as a command from God?

SHARE ...

According to what you have learned from II Kings:

- With your family, read II Kings 22 and 23. There a renewal took place under King Josiah. Talk about the elements of that renewal and what needs to take place today for the Church to be renewed.

- One of the greatest barriers for people coming to the Church is that they think it is judgmental toward them. Share with someone who thinks like this the truth of II Kings, that it is the people of God who are judged by their God. Judgment starts with the house of God.

II Kings:
Prophets and Kings

INTRODUCTION

God has always been about calling godly leaders for His people. That leadership could be in the form of a patriarch (Abraham) or a judge (Samuel); a priest (Aaron) or a military leader (Joshua); a prophet (Elisha) or a king (David). God would raise up His leaders from birth (Moses), from a family (Joseph) or from nowhere (Elijah). The standard was always high and the impact impressive.

Not all the leaders of Israel, though, were godly. Patriarchs schemed like Jacob. Judges could be sensual like Samson. Priests thought only of themselves, like the sons of Aaron and Eli. Kings built their personal wealth and comfort, like Solomon. Prophets proclaimed only what the people wanted to hear. Military leaders could become bloodthirsty.

Even though God called leaders, not all leaders were pleasing to Him.

This is the story of II Kings. Leaders are everywhere. Prophets and kings are paraded in II Kings. Page after page presents new men taking positions of leadership over Israel: prophets bringing messages to kings and the people, and kings leading the people in the affairs of state.

Not all of the prophets and kings, though, were godly. Some of the prophets were false and most of the kings "did what was evil in the sight of the Lord."

Godly leadership ... what does it look like? This is something about which II Kings provides instruction.

THEME VERSE

And Hezekiah prayed to the LORD: "O LORD, God of Israel, enthroned between the cherubim,
you alone are God over all the kingdoms of the earth. You have made heaven and earth.
Give ear, O LORD, and hear; open your eyes, O LORD, and see. ..."
II Kings 19:15, 16

I. THE MINISTRIES OF ELIJAH AND ELISHA (1 – 8:15)

Elisha succeeds Elijah. His name means "God is salvation." He is trained by Elijah and witnessed the unforgettable event when Elijah was taken into heaven by a chariot of fire and a whirlwind. Elisha's ministry lasted 50 years and was marked by some of the greatest miracles found in the Bible. Elisha was effective in his work with many kings and was crucial in stopping the Baal worship introduced by Jezebel.

Elijah and Elisha were a remarkable pair of prophets. Elijah was more severe and judgmental in his ministry, while Elisha was more tender and loving. They both, however, provided hope that the Lord was not giving up on His people when they rebelled against Him.

Yet Elijah represented a lasting hope for another prophet to come. Part of the messianic hope was for the prophet Elijah to return. He left in such a dramatic way that it was expected he would return one day in a similar fashion. The last words of Malachi spoke of the return of the Prophet Elijah, and the longing was still evident at the start of the New Testament, when John the Baptist was thought to be Elijah. The appearance of Elijah with Moses on the Mount of Transfiguration demonstrated that Elijah was a significant man of God from the Old Testament.

II. THE DIVIDED KINGDOM – THE SECOND PHASE (8:16, 17)

The decline of the two nations intensifies. Rebellion, idolatry, immorality and war are commonplace. It becomes the way of life for Israel and Judah, and they are both heading toward their downfall.

All 19 kings of Israel, the Northern Kingdom, were ungodly. Only eight out of 20 kings of Judah walked with God, and the rest did evil in the sight of the Lord.

It all ends with Israel being carried into captivity by Assyria, which had been forewarned by many a prophet. The Assyrians were cruel invaders who had built their kingdom by pillaging other countries and treating their captives horribly. The year was 722 B.C.

III. THE SOUTHERN KINGDOM – JUDAH (18 – 25)

The Southern Kingdom, Judah, continued to exist, even after their cousins in the north had been destroyed. But their end, even though delayed, was inevitable because they remained unfaithful to God.

There were periods of renewal called for by the prophets and led by kings.

Good King Hezekiah removed the high places (idolatrous worship) and sought to restore godly worship, but during his reign, Jerusalem was threatened. It was surrounded by the Assyrian army under the leadership of Sennacherib, and it looked like Judah was doomed. The Lord spoke through the Prophet Isaiah, however, and Hezekiah held true. The angel of the Lord fought for them, putting to death 185,000 Assyrians (19:35).

Another renewal occurred during the reign of King Josiah, who became king at the age of eight. When he was 26, the high priest found the Book of the Law in the temple and Josiah called for it to be read and followed. It was said of Josiah:

Neither before nor after Josiah was there a king like him who turned to the LORD as he did –
with all his heart and with all his soul and with all his strength, in accordance with all the Law
of Moses. (23:25)

The renewal, however, did not last. The kings who followed Josiah did what was evil in the sight of the Lord, and the doom was set.

The fall of Jerusalem depicted in the last chapter of II Kings is the most devastating event in the history of Israel in the Old Testament. It is hard to imagine the hurt and loss. Something that was unimaginable happened. King Nebuchadnezzar of Babylon set fire to the temple, tore down the walls and took into exile those who remained in the city.

II Chronicles 36:15-17 puts it this way:

The LORD, the God of their fathers, sent word to them through His messengers again and
again, because He had pity on His people and on His dwelling place. But they mocked God's
messengers, despised His words and scoffed at His prophets until the wrath of the LORD was
aroused against His people and there was no remedy. He brought up against them the king of
the Babylonians. ... God handed all of them over to Nebuchadnezzar.

Thus started the 70-year exile in Babylon.

Lessons From II Kings

1. God calls prophets to proclaim the Word of the Lord. If there is one activity that God is always working to accomplish with His people, it is the proclamation of His Word to them. This is so important, because we are so prone to listen to other words. Even when there might be prophets who preach for profit or pleasure, God will always provide true and faithful prophets, so that His Word will continue to go forth.

2. God calls leaders to lead His people. God has always been about calling leaders – today's pastors, elders and deacons – to give godly direction to His people. II Kings is a dramatic reminder that not all leaders of God's people will give holy guidance. When a leader knows the Lord and trusts the Lord, however, then his leadership will cause God's people to accomplish much in the Kingdom.

3. God calls His people to renewal. II Kings is a very dark time in the history of God's people. There was idolatry and immorality in every corner. The covenant God, however, remained faithful to His promises. He continued to call His people to come back. Times of renewal during the ministry of Elijah and Elisha and during the reigns of Joash, Hezekiah and Josiah all reflect the hope that the dark times we have do not have to last. The refreshment of renewal is always available. Prayer and God's Word, accompanied by faith and repentance, all lead to a return to the spiritual life in the midst of spiritual death.

NOTES

Chapter Twelve: I and II Chronicles

Assignment

Read ...

I Chronicles, Chapters 1-29, or II Chronicles 1-36, selected chapters from I and II Chronicles (one a day for a week) as follows:

I Chronicles 11 – David becomes ruler over Israel.

I Chronicles 16 – David's Psalm of thanks.

I Chronicles 22 – Preparations for the temple.

II Chronicles – Solomon asks for wisdom.

II Chronicles 5 – The Ark brought to the temple.

II Chronicles 7 – Dedication of the temple.

II Chronicles 34 – Josiah's reforms.

Memorize ...

I Chronicles 4:10 – "Jabez cried out to the God of Israel, 'Oh, that you would bless me and enlarge my territory! Let your hand be with me, and keep me from harm so that I will be free from pain.' And God granted his request;"

and/or

II Chronicles 7:14 – "If my people, who are called by my name, will humble themselves and pray and seek my face and turn from their wicked ways, then will I hear from heaven and will forgive their sin and will heal their land."

Pray ...

Asking the Lord for the wisdom to see His hand in history and the Church, and that He might come and His will be done.

Committing yourself to build the Kingdom of God now, like David and Solomon gave themselves to build the temple for God.

Examining your life to see if there is anything you are doing that is "evil in the sight of the LORD."

Through II Chronicles 7:14: Humble yourself, pray to God, seek His face and turn from your sins.

APPLY ...

In the light of I and II Chronicles, what do you:

> BELIEVE about God?
>
> REPENT of as sin?
>
> OBEY as a command from God?

SHARE ...

According to what you have learned from I and II Chronicles:

- Notice the place of genealogies in I and II Chronicles. This might be the most boring and misunderstood kind of literature in Scripture. Talk with your family about your family tree. Once they have given attention to their genealogy, see if the family appreciates more about who they are and what God has done for them. Then you will understand something of the value of genealogies in the Bible.

- Ask a friend, whether he or she is in the Church or not, if he has ever heard II Chronicles 7:14. If he has not, share it with him. If he has, then talk with him about its depth and meaning to yourself, your church and your nation.

I and II Chronicles:
God and History

INTRODUCTION

History is foundational to the Christian faith. Our God has worked in space, time and history, so the understanding of the past is crucial to learning about the involvement of our God in the affairs of men.

History, though, is not exciting to all of us. Names, places, dates, genealogies, victories and defeats can become a monotonous list of unrelated moments and details that are done and over. "What does it have to do with me?" is a constant and relevant question in our minds when confronted with history.

Yet, our God has recorded history as a part of His Word. It forms the background for psalms, poetry, prophecies and preaching. It demonstrates that life in the here and now is of prime concern to our God. He has worked in history and is working in our personal histories to redeem, reform and dispatch His people for the sake of His Kingdom.

I and II Chronicles provide the perfect harmony of God and history. History is not very pretty, but God remains faithful. History is filled with a mixture of good and evil, but God provides hope in each and every situation. History is like a roller coaster ride, but God guides us on the ever-upward climb into His presence.

There are two things going on all the time: What is happening and what God is doing. Those two things obviously are not harmonious most of the time. What is happening is like a play on opening night. On the stage, the characters, the plot, the setting and the glitz are clear to all. What is happening before, behind and beyond the scenes, however, is something else. There have been authors writing, promoters marketing, supporters fund-raising, sets being constructed, actors rehearsing and money being made. So much more is going on at that moment than the action on the stage.

That is how God is with history. We observe, record, comment about and reflect on historic events, but it is from a powerless position. We know nothing about causation, providence, significance, spirituality and eternity. That is what God is doing. Both God and history are revealed in I and II Chronicles.

I and II Chronicles probably were written after the return of the exiles to Jerusalem. With the task of reinstating the Law, reforming the people and rebuilding the temple, there was a need for the people to know who they were and where they came from.

I and II Chronicles provided religious history for them to understand the covenant made by the Lord with David and his descendants.

TITLES

In our English Bibles, we have two books: I and II Chronicles. In the Hebrew Bible, though, it is just one book: Chronicles. In the Hebrew Bible, Kings and Chronicles also do not follow one another, because

Chronicles is placed at the end of all the books of the Old Testament. Our English Bible places Malachi there.

This can be seen in Luke 11:51 when Jesus is describing how the prophets were killed in the Old Testament, saying, "… from the blood of Abel to the blood of Zechariah. …" In the Hebrew Bible, one is from Genesis and the other from II Chronicles. In other words, from the beginning to the end of the Old Testament, you have killed the prophets. "From the blood of Abel to the blood of Zechariah" was a way to say "from A to Z."

THEME VERSE

> *If my people, who are called by my name, will humble themselves and pray*
> *and seek my face and turn from their wicked ways, then will I hear*
> *from heaven and will forgive their sin and will heal their land.*
> *II Chronicles 7:14*

KINGS AND CHRONICLES

I and II Kings and I and II Chronicles predominantly cover the same material, but duplication in the Scripture is not needless repetition. Having four Gospel records is better than only having one.

With Kings and Chronicles, basically the same history is covered, but in three different ways:

1. Different Authors

It is not held by all scholars, but tradition holds that Jeremiah wrote Kings and Ezra wrote Chronicles – one a prophet and one a scribe; both having their own "books" in the Old Testament. As a result, just like the different authors of the four Gospels, you have different recollections, emphases, styles and sources.

2. Different Times

What is clear is that Kings was written before Chronicles – at least 70 years earlier. Kings was written when the events at the end of Kings and Chronicles took place, specifically from the fall of Jerusalem to the conquest of King Nebuchadnezzar in 586 B.C., when the shock of God's judgment was vivid and painful. Chronicles was written after the 70 years of exile in Babylon as the exiles were beginning to return to Jerusalem and the meaning of God's judgment was more in focus.

3. Different Purposes

Kings was written as the historical record to follow the history from II Samuel. There is an emphasis on what the kings and the prophets did. It covered both the Northern Kingdom (Israel) and the Southern Kingdom (Judah). Chronicles was written as a reminder of the covenant promises of God from Adam to Abraham to David to the fall of Jerusalem so that the returning exiles to Jerusalem might know their heritage. Chronicles emphasized what God was doing during this history, focusing primarily on the Southern Kingdom (Judah) and the continuation of the promises to David.

I CHRONICLES

1. Genealogies (1 – 9)

I Chronicles opens with list after list of genealogies. The family tree of David is presented, starting with creation and going through the patriarchs and the tribes, culminating with the line of David. There is also a priestly dimension to the genealogy, which highlights the tribe of Levi and the function of the temple.

Judah, the Southern Kingdom, rather than Israel, the Northern Kingdom, is dominant in the genealogies. The covenant promises of the Lord to David and the preservation of that line, along with the provision for the functioning of the temple, are God's perspectives from these "begat" lists.

2. David (10 – 29)

When this section of I Chronicles concerning David is compared with II Samuel, which is predominantly about David, there are some striking omissions and additions.

I Chronicles omits from the life of David his sin with Bathsheba, his struggles with Saul and Absalom's rebellion. There is a very positive perspective given to David's life, even in the light of his sin and struggles.

That is exactly where the Jews were at the time of the writing of I Chronicles. They had been judged for their sin and had struggled in exile for 70 years. Their sin was obvious. What they now needed as they returned to the Law was an understanding of God's grace and forgiveness that would sustain them in this new stage of their life together.

But I Chronicles also adds some details from the life of David that are not in II Samuel. The main additions are in his preparations for the building of the temple. David was not allowed by the Lord to be the one to actually build the temple, but that did not keep him from doing all he could to prepare the way for his son, Solomon, to be successful in its construction. David is described as making plans for the temple, gathering the necessary materials and arranging for the Levites and priests to be active in the worship. I Chronicles closes with the prayer by David for the temple, the ascension of Solomon to the throne and David's death.

II Chronicles

1. Solomon (1 – 9)

The high point in the history of Israel was the glorious period of Solomon's reign. Israel was at peace with all its neighbors and united as a nation. She was prosperous in every way and the reputation of Solomon's wealth and wisdom truly was worldwide. Above all, the temple was built. The construction and dedication of the temple dominates the first part of II Chronicles. Solomon's prayer of dedication in chapter 6 is inspirational:

O Lord, God of Israel, there is no God like you in heaven or on earth. ... You have kept your
promise to your servant David my father. ... But will God really dwell on earth with men? ...
May you hear the prayer your servant prays toward this place. ... When they sin against you
... then from heaven, your dwelling place, hear their prayer and their pleas, and uphold their
cause. And forgive your people, who have sinned against you. [selected verses]

The temple is dedicated and the glory of the Lord filled the it. All of the people worshiped and gave thanks to the Lord, saying, "He is good; His love endures forever."

After days of worship and celebration, the dedication was completed and the people were sent home:

On the twenty-third day of the seventh month he (Solomon) sent the people to their homes,
joyful and glad in heart for the good things the Lord had done for David and Solomon and for
His people Israel (7:10).

But then the Lord appeared to Solomon at night, and among the many things the Lord told him, one stands out:

If my people, who are called by my name, will humble themselves and pray and seek my face
and turn from their wicked ways, then will I hear from heaven and will forgive their sin and will
heal their land (7:14).

The majesty and magnificence of Solomon's reign reached far and wide:

King Solomon was greater in riches and wisdom than all the other kings of the earth. All the
kings of the earth sought audience with Solomon to hear the wisdom God had put in his heart.
Year after year, everyone who came brought a gift – articles of silver and gold, and robes,
weapons and spices, and horses and mules (9:22-24).

Thus ends the golden era of Israel.

2. Judah – The Southern Kingdom (10 – 36)

The glory did not last long. After Solomon, a civil war broke out and the nation of Israel was divided: one kingdom in the north (Israel) and one in the south (Judah). II Chronicles gives exclusive attention to Judah (the Southern Kingdom) because of the Davidic line and temple worship.

All of the kings of Israel were evil, but Judah was mixed. Twelve of the kings of Judah were evil and eight were good. What is interesting in demonstrating the spiritual commentary in II Chronicles is that most of the attention is given to the good kings of Judah. Specifically, five of the good kings are recorded in more detail than they were in Kings:

- Asa (14, 15).

- Jehoshaphat (17 – 20).

- Joash (23:16 – 24:16).

- Hezekiah (29 – 32).

- Josiah (34 – 35).

Every one of these good kings led spiritual reformations in Judah and their reforms restored worship at the temple, reverence for the Law of God and prayers of confession.

Lessons From I And II Chronicles

1. God is always at work in history. Nothing ever surprises the Lord. The happenings of history always include the affairs of men, but never at the exclusion of the grace and judgment of God. God's work in history is not always pleasant. He can visit in judgment and He can visit in grace – but one undeniable truth is that God is at work.

2. God is always faithful to His promises. The covenantal promises of the Lord to David are kept. The promise to build the temple and perpetuate the lineage of David on the throne is upheld by the Lord, culminating in the glory of Solomon's reign. We can be confident of the faithfulness of the Lord. It is our faithfulness that is in question.

3. God is always calling for reform. Even in the light of the Lord's faithfulness to His promises, His people sin and rebel. They turn to other gods and live for themselves. In the midst of the idolatry and immorality of the people of God, however, the Lord calls for reform, responds to repentance and blesses new obedience. That reform, as seen in the good kings of Judah in II Chronicles, will include the restoration of true worship, repentant prayer, faithful reading of and obedience to the Word of God.

NOTES

CHAPTER THIRTEEN: EZRA

Assignment

READ ...

Ezra, Chapters 1-10, or selected chapters from Ezra (one a day for a week) as follows:

Ezra 1   –   The exiles beginning to return to Jerusalem.

Ezra 3   –   The rebuilding of the temple.

Ezra 4   –   Opposition to rebuilding the temple.

Ezra 6   –   The completion of the temple.

Ezra 7   –   Ezra's return to Jerusalem.

Ezra 9   –   Ezra's confrontation of sin.

Ezra 10   –   The people's confession of sin.

MEMORIZE ...

Ezra 9:10 – "But now, O our God, what can we say after this? For we have disregarded the commands you gave through your servants the prophets."

PRAY ...

Asking the Lord for a revival in America. Even as the exiles returned to their land and desired reform, let us desire revival and reformation in the United States.

Committing yourself to the task of building the Kingdom of God right where you are. Even if many things are not what they should be, be sure you are who you should be, just like Ezra.

Examining your life to see if there is anything that displeases Him. Repentance is never easy or pleasant. It is the plucking out of the right eye or the cutting off of the right hand.

APPLY ...

In the light of Ezra, what do you:

> BELIEVE about God?
>
> REPENT of as sin?
>
> OBEY as a command from God?

SHARE ...

According to what you have learned from Ezra:

- Put yourself in the place of these exiled people of God. What if you lost everything you thought was good and beautiful? Do you think you would still remain faithful to the Lord? Talk to your family about hard times and how you might respond if these hard times hit your home. You might even speculate about how your family would have reacted if your home had been lost in a tornado or fire.

- Share with a friend about a time when you were confronted with something wrong in your life and how difficult it was to repent. Then, share about the blessings in your life now that the pain is gone.

Ezra:
Man of the Word

INTRODUCTION

We are all in need of a word – truth and wisdom beyond ourselves. We do not all believe that a word is what we need. We can be convinced that all we need is to dig deeper into our own hearts, minds and wills. We also can be convinced that all we need is something more material and concrete to meet our needs.

A word just seems too impersonal and too impotent.

To know God and to be right with God, however, a word is what we need – a Word from Him. Ezra is about a man of the Word of God.

TITLE

Ezra means "Yahweh helps."

Ezra was a scribe, which was a student of the Law. The scribe was not a priest who would offer sacrifices, and he was not an official who was a political leader. The scribe's function was to study the Law and devote himself to personally being a keeper of the Law. He was something of a "holy man." The scribe also had corporate responsibilities of prayer for the people (9:1) and in the public reading of the Law for the whole community (Nehemiah 8:1ff).

Ezra reminds us that we are to be People of the Word. We are not left to our own imaginations, opinions, culture or desires. God has spoken. He has not been silent. He has revealed His will and we find it in His Word.

Some scholars believe that Ezra was so much a "man of the Word" that he was the author of the greatest portion of Scripture on the Law of God – Psalm 119.

THEME VERSE

For Ezra had devoted himself to the study and observance of the
Law of the LORD, and to teaching its decrees and laws in Israel.
Ezra 7:10

BACKGROUND

Ezra takes up where II Chronicles left off. As a matter of fact, the last verses of II Chronicles are identical to the first verses of Ezra. In other words, the time is at the end of the Babylonian captivity – a 70-year period of exile after the fall of Jerusalem – when exiles were beginning to return to Jerusalem.

There were three returns:

- Under Zerubbabel (538 B.C.), by the order of King Cyrus of Persia, who overthrew Babylon. Zerubbabel led in rebuilding the temple.

- Under Ezra (457 B.C.), by the order of King Artaxerxes. Ezra's unique contribution was rebuilding the people spiritually and morally by teaching the Law and calling for repentance.

- Under Nehemiah (444 B.C.), also under King Artaxerxes. Nehemiah led in the rebuilding of the walls of Jerusalem.

During this period of return from captivity, other significant religious and philosophical movements were happening elsewhere in the world:

- Gautama Buddha (560 – 480 B.C.) in India.

- Confucius (551 – 479 B.C.) in China.

- Socrates (470 – 399 B.C.) in Greece.

Ezra is a man of the Word during a time when God is restoring His people to their covenant land. It is a time for rebuilding, reforming and renewing. At the heart of this spiritual restoration is the Word of God – hearing it and responding to it.

I. Rebuilding the Temple (1 – 6)

Builders of the Temple (1, 2)

Cyrus, king of Persia, made a proclamation that allowed the first wave of Jewish exiles to return to Jerusalem. This return was with a purpose: to rebuild the temple of the Lord. Those returning are listed to record this significant period of history for Israel.

Lists are significant in Ezra because this is a new beginning for the Jews. These lists become official documentation for this return and rebuilding. They become historical records of this pioneering group returning to Jerusalem which will be remembered for generations.

Ezra 2:64 gives the numbers:

42,360	–	all the people
7,337	–	manservants
200	–	singers
49,897	–	total

The Jewish population in exile was estimated at 2-to-3 million, so this first return was a small percentage of those in Babylon. The trip from Babylon to Jerusalem was a dangerous 900-mile journey.

Building the Temple (3 – 6)

The high, even mixed, emotions of rebuilding the temple are given in 3:10-13. At the laying of the foundation, there was worship with shouts of praise and weeping in remembrance of the past. This was a unique time of remembering the harshness of the judgment in the loss of Solomon's temple and celebrating the mercy of the Lord in starting work on a new temple.

There were those who opposed the rebuilding of the temple. Local residents tried to deceive Zerubbabel and Jeshua, the high priest, by making offers to help, but they were told "No," because they had no part with the returning exiles. The active opposition begins in a way familiar to us today – lobbying the politicians.

Official communications (red tape) are exchanged and the end result is that construction is halted for 15 years. Two prophets of the day, Haggai and Zechariah whom we know as Minor Prophets, got things going by their prophesies and help.

King Darius, who replaced King Cyrus, offers a decree to continue the rebuilding, and the day arrives for the completion and dedication of the new temple. This was an occasion of great joy and worship for Judah, and they did something Israel often did at a significant new beginning – they reinstituted the Passover.

II. Rebuilding the People (7 – 10)

Buildings, even if they are temples, are not enough. God is not about rebuilding temples alone. He is about rebuilding His people. Ezra focuses on this, and on how God begins by sending spiritual leaders.

Ezra leads the second wave of returning exiles 80 years after Zerubbabel. This was 58 years after Esther's time.

What was unique about Ezra?

- 7:6 – He was well-versed in the Law of Moses.

- 7:9 – "The gracious hand of God was on him."

- 7:10 – He was devoted to the study, obedience and teaching of the Law.

- 7:28 – Because the hand of the Lord was on him, he took courage to bring the people back with him.

This was an unbeatable combination: Ezra had God's hand on him and God's Word in him.

The rebuilding of the people of God, however, goes deeper than being taught the Word by godly leaders. There is the deep and difficult matter of repentance. In chapters 9-10, Ezra confronts what was the besetting sin of God's people in the land – intermarriage with foreign women. This sin is not racially based, but religiously based. The sin was not marrying someone of another race. The sin was marrying someone of another religion that led you away from your religion to theirs. The sin was idolatry.

Ezra's reaction to the sin was deep grief and prayer. His prayer in 9:6-15 is a moving prayer of confession. Ezra identified with the sin of the people; he did not see himself above it, He prayed with fervency, remembering the covenant promises and commands and admitting that a great sin had been committed.

It is one thing to lead people in confession. It is quite another for them to follow. The people recognized their sin and repented of it, and the Book of Ezra ends with a listing of all the men who had been guilty of intermarriage with foreign women.

Lessons From Ezra

1. The Word of God can move anyone to do God's bidding. The pagan King Cyrus heard the Word of God instructing him to let a remnant from Israel go back to Jerusalem and Judah. God is never limited to just His people to do His work.

2. The Word of God is to be studied and proclaimed. Ezra, as a scribe, knew this and it was the passion of his life. The Word of God gives direction for life that is sure and certain. That Word calls for the allegiance of any who claim to bear the covenant God's name.

3. The Word of God always calls for repentance. The people of Judah had a dominant sin in their lives and they were confronted with that sin by the Word of God. They confessed that sin according to the Word of God and repented of that sin because of the Word of God.

NOTES

CHAPTER FOURTEEN: NEHEMIAH AND ESTHER

Assignment

READ ...

Nehemiah, Chapters 1-13, and Esther, Chapters 1-10, or selected chapters from Nehemiah and Esther (one a day for a week) as follows:

Nehemiah 1	–	Nehemiah's prayer.
Nehemiah 2	–	Nehemiah's return to Jerusalem.
Nehemiah 3	–	Building the wall.
Nehemiah 8	–	Ezra's reading of the Law.
Nehemiah 9	–	The confession of the people.
Esther 2	–	Esther made queen.
Esther 7	–	Esther's request.

MEMORIZE ...

Nehemiah 4:14 – "Don't be afraid of them. Remember the LORD, who is great and awesome, and fight for your brothers, your sons and your daughters, your wives and your homes;"

and/or

Esther 4:14 – "And who knows but that you have come to royal position for such a time as this?"

PRAY ...

Asking the Lord for wisdom about what needs to be rebuilt in your life, or your church, or your nation. God is always about rebuilding what has been torn down.

Committing yourself to the task of building the Kingdom of God right where you are. Even if many things are not what they should be, be sure you are who you should be, just like Ezra and Nehemiah.

Thanking the Lord for His providential care for you. Even when you are not aware of the Lord's love and protection, know that you are His child under His care.

Confessing your sins. It was crucial for the returning exiles to take their sin seriously and repent, no matter how painful it was.

APPLY ...

In the light of Nehemiah and Esther, what do you:

> BELIEVE about God?
>
> REPENT of as sin?
>
> OBEY as a command from God?

SHARE ...

According to what you have learned from Nehemiah and Esther:

- Imagine the worst thing happening to you and your family. Get the family to think about this together. This is not a pleasant exercise, but it can help to identify what is most important in your lives when everything falls apart. This was the situation for Israel while in exile, but God brought them out of exile back to their home to rebuild and reform.

- The providence of God is when God cares for us as His children all of the time. Share with a friend where you have seen the hand of God working in your life recently.

Nehemiah:
Prayer and Work

William Booth, father of the Salvation Army movement, once said: "Work as if everything depended upon your work, and pray as if everything depended upon your prayer."

There are some problems with that statement but, getting beyond those, Booth was seeking to encourage the teamwork of prayer and work. Trusting God does not lead to doing nothing. Working for God does not lead to not trusting Him.

With Nehemiah, the perfect balance of prayer and work are portrayed. He trusted God every step of the way. He worked hard and faithfully.

THEME VERSE

So we rebuilt the wall till all of it reached half its height, for the people worked with all their heart.
Nehemiah 4:6

I. REBUILDING (1 – 7)

Conception Phase of Rebuilding the Walls (1, 2)

Nehemiah models the way to accomplish something great for God. He demonstrates seven things that must happen in order to step out on an adventure for God.

1. Burden

Nehemiah is the cupbearer in the court of King Artaxerxes, where he learns of the condition of the walls and gates in Jerusalem – the walls are torn down and the gates are burned. Nehemiah's heart is broken. Godly burdens are based on truth (accurate information) and spirit (acute interaction). A burden never feels good. It is heavy and it is something that can't be put aside.

2. Prayer

The first thing Nehemiah did when he was burdened was pray. His prayer in 1:5-10 is a great prayer of praise and dependence upon the Lord. He basically asked for the Lord to give him favor in the presence of the king.

3. Patience

Then Nehemiah waits. As a matter of fact, he waits four months, but he was ready when the time came. The king asked him about what was making him sad and Nehemiah told him. The king responded with all the help Nehemiah needed to return and rebuild the walls. Nehemiah knew that it was the Lord who had worked for him.

4. Action

Nehemiah kicked into action. After he was burdened and prayed and the Lord provided, he moved out. His activity was based on what God had done in his life and in the circumstances around him. Nehemiah was not just a man of action. He was a man of action based on how God had acted.

5. Expect Opposition

Opposition is never far from work for God. Nehemiah experienced the opposition of those in the land who were threatened by Jerusalem regaining its old glory, but this did not stop Nehemiah. He knew who was for him and nothing could stop him now.

6. Evaluate

When Nehemiah got to Jerusalem, he personally inspected the walls and evaluated the plan. Nehemiah only had heard of the condition of the walls secondhand. He evaluated the situation on his own and found it to be desperate and the burden true.

7. Bring In Others

Nehemiah knew he could not rebuild the walls on his own. A true plan of God will include the people of God. He needed others to help. So he shared with the leaders in Jerusalem his vision and burden and gave the invitation, "Come, let us rebuild the walls of Jerusalem, and we will no longer be in disgrace." And they responded, "Let us start rebuilding."

Construction Phase of Rebuilding the Walls (3, 4)

The construction begins. The work is delegated, as sections of the wall and different gates are assigned. The workers are also dedicated, and it is made certain that they had the ability to do the work required.

Opposition from the non-Jewish residents, however, again raised its ugly head – this time more intense and threatening. Verbal opposition was sarcastically expressed, and then a plot was put together that could lead to violence. In each case, the opposition was met with prayer and action:

But we prayed to our God and posted a guard day and night to meet this threat (4:9).

Notice the balance in Nehemiah's leadership. He exhorted them (4:14), "Don't be afraid of them. Remember the Lord, who is great and awesome, and fight for your brothers, your sons and your daughters, your wives and your homes." Remember the Lord … and fight. From that day on, the work on the walls proceeded with half of the men working on the wall and half with swords ready to fight.

Completion Phase of Rebuilding the Walls (5 – 7)

During the construction of the walls, Nehemiah faced a problem with the poor in Jerusalem being mistreated. He faced that injustice head on and then returned to the construction.

The opposition intensified and came in wave after wave, but in each case Nehemiah stood like a "wall" against it.

The walls were completed in 52 days (incredible!); the opposition now was afraid and all the glory went to God (6:15, 16).

II. Revival (8 – 13)

Construction of the walls was followed by the consecration of the people. An older Ezra leads in this revival. As the Law is read, the people confess their sin and the covenant is renewed. The walls are dedicated with pomp and circumstance.

The book ends with Nehemiah leading in other reforms, which is a reminder that there is always a need for reform. A slogan of the Protestant Reformation is, "Reformed and always reforming according to the Word of God." Nehemiah knew that the completion of such a great task like rebuilding the walls would need to be followed with continual attention to the people's walk with their God.

Esther:
A Case Study in Providence

INTRODUCTION

Providence is the care, protection, guidance and work of God even when He isn't asked, recognized or desired. Providence is the work of God, even when He doesn't get the headlines. Christians should know that their lives are not controlled by luck, fate or knocking on wood. God is giving His providential, fatherly care through the extremes of life.

The most well-known providential verse is Romans 8:28: "And we know that in all things God works for the good of those who love Him, who have been called according to His purpose." This verse is illustrated in the Book of Esther.

Esther is a case study in providence. A unique feature of this book is that the name of God is never mentioned and Esther is never quoted in the New Testament. That, though, is how providence is. In writing about the Book of Esther, Matthew Henry said, "If the name of God is not here, His finger certainly is."

Providence is the "finger of God" in the lives of His people.

THEME VERSE

These are the words of Mordecai to Esther (4:14):

> ... who knows but that you have come to royal position for such a time as this?

BACKGROUND

Esther is a story about the Jews who stayed in exile in Persia, formerly Babylon. To understand the story, you need to know the main characters:

- Xerxes is the king of Persia, the most powerful man in his day.

- Vashti is the queen, who is very beautiful and independent.

- Haman is a Jew-hating Persian who is an ambitious politician looking for a way to grow in power.

- Mordecai is a righteous Jew who is a leader in the exiled Jewish community and who is the guardian of a young woman – Esther.

- Esther is a beautiful Jewess who becomes queen and is placed in the right place at the right time.

It is interesting to contrast Ruth and Esther:

Ruth	Esther
Gentile who married a Jew	A Jew who married a Gentile
Woman of the fields	Woman of the court
Time of the judges	Time of the exile
Faithful	Faithful

I. GRAVE DANGER (1 – 4)

King Xerxes called for a banquet that lasted 180 days. There are many banquets in the Book of Esther, which gives an insight into life in the courts of Persia at this time.

At one of these banquets, the king gets drunk and wants to show off all his possessions, one of them being his beautiful wife, Vashti. She says no to the king and Vashi is banished from the king's court.

Now there is a need for a new queen. The decision is made to have a "beauty contest" to decide who the next Miss Persia will be. Enter Esther. Mordecai, her guardian, tells her not to reveal that she is Jewish. She wins the contest and is made the first lady of Persia.

Guess what they do? They have another banquet. During this time, Mordecai hears of an assassination plot to kill the king, tells Esther about it and the assassination is averted. This incident then is put in the annals of the king. This seems to be a meaningless detail, but remember that God's providence is at work.

Haman, a Persian, was promoted to a high position in the court of King Xerxes and he wanted all the respect and honor due his position. Mordecai, though, refused to pay him honor. Haman was so upset that he plotted to exterminate all the Jews. He cast lots to select a day to massacre the Jews. The word for casting lots in the Hebrew is *purim*, which today is a special Jewish holiday remembering the protection of God over the Jews.

Haman presents his plan (plot) to the king. The king agrees to the plan, and a date is set for the annihilation of the Jews.

Mordecai learns of the plot and challenges Esther to use her position as queen to help. This is where our theme verse occurs, when Mordecai tells Esther that maybe it was for "such a time as this" that she became queen. This is providence talking.

Esther had a sense of destiny and she asked for prayer, saying, "If I perish, I perish."

II. GREAT DELIVERANCE (5 – 10)

Esther woos the king and humbly waits for the king to notice her. The king gives her an open door, and she requests another banquet, but Haman was sure to be present. There is another banquet, and it leads only to Haman's rage intensifying against Mordecai. His hatred grows so strong that he has a gallows built to hang Mordecai.

This is where God is present in the Book of Esther, even though He is not named. It is in an act of providence that Esther did not control. King Xerxes could not sleep, so he did what many people do – he got something to read. He read the king's annals about Mordecai, when he uncovered the earlier assassination plot.

The king finds out that Mordecai had not been recognized for such a good deed, so he determines to honor Mordecai and asks Haman to carry it out! Imagine the humiliation for Haman.

At the banquet, Esther reveals Haman's devious deeds, her nationality and her request. The king calls for Haman to be hanged on the gallows he had made for Mordecai, and the Jews are saved.

The final chapters of Esther have the Jews in captivity celebrating their triumph, the observing of *purim* and the honoring of Mordecai.

Lessons From Nehemiah and Esther

1. God calls His people to work in His Kingdom. This is the message of Nehemiah as the task of rebuilding the walls involved work, opposition and repentance. The work of God's Kingdom is laborious and costly, but it is always worth it.

2. God cares for His people in His Kingdom. This care is called providence. This is the message of Esther. God cared for Israel at a very dangerous time in her history. His providential care was shown through a woman of His choosing, Esther.

NOTES

CHAPTER FIFTEEN: JOB

Assignment

READ ...

Job, Chapters 1-42, or selected chapters from Job (one a day for a week) as follows:

Job 1	–	Job's first test.
Job 2	–	Job's second test.
Job 3	–	Job's agony.
Job 18	–	A friend's confrontation.
Job 19	–	Job's defense.
Job 38	–	The Lord speaks.
Job 42	–	Job's restoration.

MEMORIZE ...

Job 1:21 – "Job said, 'Naked I came from my mother's womb, and naked I will depart. The LORD gave and the LORD has taken away; may the name of the LORD be praised;'"

and/or

Job 19:25 – "I know that my Redeemer lives, and that in the end He will stand upon the earth."

PRAY ...

Praising the Lord that He is sovereign and mighty over Satan, even when it does not feel like it.

Asking the Lord to make you a comforting friend to others who hurt and are suffering. Pray specifically for several family members and friends you know of right now who are hurting.

Bringing the most hurtful and burdensome matter in your life and seeking the Lord's strength and wisdom. Praise Him for being your God who is in control.

Thanking the Lord that He is the One who does not need to answer our question, "Why?"

Repenting of the sin in your life.

APPLY ...

In the light of Job, what do you:

> BELIEVE about God?
>
> REPENT of as sin?
>
> OBEY as a command from God?

SHARE ...

According to what you have learned from Job:

- Share with your family some of the times in your life when you have hurt, been troubled or buried in a problem. As you look back with 20/20 hindsight, communicate how you can now see the hand of God during and after those times of suffering.

- People are hurting all around us. Think of someone you know, possibly someone who is not a Christian, who is hurting. Go to that person and be a comforting friend. Mourn with those who mourn.

Job:
Sovereignty and Suffering

INTRODUCTION

The Book of Job holds a fascination that lifts it above the rest of the books of the Bible.

Almost everyone knows that Job is about suffering, but it is supremely about sovereignty—the sovereignty of God over suffering. God is in control over all things and – this is the hard part – sovereignty is not always comfortable.

Suffering is never to be belittled. It is real and it hurts. Suffering, though, always has a context. There is no greater question raised in the human experience than, "Why do we suffer and, in particular, why do the righteous suffer?"

There is no easy answer. That, however, does not mean there is no answer. Not even Job will satisfy many people who want a pat answer or immediate relief or simple blame. The answer goes to the very heart of our relationship with the Lord, who is Almighty and sovereign.

THEME VERSE

> *Job said, "Naked I came from my mother's womb, and naked I will depart.*
> *The Lord gave and the Lord has taken away; may the name of the Lord be praised."*
> *Job 1:21*

TITLE

The name Job can come from two languages meaning two different things: the Hebrew meaning is "persecuted one" and the Arabic meaning is the "repentant one."

The title describes the main character, not necessarily the author. The author of Job is a mystery. There have been many suggestions: Job, Elihu, Moses, Solomon, Isaiah, Hezekiah, Jeremiah and Ezra.

BACKGROUND

Job begins a new section of the Old Testament – the Writings.

Job is probably the depiction of the life of a man in the patriarchal period (around 200 B.C.) who was a godly man, but not a Hebrew. There are no references in Job to the Law, the tabernacle, Israel, the Exodus, or any other Old Testament character.

The most common name for God in Job is *Shaddi* – "the Almighty" – which occurs 31 times. This is the most characteristic name for God by the patriarchs (Abraham, Isaac and Jacob).

In Job, there is also a great emphasis on God as the Creator.

I. INTRODUCTION TO SUFFERING (1, 2)

Job opens with five scenes that provide the backdrop for the story. The scenes alternate between heaven and earth as the divine perspective is given to the human predicament.

Scene 1 (1:1-5) Earth

Job is introduced. He is a wealthy man with seven sons and three daughters, to whom he is very close; Job was a godly father.

Scene 2 (1:6-12) Heaven

There is communication between God and Satan. God brags on Job and Satan asks, "Does Job fear God for nothing?" Basically, Satan is questioning Job's genuineness. God allows Satan to bring harm to Job's possessions. Now, why did God do this? I do not know! He is sovereign and He can do what He wants.

Note two actions where God remains sovereign:

- He permits – Satan could only do what God permitted. God did not do the evil. He allowed it.

- He restricts – Satan was limited. He could not physically touch Job.

Scene 3 (1:13-16) Earth

Job suffers a great loss. His servants, his sheep and camels, and his sons and daughters are all violently taken from him. We can feel the devastation.

Job's reaction humbles us. It is revealed in the theme verse:

Job said, "Naked I came from my mother's womb, and naked I will depart. The LORD gave and the LORD has taken away; may the name of the LORD be praised" (1:21).

Scene 4 (2:1-6) Heaven

This is a repeat of Scene 2, but this time Satan was given the strange permission to intensify Job's suffering by causing bodily harm. Still God permits and restricts.

Scene 5 (2:7-10) Earth

Job's affliction is complete. The misery of his condition is made clear in verses 8-9:

Then Job took a piece of broken pottery and scraped himself with it as he sat among the ashes. His wife said to him, "Are you still holding on to your integrity? Curse God and die!"

Once again, Job's response (10) is instructive:

He replied, 'You are talking like a foolish woman. Shall we accept good from God, and not trouble?' In all this, Job did not sin in what he said.

II. DISCUSSION OF SUFFERING (3 – 31)

Job then is visited by three friends:

- Eliphaz – "God is gold" or "God dispenses judgment."

- Bildad – "Son of Contention."

- Zophar – "Rough" or "Chirper."

These are not the most spiritual or encouraging names.

These friends came to Job and at first showed their sympathy:

*Then they sat on the ground with him for seven days and seven nights. No one said a word to
him, because they saw how great his suffering was (2:13).*

They could not, however, stay silent any longer. Chapters 3-31 are filled with their insights into the
reasons for Job's suffering, and Job responds to them.

One thing needs to be said about the friends and their words to Job. In most cases, their advice is
orthodox. Read what the friends say and you will find yourself agreeing with them. They were right in their
thinking. They were not evil.

Where they missed the boat, though, was that they were orthodox (they were right), but they were not
relevant (it did not apply to Job's situation). There is a common bumper sticker today that says, "Jesus is the
Answer! Now, what is the question?" It could have been on the car (or chariot) of one of Job's friends.

A deeper analysis of this section could be done, but for the sake of simplicity, here is how the discussion
went:

The friends told Job, "You must have sinned big to suffer so much."

Job responded. "You are not my judge. The Lord is."

These theologically astute and spiritually sensitive friends were no help to Job whatsoever. They were
more of a hindrance than a help for two reasons:

- They thought they spoke for God, but they did not know what God was doing. We have evidence they
  did not in Job 1-2.

- They thought they were doing what was best for Job, but they were really adding to his suffering. Their
  words to him were of no comfort whatsoever.

There are no easy solutions to extreme tragedies and suffering.

Listen to what Joseph Bayly writes in his excellent book on grief, *A View from a Hearse*[1]:

*When Job's friends came to see him after his children died and he had suffered in so many
other ways, they missed the opportunity to go down in history as uniquely sensitive and
understanding. There they sat on the ground with him for seven days and nights, and they didn't
say a word because they saw how utterly grief-stricken he was. But then they began to talk and
spoiled it all. Sensitivity in the presence of grief usually makes us more silent, more listening.
"I am sorry" is an honest statement. "I know how you feel" usually isn't. Even though you may
have experienced the death of a person who had the same familial relationship to you as the
deceased person had to the grieving one, if the person feels that you can understand, he'll tell
you, then you may want to share your own honest, not prettied-up, feelings in your personal
aftermath with death. Don't try to prove anything to a survivor. An arm about the shoulder, a
firm grip on the hand, a kiss, these are the proofs grief needs – not logical reasoning. I was
sitting torn by grief. Someone came and talked to me of God's dealings, of what had happened,
of hope beyond the grave. He talked continually; he said things I knew were true. I was
unmoved except to wish he'd go away. He finally did. Another came and sat beside me. He didn't
talk, he didn't ask leading questions, he didn't preach, he just sat beside me for an hour and
more, listened when I said something, answered briefly, prayed simply, and left. I was moved, I
was comforted, I hated to see him go.*

III. Solutions for Suffering (32 – 41)

A fourth friend comes onto the scene. His name is Elihu, which means, "He is my God." He is a young
man who also was a friend, but he offered more sound advice than the other three. He tells Job that he needs
to humble himself before God and submit to what God is doing through the suffering.

This advice was needed and closer to the truth than that of the other friends, but still Job was not helped.
Job was showing signs of becoming self-righteous because he knew he did not deserve the suffering. What

---

1   Bayly, Joseph, *A View from a Hearse* (Colorado Springs: David C. Cook, 1973).

he needed was a confrontation with God, and that is what happened (38:1).

> *Job asked the question "Why?" in a hundred different ways. His friends told him their answers to the "why" question, but Job was not satisfied. He was about to get satisfaction, but it is not what he expected.*

When the Lord answered Job, He did not answer the question "Why?" He asked his own questions of Job. God's questions (38-39) are like hammer blows making one simple point: Job, you are not God. God is God. His ways are not our ways.

In this entire section, Job is silent.

IV. SUBMISSION TO SUFFERING (42:7-17)

Finally, Job speaks and he does two things:

- He recognizes God's sovereignty: "I know that you can do all things; no plan of yours can be thwarted" (42:2).

- He repents of his sin: "My ears had heard of you but now my eyes have seen you. Therefore I despise myself and repent in dust and ashes" (42:5, 6).

V. RESTORATION FROM SUFFERING (42:7-17)

Job's friends are rebuked (all except Elihu). The word of the Lord is given to them and they are told, "You have not spoken of me what is right, as my servant Job has." They were commanded to offer sacrifices, Job prayed for them and the Lord forgave them.

Job's worldly goods are restored two-fold (42:12, 13).

Lessons From Job

1. Trust God … no matter what. "God does not give you more than you can bear." This is a common saying, but the ultimate response to such wisdom is, "I can bear under this. I can take it." Well, that is pretty self-centered. The more exact truth is "God gives us what we cannot bear so that we might trust Him and only Him." Job responded to his intense suffering, "Even if He slay me, yet will I trust Him." No matter what happens, we are to trust God who never is surprised by our pain and is even using "all things for our good."

2. Love one another … no matter what. God wants us to love one another during times of trials and hurt. Platitudes, preaching and even personal experiences are limited in their impact. If they make you feel better than your suffering friend, then they were selfish, misapplied and no comfort whatsoever. The best thing we can do for those who hurt is to pray … be present … be ready to respond to the needs of those who are grieving.

NOTES

Chapter Sixteen: Psalms

Assignment

READ ...

Psalms, Chapters 1-150, or selected chapters from Psalms (one a day for a week) as follows:

Psalm 1	–	A beatific Psalm.
Psalm 22	–	A messianic Psalm.
Psalm 23	–	A pastoral Psalm.
Psalm 27	–	A confident prayer.
Psalm 46	–	A celebration Psalm.
Psalm 51	–	A confessing Psalm.
Psalm 103	–	A Psalm of personal praise.

MEMORIZE ...

Psalm 119:11 – "I have hidden your word in my heart that I might not sin against you;"

and/or

Psalm 46:1 – "God is our refuge and strength, an ever present help in trouble;"

and/or

Psalm 19:14 – "May the words of my mouth and the meditation of my heart be pleasing in your sight, O Lord, my rock and my Redeemer."

PRAY ...

Seeking to worship the Lord in every situation in your life. Make praising God the central act of your life.

Giving to the Lord every conflict in your life, including those with your enemies. Leave ultimate judgment in the hands of God.

Using Psalm 51 as a guide to confess your sin.

Thanking the Lord for every good and perfect blessing in your life. Remember those times He delivered and restored you.

Asking that praise would be central to your Christian walk.

APPLY ...

In the light of Psalms, what do you:

>   BELIEVE about God?

>   REPENT of as sin?

>   OBEY as a command from God?

SHARE ...

According to what you have learned from Psalms:

- Talk with your family about what worship means to you. Recollect some of the times in the past when you felt close to God in worship. Talk about the Sunday morning worship service and reflect on how each part points you toward the Lord in worship.

- Share with someone who does not regularly go to church what the worship at church means to you. Go beyond something learned in a sermon or enjoyed in the music. Reflect on your experience of sensing the closeness and majesty of God. You may find him or her desiring something that you have experienced.

Psalms:
A Biblical Hymnal

INTRODUCTION

There came a point in Martin Luther's spiritual journey when the teaching of the Church was not providing peace with God, so he took the radical step of going to the Bible alone to discover the truth. He started this Bible study commitment with the Psalms.

The main concept from Psalms that both stirred and disturbed him was the righteousness of God. How can one be a sinner, but also be righteous before Him? It was his later study of Paul's Epistle to the Romans that touched his soul – the concept of justification by faith alone in Jesus Christ.

After this focus on the study of the Word of God which began in Psalms came the Reformation … the greatest revival in the history of the Church.

Martin Luther felt that the Reformation would not be completed until two things happened:

- The Bible was available in the common man's language.

- A hymnal (psalter) was in every home.

These two things would provide Biblical understanding of the faith and an expression of the faith. The Bible and the hymnal go together. Psalms is the Biblical hymnal:

- The Psalms are very musical.

- They are very emotional.

- They are very worshipful.

Psalms is not only the longest book of the Bible, but it also may be the most turned to book in the Bible.

THEME CHAPTER

Praise the LORD.
Praise God in His sanctuary;
praise Him in His mighty heavens.
Praise Him for His acts of power;
praise Him for His surpassing greatness.

Praise Him with the sounding of the trumpet,
praise Him with the harp and lyre,
praise Him with tambourine and dancing,
praise Him with the strings and flute
praise Him with the clash of cymbals,
praise Him with resounding cymbals.
Let everything that has breath praise the Lord.
Praise the LORD.
Psalm 150

TITLE

Psalms in Hebrew means "praises" (plural). It is a collection of individual Psalms. There are a variety of authors of the Psalms.

AUTHORS

Who wrote the Psalms?

- 73 (almost half) were written by David.

- 12 by Asaph ("collector," probably a priest who was the head of musical worship in the temple).

- 10 by the sons of Korah (a guild of singers).

- Two by Solomon (72, 127).

- One by Moses (90).

- One by a Levite, Ethan (89).

- More than 50 are anonymous (some are attributed to Ezra).

SUPERSCRIPTIONS

One hundred and sixteen Psalms have superscriptions. Most superscriptions give editorial comments, authorship or musical direction. Some give historical context:

- Psalm 51 (II Samuel 11:1 – 12:25) – "When the prophet Nathan came to him after David had committed adultery with Bathsheba."

- Psalm 52 (I Samuel 22:9, 10) – "When Doeg the Edomite had gone to Saul and told him: 'David has gone to the house of Ahimelech.'"

- Psalm 3 (II Samuel 15:13 – 17:22) – "When David fled from his son Absalom."

- Psalm 18 (II Samuel 8:1-14) – "David sang to the Lord the words of this song when the Lord delivered him from the hand of all his enemies and from the hand of Saul."

Some superscriptions give one-word designations (the numbers in parentheses are the number of times the word occurs in the superscriptions):

- *Mizmor* (57) – usually translated "psalm." Refers to a song accompanied by a string instrument.

- *Shir* (29) – "song" (Psalm 88).

- *Maskil* (13) – a contemplative poem (Psalms 32, 42).

- *Miktam* (6) – unknown, but it usually marks Davidic prayers occasioned by great danger (Psalms 16, 56, 58, 59, 60).

- *Tepillah* (5) – "prayer" (Psalm 17).

- *Tehillah* (1) – "praise" (Psalm 145).

Various unknown or unclear words that probably refer to the use of particular musical instruments, movements or tunes occasionally are used:

- *Mahalath* – Psalm 53, a specific tune.

- *Alamoth* – Psalm 46, maidens playing tambourines.

- *Sheminith* – Psalm 6, 12, an eight-stringed instrument.

- *Shiggaion* – Psalm 7, a musical term unknown today.

Some superscriptions speak of the occasion for the Psalm, like Psalm 30, "for the dedication of the temple," or Psalm 55, "for the choir director."

Selah is not a superscription because it is interspersed in the text. It occurs 71 times and marks a pause or a musical interlude. It is a call to reflect or meditate. The exact meaning of *selah* is uncertain.

CLASSIFICATION OF PSALMS (11 GROUPS)

It is difficult to give a survey of Psalms because it is not telling a story or presenting a singular message. Psalms, though, can be understood as a collection of many different songs of praise for many different situations in life. Here are some of the classifications of the Psalms:

- Individual Lament Psalms are addressed to God and are very personal in their expression. These Psalms usually call for God to rescue the author. Examples are Psalms 40 and 51.

- Communal Lament Psalms are addressed to God and are corporate expressions for the nation or the people of God. Once again, there is a call for God to rescue the nation in a time of danger. Examples are Psalms 60, 80 and 90.

- Individual Thanksgiving Psalms are expressions of thanks for what God had done or will do for a particular person. Examples are Psalms 32 and 34.

- Communal Thanksgiving Psalms are expressions of thanks for what God had done or will do for the nation. Examples are Psalms 124 and 129.

- General Praise Psalms revolve around many expressions of praise that uplift the greatness of God. Hallelujah (meaning "praise the Lord") occurs often. Examples are Psalms 8, 103 and 150.

- Descriptive Praise Psalms praise God for specific attributes of God or acts by God. Examples are Psalms 33 and 36.

- Enthronement Psalms uphold God's sovereignty to reign over all. Examples are Psalms 47 and 93.

- Pilgrimage Psalms, which are known as "Songs of Zion," are sung by pilgrims traveling to Jerusalem for annual feasts like Passover, Pentecost or Tabernacles. Examples are Psalms 43, 46 and 76.

- Royal Psalms have an emphasis on the earthly, as well as the heavenly, reign of the King. Examples are Psalms 2, 45 and 72.

- Wisdom and Didactic Psalms give instructions in the way of righteousness. They teach about how to live for God. Examples are Psalms 1 and 119.

- Imprecatory Psalms call down a curse upon enemies and call for Divine judgment. Examples are Psalms 7, 35, 40, 55, 58, 59, 69, 79, 109, 137, 139 and 144. To "politically correct" ears, these Psalms seem unreasonably harsh, but a few things need to be kept in mind:

  a. They call for Divine justice, rather than human vengeance.

  b. They ask God to punish the wicked, and thus vindicate His righteousness.

  c   They condemn sin (in the Hebrew mind, there was no sharp distinction between the sin and the sinner).

Even Jesus called down a curse on several cities and told His disciples to curse cities that did not receive the Gospel (Matthew 10:14, 15).

The Psalms can be divided into five books that parallel the Pentateuch. Each book has a distinctive message and closes with a doxology. Here is a description of each book and the general message in them.

Book 1 (1 – 41)

David is the main author of these Psalms that focus on the human condition as a theme. These Psalms are generally very personal. Book 1 parallels Genesis. The doxology is in Psalm 41:13.

Book 2 (42 – 72)

David and Korah are the main authors of these Psalms, whose main theme is deliverance. Book 2 parallels Exodus. The doxology is in Psalm 72:18, 19.

Book 3 (73 – 89)

These Psalms are known as Sanctuary Psalms because they are very liturgical. Book 3 parallels Leviticus. The doxology is in Psalm 89:52.

Book 4 (90 – 106)

These Psalms focus on the wanderings and conflicts of life on earth. Book 4 parallels Numbers. The doxology is in Psalm 106:48.

Book 5 (107 – 150)

These Psalms stress the Word of God and the praise of God. Book 5 parallels Deuteronomy. The doxology is Psalm 150.

PRACTICALITY OF THE PSALMS

The Book of Psalms is meant to impact our lives at the point of our needs and cause our eyes to be lifted beyond our needs. In the Psalms, we find the heart of Biblical worship, prayer and genuine faith.

Psalms will help you with personal needs:

- Psalm 23 – There is no other Psalm that ministers like more than "The LORD is my shepherd, I shall not want. …"

- Psalm 27 – "The LORD is my light and my salvation – whom shall I fear? The LORD is the stronghold of my life – of whom shall I be afraid?"

- Psalm 40 – "I waited patiently for the LORD; He turned to me and heard my cry."

- Psalm 46 – "God is our refuge and strength, an ever-present help in trouble."

- Psalm 51 – "Have mercy on me, O God, according to your unfailing love; according to your great compassion blot out my transgressions."

- Psalm 121 – "I lift up my eyes to the hills – where does my help come from? My help comes from the LORD, the Maker of heaven and earth."

- Psalm 139 – "O LORD, you have searched me and you know me. You know when I sit and when I rise; you perceive my thoughts from afar."

The Psalms will lead you to deeper praise and worship:

- Psalm 100 – "Make a joyful noise unto the Lord, all ye lands."

- Psalm 34 – "I will extol the LORD at all times; His praise will always be on my lips."

- Psalm 75 – "We give thanks to you, O God, we give thanks, for your Name is near; men tell of your wonderful deeds."

- Psalm 89 – "I will sing of the LORD's great love forever; with my mouth I will make your faithfulness known through all generations."

- Psalm 103 – "Praise the LORD, O my soul; all my inmost being, praise His holy name. Praise the LORD, O my soul, and forget not all His benefits."

- Psalm 106 – "Praise the LORD. Give thanks to the LORD, for He is good, His love endures forever."

- Psalm 145 – "I will exalt you, my God the King; I will praise your name for ever and ever. Every day I will praise you and extol your name for ever and ever."

The Psalms will provide clearer insight into your life and the world:

- Psalm 1 – "Blessed is the man who does not walk in the counsel of the wicked or stand in the way of sinners or sit in the seat of mockers. But his delight is in the law of the LORD. ..."

- Psalm 19: –"The heavens declare the glory of God; the skies proclaim the work of His hands."

- Psalm 42 – "As the deer pants for streams of water, so my soul pants for you, O God."

- Psalm 90 – "LORD, you have been our dwelling place throughout all generations. Before the mountains were born or you brought forth the earth and the world, from everlasting to everlasting you are God."

- Psalm 119 – "Blessed are they whose ways are blameless, who walk according to the law of the LORD."

- Psalm 127 – "Unless the LORD builds the house, its builders labor in vain. Unless the LORD watches over the city, the watchmen stand guard in vain."

NOTES

CHAPTER SEVENTEEN: PROVERBS

Assignment

READ ...

Proverbs, Chapters 1-31, or selected chapters from Proverbs (one a day for a week) as follows:

Proverbs 1	–	Introduction to Proverbs.
Proverbs 3	–	The benefits of wisdom.
Proverbs 9	–	The personification of wisdom.
Proverbs 15	–	General Proverbs.
Proverbs 20	–	General Proverbs.
Proverbs 27	–	General Proverbs.
Proverbs 31	–	A virtuous woman.

MEMORIZE ...

Proverbs 1:7 – "The fear of the LORD is the beginning of knowledge, but fools despise wisdom and discipline;"

and/or

Proverbs 3:5, 6 – "Trust in the LORD with all your heart and lean not on your own understanding; in all your ways acknowledge Him, and He will make your paths straight;"

and/or

Proverbs 15:1 – "A gentle answer turns away wrath, but a harsh word stirs up anger."

PRAY ...

Asking for wisdom in your life, like the wisdom shown in Proverbs.

Confessing those times in your life when you have been foolish, lazy, prideful, sensual and selfish.

For the fear of the Lord to be more a part of your Christian life.

Thanking the Lord for wise people who have influenced your life and provided good examples of godly living.

For the leaders of your church, community and country that they might have a wisdom beyond themselves.

Thanking God for the godly women in your life like the one portrayed in Proverbs 31.

APPLY ...

In the light of Proverbs, what do you:

> BELIEVE about God?
>
> REPENT of as sin?
>
> OBEY as a command from God?

SHARE ...

According to what you have learned from Proverbs:

- Around the breakfast or dinner table one day, get into a family discussion about wise and foolish people. Ask the family whom they respect as wise and then get them to describe what they mean. Then take Proverbs and read some of the general Proverbs in chapters 10-29 and ask the family to talk about what they mean.

- Strike up a conversation with someone you do not know well. It may be someone you meet in a store, or in your neighborhood, or at work. Look for an opportunity to share with him or her your reading of Proverbs and share one Proverb with him. Say something like this. "I read the other day, 'An anxious heart weighs a man down, but a kind word cheers him up' (12:25). What do you think that means?" Go where the conversation leads.

Proverbs:
Practical Religion

INTRODUCTION

Many Americans do not believe that Christianity is relevant or practical. The accusation that the main message of the faith is "pie-in-the-sky-in-the-bye-and-bye" is evidence of this. We too often think that the Church can be "so heavenly minded that we are of no earthly good." The connection of spiritual things to everyday life is never made in the minds of many people.

Proverbs is the most intensely practical and earthy book in the Old Testament. Under the general umbrella of wisdom, practical issues like marriage and family, money management, sexual temptation, drunkenness, the discipline of children, the value of friendship, the destructiveness of gossip and the integrity of life are presented in the context of living a full and joyful life.

THEME VERSE

The fear of the LORD is the beginning of knowledge,
but fools despise wisdom and discipline.
Proverbs 1:7

TITLE

The Hebrew word for "proverb" means "comparison," "similar" or "parallel." This refers to a literary style of using a comparison or a figure of speech to make an observation about life. Proverbs gives word pictures of truths that are important to living life to its fullest.

AUTHOR

Solomon wrote most of Proverbs – to be exact, Proverbs 1-29. The unknown Agur wrote Proverbs 30 and the unknown Lemuel wrote Proverbs 31.

BACKGROUND

The connection between wisdom and King Solomon was no mistake. The story from I Kings gives the account of when Solomon first replaced his father, David, as the king of Israel. God told him to ask for whatever he wanted, and Solomon asked for wisdom (I Kings 3:5-9). This was elaborated on later when it was stated that God gave Solomon the greatest wisdom in the world (I Kings 4:29, 30).

Solomon wrote 3,000 proverbs and 1,005 songs (I Kings 4:32). There are 800 proverbs in the Book of Proverbs. People came from all over the world to listen to Solomon's wisdom (I Kings 4:34). The queen of Sheba came to hear Solomon's wisdom and to see Solomon's wealth (I Kings 10:1-13).

It is interesting to do a comparison of Psalms and Proverbs:

Psalms	**Proverbs**
Written by David	Written by Solomon
How to get along with God	How to get along with one another
How to live in private	How to live in public
How to praise	How to be practical

I. PREPARATION FOR WISDOM (1 – 9)

Prologue (1:1-7)

The purpose and theme of the book is given in our theme verse (1:7):

The fear of the LORD is the beginning of knowledge, but fools despise wisdom and discipline.

Three distinctions are made in this verse: knowledge, wisdom and discipline.

- Knowledge is consciousness of the truth. Knowledge relates to facts and understanding. This knowledge begins with God and our proper fear (reverence) of God. Knowing anything begins with knowing God.

- Wisdom is the practice of the truth. Wisdom relates to life and morality. The truth is to become something we do and not just something we know.

- Discipline is growth in the truth. Discipline relates to learning the truth by mistakes and getting stronger. The truth is not something we instantly and easily grasp. It takes discipline, self-control and self-denial to be godly.

Exhortation (1:8-9)

Ten exhortations are given, all starting with "my son." These emphasize a father's efforts to persuade his son to pursue the path of wisdom in order to achieve godly success in life.

These exhortations (or warnings) deal with such practical issues as crime, foolishness, immorality, adultery and laziness.

There are three highlights in this section:

Trust in the LORD with all your heart and lean not on your own understanding; in all your ways acknowledge Him, and He will make your paths straight. (3:5, 6)

There are six things the LORD hates, seven that are detestable to Him: haughty eyes, a lying tongue, hands that shed innocent blood, a heart that devises wicked schemes, feet that are quick to rush into evil, a false witness who pours out lies and a man who stirs up dissension among brothers. (6:16-19)

Without reading the whole passage of Proverbs 7:1-27, let it suffice to say that this section captures the enticing temptation of a young man to commit sexual sin and the destructive nature of adultery.

II. PROVERBS ON WISDOM (10 – 29)

This section is predominantly made up of one-verse couplets that stand alone. Any one of them deserves to be on a bumper sticker or in needlepoint.

There are three kinds of couplets:

- The Contrastive Couplet, which uses the conjunction "but."
     a. 10:4 – "Lazy hands make a man poor,
               BUT diligent hands bring wealth."

     b. 11:4 – "Wealth is worthless in the day of wrath,
               BUT righteousness delivers from death."

     c. 12:25 – "An anxious heart weighs a man down,
               BUT a kind word cheers him up."

     d. 13:4 – "The sluggard craves and gets nothing,
               BUT the desires of the diligent are fully satisfied."

- The Completive Couplet, which uses the conjunction "and."
     a. 14:13 – "Even in laughter the heart may ache,
               AND joy may end in grief."

     b. 15:23 – "A man finds joy in giving an apt reply –
               AND how good is a timely word!"

     c. 16:3 – "Commit to the LORD whatever you do,
               AND your plans will succeed."

- The Comparative Couplet, which uses "like," "then" or "better."
     a. 15:16 – "BETTER a little with the fear of the LORD
               than great wealth with turmoil."

     b. 11:22 – "LIKE a gold ring in a pig's snout
               is a beautiful woman who shows no discretion."

     c. 25:11 – "A word aptly spoken
               is LIKE apples of gold in settings of silver."

     d. 25:25 – "LIKE cold water to a weary soul
               is good news from a distant land."

III. PRECEPTS OF WISDOM (30, 31)

This section is like an appendix by two unknown sages, Agur in chapter 30 and Lemuel in chapter 31. I Kings 4:31 gives us a little insight: "Solomon was wiser than any other man, including Ethan the Ezrahite – wiser than Heman, Calcol and Darda, the sons of Mahol." There were many "wise men" during the time of Solomon and probably Agur, son of Jakeh, was one of them. Lemuel is called a king and some think this is wisdom from a non-Israelite source that Solomon admired.

The Value of Proverbs

- Teaches us about human nature.

- There are 187 different kinds of people described in Proverbs – 46 of them are men and 23 are women, while the rest could be either. They are described as:
     1. foolish/wise
     2. proud/humble
     3. worthless/lazy
     4. kings/slaves

5. angry/merciful
6. strong/stubborn
7. intellectual/slothful
8. contentious/good
9. diligent
10. needy / rich
11. prudent
12. fearful

- To know Proverbs is to know people. To know Proverbs also is to know yourself.

- Teaches us about problem-solving.

- Proverbs tells us to face problems, not to run from them. Its insights help us to see real problems, not imaginary ones. They give hope, no matter the problem. They hit problems head on and do not offer excuses.

- Problems are confronted as being the result of faulty thinking, slothful living, selfish desires and godless reasoning.

- Teaches us about morality.

If you want to know what is right and wrong, Proverbs is for you. Its verses do not hesitate to hit head-on on some of the most sensitive issues of our day and then give black-and-white wisdom.

Issues like money, sex, pride, laziness, anger and addiction (20:1) are handled with a bluntness that is refreshing and needed.

If you desire to be holier, more righteous, more like Christ, then Proverbs is for you.

Notes

CHAPTER EIGHTEEN: ECCLESIASTES

Assignment

READ ...

Ecclesiastes, Chapters 1-12, or selected chapters from Ecclesiastes (one a day for a week) as follows:

Ecclesiastes 1	–	Everything is meaningless.
Ecclesiastes 3	–	A time for everything.
Ecclesiastes 5	–	Being in awe of God.
Ecclesiastes 7	–	The value of wisdom.
Ecclesiastes 9	–	Our common destiny.
Ecclesiastes 11	–	Cast your bread upon the waters.
Ecclesiastes 12	–	The conclusion of the matter.

MEMORIZE ...

Ecclesiastes 1:2 – "'Meaningless! Meaningless!' says the Teacher. 'Utterly meaningless! Everything is meaningless;'"

and/or

Ecclesiastes 3:1 – "There is a time for everything, and a season for every activity under heaven;"

and/or

Ecclesiastes 12:13 – "Fear God and keep His commandments, for this is the whole duty of man."

PRAY ...

Getting honest with God about how meaningless some of the things in your life might be.

Asking the Lord to give meaning and significance to every area of your life.

Confessing how you have lived for such things as money, pleasure or knowledge rather than for God.

Asking for wisdom about what it means to "fear God."

APPLY ...

In the light of Ecclesiastes, what do you:

> BELIEVE about God?
>
> REPENT of as sin?
>
> OBEY as a command from God?

SHARE ...

According to what you have learned from Ecclesiastes:

- Have a conversation with your family about what parts of your lives together are significant and meaningful. Work on a "Top Ten" list of those things most meaningful and valuable to you as a family, starting with the most meaningful and ending with the least meaningful. Don't worry if you can't name 10 meaningful things in your life.

- Share with someone not in church Ecclesiastes 1:2: "'Meaningless! Meaningless!' says the Teacher. 'Utterly meaningless! Everything is meaningless.'" Ask him what he thinks it means and see where the conversation goes. Be ready to share the meaning in your life through your relationship with Jesus Christ.

Ecclesiastes:
Confessions of a Cynic

INTRODUCTION

Psalms, Proverbs and Ecclesiastes form a trinity of Biblical literature that is unique and powerful in its diversity and the impact it has on lives. The distinctives of the three books can be understood in this way:

- Psalms – songs to God.

- Proverbs – sayings to others.

- Ecclesiastes – philosophy to yourself.

Ecclesiastes can be called the "Confessions of a Cynic" because it conveys someone who is struggling with life, questioning everything about life, doubting the value of life itself – and he does it in a sarcastic, cynical, even hyperbolic manner.

There is a little bit of a cynic in everyone. There can be pessimism about everything and sometimes one only sees a glass half-full. Being negative about things comes a whole lot easier than today's popular positive thinking.

Some people believe that Solomon was having a mid-life crisis when he wrote Ecclesiastes. To him, everything was tainted and nothing seemed to be worth the effort and bother.

THEME VERSES

"Meaningless! Meaningless!" says the Teacher.
"Utterly meaningless! Everything is meaningless."
Ecclesiastes 1:2

Now all has been heard; here is the conclusion of the matter:
Fear God and keep His commandment, for this is the whole duty of man.
Ecclesiastes 12:13

TITLE

The Hebrew word *qoheleth* means "preacher," "teacher" – "one who addresses an assembly." It also can mean "master of ceremonies."

The Greek translation of this Hebrew word is Ecclesiastes. We get our English word, "ecclesiastical," which refers to anything relating to the church or the clergy.

The teacher is probably Solomon. He is thought by most scholars to be the author, but there are those who doubt it. Solomon was a man who truly had everything, so he was well-equipped to come to the conclusions of Ecclesiastes. I Kings 10:23 tells us:

King Solomon was greater in riches and wisdom that all the other kings of the earth. The whole world sought audience with Solomon to hear the wisdom God had put in his heart.

Ecclesiastes is the most secular of all the books of the Bible. Money, books, knowledge, wine, work, humor, success, sex, pleasure and friends are given as a part of life, but they do not satisfy. The message of Ecclesiastes strikes you as being depressing, realistic, contemporary and honest.

I. EXCLAMATION (1:1-11)

Ecclesiastes 1:2 – "'Meaningless! Meaningless!' says the Teacher. 'Utterly meaningless! Everything is meaningless.'"

In the King James Version, "Vanity, Vanity. All is vanity." He is not speaking about bedroom furniture. This word "vanity" or "meaningless" occurs 35 times in Ecclesiastes and only one other time in all the rest of Scripture, in Job 27:12.

Here are other words with the same meaning:

- futility.

- vain.

- hollow.

- pointless.

- worthless.

- meaningless.

- emptiness.

- uselessness.

- ineffectiveness.

It is a common experience to think that nothing is working out, that nothing that has been done ever accomplishes the desired goal. This kind of struggle today might be diagnosed as clinical depression, and that can be the case with some people. But there is a very human condition that is not abnormal or sick in which we struggle with the value of the stuff of our lives. Sometimes reality is tough.

Meaninglessness is the verdict on all things apart from God. The phrase "under the sun" occurs 29 times in Ecclesiastes, and it shows the perspective of the book. It is a secular perspective, an earthly perspective. Heaven is not part of the consideration. If we live just for what we see, hear, feel, taste and smell, then everything is meaningless!

II. EXPERIENCE (1:12 – 2:26)

The "teacher" or "preacher" describes his experiences in seeking for meaning. He is very personal here. He uses the first person pronoun "I" throughout this section to speak of his existential experience of futility. He tried everything and he goes into detail about what he tried:

1. Wisdom and Knowledge (1:12-18) – He speaks of his study and his growth in wisdom and knowledge and how it consumed his life. He comes to this conclusion:

    For with much wisdom comes much sorrow; the more knowledge, the more grief (18).

2. Pleasures (2:1-3) – He gave himself to pleasure – laughter and wine.

3. Work and Wealth (2:4-11) – He took on great projects to accomplish something great and build something lasting, but he came to the same conclusion:

    ... everything was meaningless, a chasing after the wind; nothing was gained under the sun (11).

4. Wisdom and Folly (2:12-16) – He compared wisdom and folly and said wisdom always was best, but still he was not convinced.

Then, for the first time, he brings God into the discussion at the end of chapter 2, but in an unconvincing manner. The teacher reaches the most positive conclusion he could in verse 2:24 – "A man can do nothing better than to eat and drink and find satisfaction in his work. This, too, I see, is from the hand of God." In just a few more verses, however, he comes to the same conclusion: "This, too, is meaningless, a chasing after the wind."

III. EXPLORATION (3 – 6)

The teacher changes from personal experiences to a broader exploration of the matter. Philosophy comes to the Bible as the author explores some great truths in the human experience.

-   Time (3:1-15) – There is a time for everything, and we have one of the most revered passages of Scripture. "There is a time for everything, and a season for every activity under heaven. ..." and he covers many of the events of humanity. His conclusion, though, still is the same.

-   Death (3:16-22) – He struggles with the fate of man and sees it like the fate of the animals. We all will die and become dust. "... All come from dust, and to dust all return."

-   Injustice (4:1-3) – He saw injustice in the world, where many people were oppressed, and wondered if anything ever could be done.

-   Loneliness (4:8-12) – He pictures someone all alone and how depressing that is. He gives the proposition that "Two are better than one," and speaks of the great comfort of having a partner in life.

-   Youth (4:13-16) – He wonders if youth might be the answer to the problems he is seeing. Can it be that the next generation can do it better? Even this, though, is seen as "a chasing after the wind."

-   Being Religious (5:1-7) – He brings God into the thought and confesses that too many people are saying too many words before God, whether praying or making vows. He suggests that we need to listen more in the presence of God. Being religious with many words is seen as meaningless and the teacher gives this advice: "Stand in awe of God" (5:7).

-   Riches (5:8 – 6:12) – Even the best this life can offer in wealth, possessions and material things cannot bring meaning. It is another evil under the sun. All these things we can enjoy for a season, but they can be stolen and taken away quickly.

IV. EXHORTATIONS (7:1 – 12:7)

So, what is one to do? If everything is so bad, then end it all. Take your own life. That, however, is not the direction in which Ecclesiastes goes.

There are a couple of general exhortations from this section:

1. We all struggle with meaninglessness and insignificance at some point in our lives. There are some lessons to be learned that can help one cope with meaninglessness and insignificance at the moment. Kenneth Boa summarizes the teachings in chapters 7-9 with these words:

Levity and pleasure-seeking are seen as superficial and foolish; it is better to have sober depth of thought. Wisdom and self-control provide perspective and strength in coping with life. One should enjoy prosperity and consider truth in adversity – God made both. Avoid the twin righteousness and immorality. Sin invades all men, and wisdom is cut short by evil and death. The human mind cannot grasp ultimate meaning. Submission to authority helps one avoid unnecessary hardship, but real justice often is lacking on earth. The uncertainties of life and certainty of the grave show that God's purposes and ways often cannot be grasped. One should therefore magnify opportunities while they last because fortune suddenly can change.[1]

2. We all need to go on an adventure of faith. "Cast your bread upon the waters, for after many days you will find it again" (11:1).

For a Jew, the most adventurous thing was sea travel. It was not a natural part of his nomadic shepherd/farmer's life. For him to "cast his bread upon the waters" was like our "heading for the mountains" or "taking a risk with a new business venture" or "buying a motorcycle and hitting the road" or "getting a makeover." In other words, take a risk. Get out of your rut. Do something different. Go on an adventure. Don't always play it safe. Get in touch with your wild side. Then, maybe you will find yourself.

V. EPILOGUE (12:9-14)

Ecclesiastes concludes with two simple, yet profound, truths:

1. Be faithful to God (13) – "Now all has been heard; here is the conclusion of the matter: Fear God and keep His commandments, for this is the whole duty of man."

The God-centered way of living is the way to live. Be focused on God and fear Him (revere Him). Everything else will disappoint us and complicate our lives, but we always need to come back to His Word and make sure we are in tune with Him.

2. Leave everything to God (14) – "For God will bring every deed into judgment, including every hidden thing, whether it is good or evil."

God is going to take care of the mess and the meaninglessness. Ultimately, it is not of our concern. In this life, everything does not make sense. If we expect clarity in everything, not only will we be frustrated, but we also will be wrong. This life was meant to be lived by faith in the God who will judge all things and will take care of all things.

Lessons From Ecclesiastes

1. There are limitations to the meaning of life found in creation.

2. There are no limitations to the meaning of life found in the Creator.

---

1   Boa, Kenneth *Talk Through the Old Testament* (Carol Stream: Tyndale House Publishers, 1980), p. 133.

NOTES

CHAPTER NINETEEN: SONG OF SOLOMON

Assignment

READ ...

Song of Solomon, Chapters 1-8, or selected chapters from Song of Solomon (one a day for a week) as follows:

       Song of Solomon 1   –   A passionate love.

       Song of Solomon 6   –   A persistent love.

MEMORIZE ...

Song of Solomon 8:6:

> *Place me like a seal over your heart,*
> > *like a seal on your arm;*
> > *for love is as strong as death,*
> > *its jealousy unyielding as the grave.*
>
> *It burns like blazing fire,*
> > *like a mighty flame.*

PRAY ...

Thanking God for human love. Get specific and thank God for all the relationships in your life where love is central.

Thanking God for His love for you that is greater than any human love (John 3:16).

Confessing where you have not loved God and others as you ought. Ask God for a new passion in your life for Him and others.

Thanking God for your spouse and the love you share.

APPLY ...

In the light of the Song of Solomon, what do you:

> BELIEVE about God?
>
> REPENT of as sin?
>
> OBEY as a command from God?

SHARE ...

According to what you have learned from the Song of Solomon:

- Have a conversation in your family about sex. Father and mother need to talk this out to decide on the best way to have this conversation with the children. Care needs to be taken to be specific, but not overly so. Special attention needs to be given to particular questions the children might have in regard to sex.

- Be careful with this one. Be sure to have this conversation only with someone of your own sex. With those warnings, though, ask someone who is skeptical of or critical about the Church what they think God says about sex. Once again, be careful here. Don't feed any evil desires. It is often very telling, however, that many people think sex is always evil and God is opposed to it. The Song of Solomon emphasizes the truth that sex is a gift of God, and it is meant for pleasure and fulfillment within marriage.

Song of Solomon: A Love Song

THEME VERSE

We rejoice and delight in you; we will praise your love more than wine.
Song of Solomon 1:4

INTERPRETATIONS

How to interpret the Song of Solomon has been a raging debate over the centuries. There have been three different ways that it has been understood:

- Fictional: It is just a love story that is literature. No historical truth. No deeper meaning. It simply is a piece of fiction showing the private life of a king.

- Allegorical: An allegory is a story that is not historical, but illustrates a deeper truth. The deeper truth of the Song of Solomon is the love that God has for His people. We need to know that the Bible does show a strong parallel between God's covenant relationship with the Church and the marriage covenant between a man and a woman. (Ezekiel 16:23; Hosea 1-3; and Ephesians 5:22ff.)

- Historical: A poetical record of Solomon's actual romance with his wife. It may be applicable as an illustration of God's love for us, but its literal purpose is showing the love that a husband and a wife share – and it is very sensual and sexual.

TITLE

- 1:1 – "Song of Songs."

- Traditional – "Song of Solomon."

- Latin – "Canticles."

Solomon wrote 1,005 songs (I Kings 4:32). This is the "Song of Songs," which probably means it was considered the best of all of the songs written by Solomon.

An interesting observation is that Ecclesiastes, the most secular book in the Bible, is followed by the Song of Solomon, which is the most sensual book in the Bible.

PROBLEM

Solomon had a problem with women. I Kings 11:1-4 records that Solomon had 700 wives and 300 concubines. Something was out of line here.

Is Solomon the best person to write about monogamous, faithful and godly love in marriage? Good question.

Some reasons to uphold that Solomon had integrity in writing the Song of Songs:

- The bulk of Solomon's marriages were political arrangements. This was the way things were done. If a treaty was made with another country, that treaty was ratified by way of a marriage between the two countries.

- The Song of Songs itself recognizes that Solomon had a harem:

    Sixty queens there may be, and eighty concubines, and virgins beyond number; but my dove, my perfect one, is unique, the only daughter of her mother, the favorite of the one who bore her. The maidens saw her and called her blessed; the queens and concubines praised her (6:8, 9).

This explains, within the context of a harem, that Solomon was devoted to one woman and everyone else was devoted to her, as well.

Solomon probably wrote the Song of Songs while he was a young man in the more faithful and godly time of his life, while the temple was being built and the favor of God was upon him. It was later in life that his many wives stole his heart away to idols.

The situation portrayed with purity and passion in the Song of Songs only shows how far Solomon fell later on in life into impurity in his relationships with women.

There is no easy way to outline the Song of Solomon. It is like a one-act play. We need to begin by knowing the characters. They are:

- The bride (the beloved), shown by the feminine pronouns.

- The groom (the lover), shown by the masculine pronouns.

- The chorus (friends), shown by the plural pronouns.

I. FALLING IN LOVE (1 – 3)

The courtship is described in a way that almost makes us blush:

"Let him kiss me with the kisses of his mouth – for your love is more delightful than wine" *(1:1).*

"How beautiful you are, my lover! Oh, how charming! And our bed is verdant" (1:10).

"His left arm is under my head, and his right arm embraces me" (2:6).

"My lover is mine and I am his" (2:16).

The admiration of one another is mutual and inclusion of the "friends" emphasizes that this relationship was known by everyone.

II. UNITED IN LOVE (4 – 5:1)

The admiration continues (4:1-5):

How beautiful you are, my darling! Oh, how beautiful!
Your eyes behind your veil are doves.

Your hair is like a flock of goats descending from Mount Gilead.
Your teeth are like a flock of sheep just shorn, coming up from the washing.
Each has its twin; not one of them is alone.
Your lips are like a scarlet ribbon; your mouth is lovely.
Your temples behind your veil are like the halves of a pomegranate.
Your neck is like the tower of David, built with elegance;
on it hang a thousand shields, all of them shields of warriors.
Your two breasts are like two fawns, like twin fawns of a gazelle that browse among the lilies.

Whew!

III. STRUGGLING IN LOVE (5:2-6)

There is a dream by the woman wherein she fears that the man has left her. She describes it this way: "I slept but my heart was awake." The fear of her dream grips her: "I looked for him but did not find him. I called him but he did not answer."

The admiration between the couple continues, but there is some anxiety in the relationship.

IV. GROWING IN LOVE (7 – 8)

Even with some jealousy and separation in their relationship, they do not let it keep them apart. The Song of Solomon ends with the relationship between the man and the woman being strong and faithful.

Lessons From the Song of Solomon

1. Sexuality is not innately sinful. Sex is a gift of God.

2. Sexuality in marriage is meant to be pleasant and beautiful. This might be one of the greatest lessons we can teach our children.

NOTES

CHAPTER TWENTY: ISAIAH

Assignment

READ ...

Isaiah, Chapters 1-66, or selected chapters from Isaiah (one a day for a week) as follows:

Isaiah 1	–	Confrontation of a sinful nation.
Isaiah 2	–	The day of the Lord.
Isaiah 6	–	Isaiah's vision of the Lord.
Isaiah 9	–	Unto us a child is born.
Isaiah 40	–	Comfort for God's people.
Isaiah 53	–	The suffering servant.
Isaiah 55	–	His ways are not our ways.

MEMORIZE ...

Isaiah 1:18 – "'Come now, let us reason together,' says the LORD. 'Though your sins are like scarlet, they shall be as white as snow; though they are red as crimson, they shall be like wool;'"

and/or

Isaiah 9:6 – "For to us a child is born, to us a son is given, and the government will be on His shoulders. And He will be called Wonderful Counselor, Mighty God, Everlasting Father, Prince of Peace;"

and/or

Isaiah 55:6 – "Seek the LORD while He may be found; call on Him while He is near."

PRAY ...

Confessing the sins we can commit as religious people.

Worshipping the Lord as the one who is Holy, Holy, Holy.

Thanking God for the promise of the Messiah, who would be called Immanuel.

Marveling in the truth that the Lord's ways and thoughts are not our ways and thoughts.

Longing for the new heavens and the new earth when the reign of the Lord will be clear and comprehensive.

APPLY ...

In the light of Isaiah, what do you:

>   BELIEVE about God?

>   REPENT of as sin?

>   OBEY as a command from God?

SHARE ...

According to what you have learned from Isaiah:

- Talk about Christmas with the family, no matter what time of the year it is. Isaiah gives us many insights into the Messiah's coming. Read together Isaiah 7:14; 9:2-7; and Isaiah 53. Isaiah 53 does not talk about a child being born, but of a Messiah who would come and be willing to suffer for our sins.

- Ask someone you know who has problems with the Church what he thinks of Isaiah 1:15, 16:

  When you spread out your hands in prayer, I will hide my eyes from you; even if you offer many prayers, I will not listen. Your hands are full of blood; wash and make yourselves clean. Take your evil deeds out of my sight!

These are the words of the Lord to religious people who are hypocritical. You may have found a point of agreement with your friend.

Isaiah:
Prince of the Prophets

INTRODUCTION

What Michelangelo is to artists, Beethoven to composers, Lincoln to presidents, Billy Graham to preachers, Vince Lombardi to football coaches and Shakespeare to writers – Isaiah is to prophets.

He is considered the best of the bunch: the best bloodline, the best educated, the best positioned in the court of the king and the most articulate.

THEME VERSE

"Come now, let us reason together," says the LORD. "Though your sins are like scarlet,
they shall be as white as snow; though they are red as crimson, they shall be like wool."
Isaiah 1:18

TITLE

Isaiah means "Yahweh is salvation." His name serves as an excellent summary of the contents of his prophecy.

The word salvation occurs 26 times in Isaiah and only seven times in the rest of the prophets combined.

- The need of salvation – judgment.

- The call to salvation – repentance.

- The way to salvation – Messiah

BACKGROUND

Isaiah 1:1 – It is made clear that Isaiah was serving kings in the capital city of Jerusalem right in the king's court. The setting is somewhat reminiscent of Peter Marshall's ministry as chaplain of the U.S. Senate, with influence over powerful people.

The dates for Isaiah are 740-680 B.C., which is during the time of the divided kingdom. He is serving the kings of the Southern Kingdom – Judah.

OVERVIEW

Isaiah has been called the Bible within the Bible:

Bible	**Isaiah**
66 books	66 chapters
39 Old Testament	1 – 39 on law and judgment
27 New Testament	40 – 66 on good news – Messiah and deliverance

I. PROPHETIC CONDEMNATION (1 – 35)

Isaiah opens his prophecy with a scathing condemnation of Judah as a rebellious nation. They were rebellious children and their rebellion affected every part of their lives, even their religious lives. The Lord made it clear:

Stop bringing meaningless offerings! Your incense is detestable to me. New Moons, Sabbaths and convocation – I cannot bear your evil assemblies. … When you spread out your hands in prayer, I will hide my eyes from you; even if you offer many prayers, I will not listen (1:13, 15).

In the midst of promised judgment, the Lord's gracious offer would always stand:

"Come now, let us reason together," says the LORD. "Though your sins are like scarlet, they shall be as white as snow; though they are red as crimson, they shall be like wool" (1:18, the theme verse).

Isaiah 6 is one of the most memorable chapters in the Bible. It is the record of Isaiah's call in the context of seeing the Lord high and lifted up in the temple. Angelic beings cry out, "Holy, holy, holy is the LORD Almighty," and Isaiah is convicted of his sin and the sins of the people around him. As the Lord forgives his sin, He then calls for someone to go in His name, and Isaiah answers, "Here am I. Send me." There is so much in Isaiah 6 about worship, conviction, forgiveness and mission. In the midst of this prophetic condemnation of Judah in chapters 1-12, glimpses of the coming Messiah are given:

- 7:14 – "The virgin shall conceive and bear a son and His name shall be called Immanuel."

- 9:6 – "Unto us a child is born, unto us a son is given."

- 11:1 – "A shoot will come up from the stump of Jesse."

This condemnation for sin, though, will start with Judah. Chapters 13-23 then give a list of other nations that also will experience the judgment of God: Babylon, the Philistines, Moab, Damascus, Cush, Egypt, Edom.

Isaiah is not yet through with the bad news. Chapters 24-35 make it clear that the judgment of the Lord will be for the whole earth:

See, the LORD is going to lay waste the earth and devastate it; He will ruin its face and scatter its inhabitants (24:1).

Isaiah takes a hop, skip and a jump around the known world at that time, and it is clear that no one will escape the wrath of God:

The LORD is angry with all nations; his wrath is upon all their armies (34:2).

So, the table is set. Judgment is coming. But is that the end? No, it is only the beginning. The Lord is about to do something magnificent. Chapters 34-35 show that shift in what the Lord will do. Chapter 34 is filled with words like wrath, death, blood and desolation; then chapter 35 is filled with words like rejoice, joy, glory and redemption. Biblically, the bad news always precedes the good news.

II. Historical Condemnation and Deliverance (36 – 39)

We then have a unique section (36 – 39) where the prophetic word tells a story from history. Parallel passages to this story can be found in II Kings 18 – 20 and II Chronicles 32. It is the historical record of when King Hezekiah was king of Judah. Isaiah knew firsthand the details, because he was in the king's court.

The danger came from the Assyrian king, Sennacherib, who already had destroyed the Northern Kingdom, Israel, in 722 B.C. He had turned his attention to Jerusalem and had every intention of wiping it out as well. Sennacherib even thought that God had told him to take Judah, so he laid siege to Jerusalem and began to slowly starve the city.

Isaiah gives a prophecy of deliverance from the Lord that simply went:

Do not be afraid. I am going to conquer Sennacherib myself, send him home, and there he will be cut down with the sword (37:6, 7).

King Hezekiah believed the Word of the Lord through Isaiah and prayed a magnificent prayer:

Now, O Lord our God, deliver us from his hand, so that all kingdoms on earth may know that you alone, O Lord, are God (37:20).

The end result gave the Lord all the glory:

Then the angel of the Lord went out and put to death a hundred and eighty five thousand men in the Assyrian camp. When the people got up the next morning – there were all the dead bodies! So Sennacherib king of Assyria broke camp and withdrew. He returned to Nineveh and stayed there (37:36, 37).

Then we are told that back in Nineveh, Sennacherib's sons killed him with the sword.

In chapter 38, we get another historical account of Hezekiah's illness, his prayer for healing and the gift of an extra 15 years of life.

III. Prophetic Consolation (40 – 66)

Then there is a radical change in Isaiah's prophecy. It is so radical that many Biblical scholars say that the same Isaiah who wrote the first part of Isaiah could not have written the second part. There must have been two Isaiahs. Some scholars even insist that there had to be three Isaiahs. All I know is that in the flow of the prophecy, the light dawns, beginning with chapter 40. The bad news of judgment is over. The historical deliverance of Judah by the Lord is remembered. There is, however, the matter of the deliverance of the whole earth.

The words have echoed throughout all of history of the Lord's doings:

A voice of one calling: "In the desert prepare the way for the Lord; make straight in the wilderness a highway for our God. Every valley shall be raised up, every mountain and hill made low. ... And the glory of the Lord will be revealed, and all mankind together will see it. For the mouth of the Lord has spoken" (40:3-5).

The truth of the Lord's comfort and consolation is about to be proclaimed.

Chapters 40 – 48 are filled with the sovereign grace of God. He has spoken. He is coming. He is the helper of Israel. He is doing a new thing. He will forgive our transgressions. He has redeemed His people. He is displaying His glory.

There are 216 verses in chapters 40 – 48 and 115 of them speak of God's power, might, grace, goodness and glory. This is the basis of our hope, even in the light of our deserving judgment.

The hope we have in the Lord, however, is made very specific with the promises of the Messiah to come. Chapters 49 – 57 begin to speak of "the servant of the Lord," "salvation to the ends of the earth," "the Sovereign Lord who helps," "the righteousness of the Lord for all generations" and "the Holy One of Israel."

Right in the middle of this section is the vivid description of the "suffering servant" in Isaiah 53. There is no Scripture like it. It is a picture of Jesus that gives depth to the Crucifixion. It is a prophecy about Jesus that places our sin right on the head of Jesus on the Cross:

> *Surely He took up our infirmities and carried our sorrows, yet we considered Him stricken by God, smitten by Him, and afflicted. But He was pierced for our transgressions, He was crushed for our iniquities; the punishment that brought us peace was upon Him, and by His wounds we are healed. We all, like sheep, have gone astray, each of us has turned to his own way; and the LORD has laid on Him the iniquity of us all (53:4-6).*

The prophecy of Isaiah concludes with a picture of future hope in chapters 58 – 66 that goes beyond the truth of the Messiah who would suffer and die. No, this Messiah also would establish a new kingdom, even a new heaven and a new earth. The glory of His kingdom will stand forever.

Lessons From Isaiah

1. Greatness is not who you are, but whose you are (1:18.) Left to our own efforts, education, resources and reputation, we are doomed. It is only as we honestly confess our sins and seek the Lord's mercy that we find purpose, peace and power.

2. Our conception of sin is molded by our understanding of God (6). When a person joins the Presbyterian Church (USA), he or she says "Yes" to this question: "Do you acknowledge yourself to be a sinner in the sight of God …?" We only know our shortcomings by seeing who God really is – the one who is "holy, holy, holy."

3. Our hope is in Christ alone (53). The truth that Christ suffered and died "for us" is made as clear as it can be made in Isaiah 53. The connection of the cross to our corruption is at the heart of the Good News of what God has done for us.

4. Everything else will fade and fail; but God's Word will stand forever:

> *As the rain and the snow come down from heaven, and do not return to it without watering the earth and making it bud and flourish, so that it yields seed for the sower and bread for the eater, so is my word that goes out from my mouth: It will not return to me empty, but will accomplish what I desire and achieve the purpose for which I sent it (55:10, 11).*

NOTES

CHAPTER TWENTY-ONE: JEREMIAH AND LAMENTATIONS

Assignment

READ ...

Jeremiah, Chapters 1-52, and Lamentations, Chapters 1-5, or selected chapters from Jeremiah and Lamentations (one a day for a week) as follows:

Jeremiah 1	–	The call of Jeremiah.
Jeremiah 7	–	The sins of religious people.
Jeremiah 17	–	The condition of the human heart.
Jeremiah 18	–	A visit to the potter's house.
Jeremiah 31	–	The promise of a new covenant.
Jeremiah 52	–	The fall of Jerusalem.
Lamentations 1	–	Despair over the fall of Jerusalem.

MEMORIZE ...

Jeremiah 1:5 – "Before I formed you in the womb I knew you, before you were born I set you apart; I appointed you as a prophet to the nations;"

and/or

Jeremiah 31:33 – "'This is the covenant I will make with the house of Israel after that time,' declares the Lord. 'I will put my law in their minds and write it on their hearts. I will be their God, and they will be my people.'"

PRAY ...

Confessing to the Lord the sin in your heart that He sees, but no one else does.

Thanking the Lord that He knew you and called you even before you were born.

Praising God as a covenant-making Lord who promises to be our God and to keep us as His people.

Expressing the grief and sorrow in your life over a great loss or hurt. Remember that weeping and mourning can be godly expressions.

Apply ...

In the light of Jeremiah and Lamentations, what do you:

> BELIEVE about God?
>
> REPENT of as sin?
>
> OBEY as a command from God?

Share ...

According to what you have learned from Jeremiah and Lamentations:

- Jeremiah very much was a prophet of the heart. He knew that the human heart was sinful, but he also knew that God changes human hearts. Have a conversation with your family or with some friends about "matters of the heart." This means to talk about that part of your lives that no one else sees ... that part known only by each person and his God.

- Talk with someone you know – Christian or not – who recently has had a great loss. Maybe it is the death of a loved one, the loss of a job, a serious illness, etc. Go to that person and "mourn with those who mourn." Jeremiah was the "weeping prophet" and he openly lamented over the great disaster of the fall of Jerusalem. Sharing in the sorrow of someone else – without preaching to him – might give you an opportunity to simply love someone who is hurting.

Jeremiah: Standing Alone

INTRODUCTION

Jeremiah probably is known by most people as the "weeping prophet."

Oh, that my head were a spring of water and my eyes a fountain of tears! I would weep day and night for the slain of my people (9:1).

But if you do not listen, I will weep in secret because of your pride; my eyes will weep bitterly, overflowing with tears, because the LORD's flock will be taken captive (13:17).

Jeremiah also wrote the Book of Lamentations, which is a book full of weeping, mourning and lament. But why did he weep? He wept because he prophesied during a time of approaching judgment for Judah. He preached and called for repentance, but the people did not listen. Jeremiah was faithful, but the people were not. Judgment was coming and Jeremiah knew it. This will cause anyone to weep.

We know that Jesus wept. We remember the shortest verse in the Bible (John 11:35) as "Jesus wept." That was at the death of Lazarus and He demonstrated His love for Lazarus. There is, however, a second time where it is recorded that Jesus wept. It is in Luke 19:41. As He approached Jerusalem, He wept over the city. He wept then because He knew the judgment of God was coming soon to Jerusalem, and the people had not heeded the call to repentance. Jesus wept there for the hardness of the people's hearts and the coming judgment.

This was the way Jeremiah wept. The people would not listen to the call to return to God and it broke his heart.

Jeremiah's weeping, though, went deeper. It was not only because of the hardness of the people, but because of the loneliness of Jeremiah's call. Jeremiah, more than most prophets, stood alone in his ministry:

- Jeremiah 16:1, 2 – The Lord told him that he was not to marry or have children.

- Jeremiah 20:14-18 – Jeremiah struggled with depression and even wished that he had never been born.

- Jeremiah 26:7-11 – The religious leaders sought to kill Jeremiah.

No wonder he wept! Ministry to a dying world or a dying people is useless until one is also willing to die. The Church is in need of a "weeping" ministry. The Church must have its heart broken before it can stand alone, as Jeremiah did.

BACKGROUND

Jeremiah's prophetic ministry covered 40 years. No other prophet had such a lengthy ministry with such little result. He gave himself to 40 years of ministry in Judah with no positive response. The nation did not change. Jeremiah preached for them to repent – he called for repentance 47 times – and there was no response. Put in the position of watching the death of his nation, Jeremiah was called to preach the funeral – over and over again. He stood alone and wept.

As Jeremiah stood alone, he was a strange mixture of toughness and tenderness. One author called him "a figure of bronze who dissolves into tears."

I. CALL OF JEREMIAH (1)

Jeremiah was a PK – a priest's kid. His ministry started under good King Josiah and spanned a 40-year period of worsening conditions.

God's call on Jeremiah's life came before conception:

Before I formed you in the womb I knew you, before you were born I set you apart; I appointed you as a prophet to the nations (1:5).

This verse shows the sovereignty of God in the calling of Jeremiah before Jeremiah had done a thing. It also shows the sanctity of life – even unborn life. God's activity is clear: "I formed you in the womb;" "I knew you in the womb;" and "I set you apart before you were born." The unborn are precious in the sight of God.

Jeremiah had an excuse, though. He could not speak because he was "only a child." The Lord reassures him:

But the LORD said to me, "Do not say, 'I am only a child.' You must go to everyone I send you to and say whatever I command you. Do not be afraid of them, for I am with you and will rescue you," declares the LORD (1:7, 8).

The Lord tells Jeremiah that his ministry would begin with a negative impact:

- To uproot.

- To tear down.

- To destroy.

- To overthrow.

Then, his ministry would lead to a positive impact:

- To build.

- To plant.

II. CONDEMNATION OF JUDAH (2 – 45)

Sins of Religious People

More than any other prophet, Jeremiah confronts the sins of religious people. Judah at this time had an active religious life. Sacrifices were being offered, prayers were being made, the temple was functioning, etc. There was no heart religion, however, only an outward observance of rituals that was not accompanied by any repentance.

Listen to some of his rebukes:

A horrible and shocking thing has happened in the land: The prophets prophesy lies, the priests rule by their own authority, and the people love it this way. (5:30, 31)

From the least to the greatest, all are greedy for gain; prophets and priests alike, all practice deceit. They dress the wound of my people as though it were not serious. "Peace, peace," they say, where there is no peace. Are they ashamed of their loathsome conduct? No, they have no shame at all; they do not even know how to blush. (6:13-15)

This is what the LORD Almighty, the God of Israel, says: "Reform your ways and your actions, and I will let you live in this place. So do not trust in deceptive words and say, 'This is the temple of the LORD, the temple of the LORD, the temple of the LORD!'" (7:3, 4)

Jeremiah speaks to the LORD about the people: "You are always on their lips but far from their hearts" (12:2b).

Jeremiah's Life Becomes Object Lessons

Jeremiah is called by God to graphically prophecy some truths in his own life. Jeremiah was told by the Lord to do several things to illustrate his message to the people:

- The wineskin (13:12-14).

- Jeremiah was told to not marry or have children (10:1-9).

- Go to the potter's house (18:1-8).

- Go buy a clay jar (19:1-13).

- The two baskets of figs (24:1-10).

- Jeremiah was to put on a yoke (27:1-11).

- Jeremiah was to buy a field (32:6-15).

- Jeremiah was to bury some stones (43:8-13).

The meanings of each of these object lessons were unique and powerful, but generally they all proclaimed that God was sovereign and holy; the people were not honoring Him as such, and judgment was coming.

III. THE LORD'S COVENANT HOPE (30 – 33)

In the middle of the confrontation of religious sins and the call of Jeremiah to preach the hard message of repentance is the promise of God about the future. The Lord promises a coming day when a new covenant will be made and the people will be more faithful than the current ones (31:33, 34).

"This is the covenant I will make with the house of Israel after that time," declares the LORD. "I will put my law in their minds and write it on their hearts. I will be their God, and they will be my people. No longer will a man teach his neighbor, or a man his brother, saying, 'Know the LORD,' because they will all know me, from the least of them to the greatest."

IV. CONDEMNATION OF NATIONS (46 – 51)

Jeremiah was called from the womb to be a "prophet to the nations." This becomes clear in chapters 46 – 51 where the nations around Judah are not going to get away from judgment. Jeremiah delivers prophetic oracles against nine nations:

- Egypt.

- Philistia.

- Moab.

- Ammon.

- Edom.

- Damascus.

- Arabia.

- Elam.

- Babylon.

V. CONSUMMATION OF JUDGMENT (52)

After 40 years of preaching that judgment would come if the people did not repent, judgment came.

The fall of Jerusalem to Babylon's forces is such a significant event in the Old Testament that it is recorded in detail four times:

- II Kings 25.

- II Chronicles 36.

- Jeremiah 39 as prophecy.

- Jeremiah 52 as history.

Lamentations:
Flip Side of Sin

INTRODUCTION

Sin is like buying an old 45 record. You buy the record for the one hit song you like but, at the same time, you buy the flip-side song that is usually not good.

Lamentations gives us the "flip side" of sin. There is no doubt that sin can be pleasant and enjoyable, but remember: There is a flip side that always, comes with the sin – judgment.

The people of Judah had chosen to follow the sensual, the idolatrous, the rebellious, the empty religious life. They had been told time and time again, especially by Jeremiah, to "repent or perish," but they never repented. The time for the "flip side" had come. Judgment had arrived. Jerusalem was destroyed.

THEME VERSE

How deserted lies the city, once so full of people! How like a widow is she, who once was great among the nations! She who was queen among the provinces has now become a slave.
Lamentations 1:1

TITLE

Lamentations is not the name of a prophet or a people. It is the name of an act, a condition. To lament is to wail, cry out, regret strongly or mourn aloud. It is the guttural sound from someone who has been deeply hurt. A lament is what one feels when the worst thing happens.

When something bad happens to us – a sickness, an accident, a storm, etc., we often say, "Well, it could have been worse." A lament is experienced when that cannot be said because the worst has happened.

BACKGROUND

Jeremiah, the weeping prophet, is the one who wrote Lamentations. He is not mentioned in the book, but traditionally he is recognized as the author, and logically he is suited to be the author because of his history and temperament.

The date is 586 B.C. – the day of infamy for the Jews. It was the day the nation died. Jerusalem was besieged and overthrown. The people suffered immensely. The temple, palace and walls were destroyed. The "cream of the crop" of the people was taken away to exile to spend the next 70 years in Babylon.

Lamentations is written in a highly stylized form following an alphabetic acrostic throughout the lament.

This means that each line begins with a different letter from the Hebrew alphabet. There are 22 in each chapter, except in chapter 3 where there are three lines in the acrostic, and in chapter 5, where there are 22 verses, but not in acrostic style.

I. Voice of the City (1)

The city referred to is Jerusalem, which was devastated by Babylon. The lament is expressed by Jeremiah:

Jerusalem has sinned greatly and so has become unclean. All who honored her despise her, for they have seen her nakedness; she herself groans and turns away (1:8).

Then, the lament is expressed by Jerusalem personified. It is as if Jerusalem is speaking:

See, O Lord, how distressed I am! I am in torment within, and in my heart I am disturbed, for I have been most rebellious. Outside, the sword bereaves; inside, there is only death (1:20).

II. The Voice of the Lord (2)

In this section, the voice of the Lord is heard. Babylon was the invading army that destroyed Jerusalem, but Babylon was only a secondary cause. The Lord was the primary cause. He brought Babylon to judge Jerusalem:

The Lord is like an enemy; He has swallowed up Israel. He has swallowed up all her palaces and destroyed her strongholds. He has multiplied mourning and lamentation for the Daughter of Judah (2:5).

This is hard to take. We can almost talk ourselves out of the eventuality of judgment. We can convince ourselves that our God would never do such a thing to us. It just doesn't sound like God.

The day of judgment, though, is coming. It will always be preceded by a period of mercy and grace, but judgment is coming. Jerusalem now knew that what brought them down was not a powerful Babylonian army, but a powerful, holy God.

III. Voice of the Prophet (3)

The third chapter is the only chapter with 66 verses. All the rest have 22. In this chapter, the prophet Jeremiah shares his thoughts and emotions:

- Jeremiah's realism about God's wrath (1-18).

- 3:1 – "I am the man who has seen affliction by the rod of His wrath."

- Jeremiah's understanding of redemption (19-39).

- 22, 23 – "Because of the Lord's great love we are not consumed, for His compassions never fail. They are new every morning; great is your faithfulness."

- 40-55 – Jeremiah's repentance (40): "Let us examine our ways and test them, and let us return to the Lord."

- 55-60 – Jeremiah's relief (55-57): "I called on your name, O Lord, from the depths of the pit. You heard my plea: 'Do not close your ears to my cry for relief.' You came near when I called you, and you said, 'Do not fear.'"

IV. VOICE OF DEVASTATION (4)

This chapter reviews the devastation and destruction. There is no quick moving forward even in the light of the Lord's ministry of comfort:

The punishment of my people is greater than that of Sodom, which was overthrown in a moment without a hand turned to help her (6).

We too often respond to terrible things in our lives with "just forget it." That is often good advice, especially if we are dwelling on something without the mercy of God. There are some things, though, we should never forget! The people of Jerusalem were to never forget what happened to them and why.

V. VOICE OF THE CAPTIVES (5)

This last chapter is in the form of a prayer. The people lament their condition before the Lord (1-18).

Remember, O LORD, what has happened to us; look, and see our disgrace. (1)

And then they pray for restoration (19-22).

Restore us to yourself, O Lord, that we may return; renew our days as of old unless you have utterly rejected us and are angry with us beyond measure. (21, 22)

Lessons From Jeremiah and Lamentations

1. God calls us to stand alone if there is no one else who will be faithful. This was the difficult call placed upon Jeremiah. He was given a message of judgment and repentance, but the people did not respond. Even the religious establishment did not stand with him. It is never easy to stand alone and be faithful, so weeping might be what God calls us to do.

2. God calls us to stand knowing we are never really alone. The worst event in the Old Testament was the fall of Jerusalem, and the message of Lamentations is that God was with them in their pain. Our weeping can be real and genuine, but it is never an end in itself. God works through our pain to demonstrate His good providence.

NOTES

Chapter Twenty-Two: Ezekiel

Assignment

Read ...

Ezekiel, Chapters 1-48, or selected chapters from Ezekiel (one a day for a week) as follows:

Ezekiel 2	–	The call of Ezekiel.
Ezekiel 3	–	The call of Ezekiel continued.
Ezekiel 13	–	False prophets condemned.
Ezekiel 33	–	Ezekiel a watchman.
Ezekiel 34	–	Prophecy against the shepherds.
Ezekiel 37	–	The vision of the valley of dry bones.
Ezekiel 43	–	The glory of God will return to the temple.

Memorize ...

Ezekiel 3:12 – "Then the Spirit lifted me up, and I heard behind me a loud rumbling sound – May the glory of the Lord be praised in His dwelling place!"

and/or

Ezekiel 18:4 – "The soul who sins is the one who will die;"

and/or

Ezekiel 37:13 – "Then you, my people, will know that I am the Lord, when I open your graves and bring you up from them."

Pray ...

Giving yourself to the Lord even if He has something difficult and painful for you to do.

Confessing your own sin, knowing that the soul that persists in sin surely will die.

For the glory of God to be real in the Church and in your life.

Longing for the day when the whole earth will be filled with the glory of God.

APPLY ...

In the light of Ezekiel, what do you:

>BELIEVE about God?

>REPENT of as sin?

>OBEY as a command from God?

SHARE ...

According to what you have learned from Ezekiel:

- Share with your family some of the difficult times you have had in your Christian life. Seek to be real and genuine about the call God has placed on our lives that is not always is pleasant. This is not complaining, but it is being honest about how heavy it is to follow the Lord.

- Ask someone who is not in the Church about what he thinks of the Church. Give him permission to be truthful about the Church's weaknesses and bad reputation. Don't get defensive, but where you can agree with the Church's problems, do so. Do bring in the message of Ezekiel 37, where the Lord brings life to the dead, dry bones in the valley. The Lord desires to bring renewal to the Church.

Ezekiel:
Weird and Wonderful

INTRODUCTION

The first question of the Shorter Catechism is:

Q. What is the chief end of man?

A. Man's chief end is to glorify God and enjoy Him forever.

How do you glorify God? In other words, what are we to do in order to bring glory to God? The child's catechism makes it as clear as it can be in the first five questions:

- Who made you? God.

- What else did God make? God made all things.

- Why did God make you and all things? For His own glory.

- How do you glorify God? By loving Him and doing what He commands.

- Why ought you to glorify God? Because He made me and takes care of me.

This is one of the keys of the Christian life – living to give glory to God.

The Bible often speaks of the glory of God. In addition to the verb – to glorify God – the noun is frequently used – the glory of God.

So there is another question: What is the glory of God?

1. Presence of God

The glory of God is other-worldly. It is not natural to us. We do not see it every day. It most often is described as a light or a brilliance or a cloud. It is called the *Shekinah* Glory. *Shekinah* is Hebrew for "dwelling," so the *Shekinah* Glory is the glory of God that comes and dwells with His people.

In the Old Testament it is connected with the Ark of the Covenant, the Holy of Holies in the tabernacle and the temple, and it is always an indicator of the presence of God.

Then the cloud covered the Tent of Meeting, and the glory of the LORD filled the tabernacle.
Moses could not enter the Tent of Meeting because the cloud had settled upon it, and the glory
of the LORD filled the tabernacle.
Exodus 40:34, 35

2. The Law of God

The glory of God is inseparably connected with the Law. God's Law is holy. It is an expression of the holiness of God and it tells us how to be holy. The Law of God cannot be easily dismissed. It is an expression of the very nature of God.

When Moses went up on the mountain, the cloud covered it, and the glory of the LORD settled on Mount Sinai. For six days the cloud covered the mountain, and on the seventh day the LORD called to Moses from within the cloud. To the Israelites the glory of the LORD looked like a consuming fire on top of the mountain. Then Moses entered the cloud as he went on up the mountain. And he stayed on the mountain forty days and forty nights.
Exodus 24:15-18

And what happened during those 40 days? Moses received the Law from God.

3. The Fear of God

There is a part of the glory of God that should cause us to tremble. The truth is that we don't know what we really are talking about when we talk about the glory of God. It is messing with fire. His glory should remind us about how unrealistic it is for us to even think that we can see God or be near to God. Our casualness, informality, buddy-buddy attitude toward God really is putting us in danger of being burned. We don't fear God enough.

Now, why all this talk about the glory of God? Well, it is because the Book of Ezekiel has as its main theme the glory of God. Stuart Briscoe has written a book on Ezekiel titled *All Things Weird and Wonderful*.[1] This is a good description of Ezekiel.

All the prophets are hard to read. It is hard to decipher the imageries and illustrations. The language seems to be saying the same thing over and over again. It is often unclear if the prophecy is about the present or the future.

Ezekiel, though, is especially hard to read. It is difficult to grasp what he is saying most of the time – but the one truth that stands out in Ezekiel is the focus on the glory of God.

THEME VERSES

Then they will know that I, the LORD their God, am with them and that they, the house of Israel, are my people, declares the Sovereign LORD. You my sheep, the sheep of my pasture, are (my) people, and I am your God, declares the Sovereign LORD.
Ezekiel 34:30, 31

To know God is to know about His glory. The glory of God stretches us beyond the common understanding of God to the uncommon, from the natural to the supernatural.

BACKGROUND

Ezekiel overlapped the end of Jeremiah's ministry and the beginning of Daniel's ministry. This means that Ezekiel was an eyewitness to the judgment of God in the fall of Jerusalem, as well as an eyewitness to many people being taken into captivity in Babylon. As a matter of fact, Ezekiel was in one of the first waves of exiles taken into captivity.

Ezekiel has more dates in the book than that of any other prophet. It is almost like he is marking the time of one of the most disturbing and significant periods in Israel's history.

We don't know anything about Ezekiel from any other source. We do know that he was a priest, which becomes obvious with the multiple references to the temple in his prophecy. This made Ezekiel unique as a prophet and priest, which usually was not the case.

---

1   Briscoe, Stuart, *All Things Weird and Wonderful* (Wheaton: Victor Books, 1977).

Ezekiel means "God strengthens."

There are some phrases that occur over and over again in Ezekiel:

- "They shall know that I am the LORD" (62 times).

- "Son of man" (92 times).

- "The word of the LORD came to me" (49 times).

- "Glory of the LORD" (17 times), second only to Isaiah in occurrence.

I. GOD'S HEAVENLY GLORY (1 – 7)

Ezekiel's Call (1 – 3)

The "weird and wonderful" characteristic of Ezekiel is demonstrated in the very first chapter. The "wheel within a wheel" vision with four living creatures is hard to understand, but Ezekiel gives the main interpretation:

This was the appearance of the likeness of the glory of the LORD. When I saw it, I fell facedown ... (1:28b).

Ezekiel then conveys his call, which was not an easy one:

Son of man, I am sending you to the Israelites; to a rebellious nation that has rebelled against me; they and their fathers have been in revolt against me to this very day. The people to whom I am sending you are obstinate and stubborn. Say to them, "This is what the Sovereign LORD says." And whether they listen or fail to listen ... they will know that a prophet has been among them. And you, son of man, do not be afraid of them or their words. Do not be afraid, though briars and thorns are all around you and you live among scorpions. Do not be afraid of what they say or be terrified by them, though they are a rebellious people (2:3-6).

This is a remarkable call!

Ezekiel's Sermons and Signs (4 – 7)

Ezekiel's sermons then begin, and many of them are punctuated with signs, visions, parables and apocalyptic descriptions of the future. The prophet becomes a personal participant in the proclamation. He was to symbolize the siege of Jerusalem by living off a meager diet of bread and lying on his side for many days out in public. In chapter 5, he was to cut his hair, then burn some of it and scatter some of it to show what would happen to the inhabitants of Jerusalem after they were destroyed.

II. GOD'S DEPARTING GLORY (8 – 24)

Vision of Departing Glory (8 – 11)

God shows Ezekiel the abhorrent idolatries being practiced in the temple. Immorality was commonplace. The glory of the Lord is seen by Ezekiel as leaving the temple:

Then the glory of the LORD departed from over the threshold of the temple and stopped above the cherubim. While I watched, the cherubim spread their wings and rose from the ground, and as they went, the wheels went with them. They stopped at the entrance to the east gate of the LORD's house, and the glory of the God of Israel was above them (10:18, 19).

Sermons of Judgment (12 – 24)

The symbols, parables and visions continue in the form of messages, one after another, that show that the judgment upon Judah is warranted because the glory of God has been violated.

Ezekiel's personal life becomes an object lesson when his wife dies. She died on the day that the siege of Jerusalem started. The Lord told Ezekiel that he was not to mourn her death until the city of Jerusalem fell … three years later.

III. GOD'S UNIVERSAL GLORY (25 – 32)

This section gives judgment on the neighboring nations of Ammon, Moab, Edom, Philistia, Tyre (three chapters), and Egypt (four chapters).

The glory of God was not only to influence a regional nation, Judah. The glory of God was universal, influencing all nations so that when the other nations were wicked, they were to be judged as well.

IV. GOD'S RETURNING GLORY (33 – 48)

God declares Ezekiel to be a watchman for the house of Israel, which meant that he was stationed in a high position to see everything that was happening, especially from God's perspective. As Israel's watchman, he declares that things are not going well and Jerusalem will fall.

There is a scathing indictment of the shepherds in chapter 34. The shepherds were the spiritual leaders of Judah and the sheep were the people. The shepherds had failed the sheep dramatically. The Lord tells them (34:10):

I am against the shepherds and will hold them accountable for my flock. I will remove them from tending the flock so that the shepherds can no longer feed themselves.

Yet, in the midst of the fall of Jerusalem and the reality of judgment, hope is given. The vision of the valley of dry bones in Ezekiel 37 is one of the most graphic passages in the entire Bible about renewal and revival.

Lessons From Ezekiel

1. We are to live for God's glory. What is the chief end of man? Man's chief end is to glorify God and to enjoy Him forever. We must be focused on what is the most important – and the glory of God is always the most important.

2. God calls us to difficult tasks. Ezekiel and Jeremiah stand as two reminders of how the call of God is often heavy and difficult. The difficulty of a call is never the reason for rejecting a call. The difficulty of a call often is the evidence it is a call from God because it is a call that only God can fulfill.

3. With God, there is always hope of renewal (37). What is clear in Ezekiel 37 is that renewal (life coming into dry bones) can only come by the Spirit of God moving and bringing life. Renewal is always our hope, even in the worst of situations. There is no situation beyond the reach of God's grace, power and love.

NOTES

CHAPTER TWENTY-THREE: DANIEL

Assignment

READ ...

Daniel, Chapters 1-12, or selected chapters from Daniel (one a day for a week) as follows:

Daniel 1 – Daniel's stand in Babylon.

Daniel 3 – The fiery furnace.

Daniel 4 – Nebuchadnezzar's dream.

Daniel 5 – The handwriting on the wall.

Daniel 6 – Daniel in the lion's den.

Daniel 9 – Daniel's prayer.

Daniel 12 – The end times.

MEMORIZE ...

Daniel 4:34, 35 – "His dominion is an eternal dominion; His kingdom endures from generation to generation. All the peoples of the earth are regarded as nothing. He does as He pleases with the powers of heaven and the peoples of the earth;"

and/or

Daniel 2:20, 21 – "Praise be to the name of God for ever and ever; wisdom and power are His. He changes times and seasons; He sets up kings and deposes them. He gives wisdom to the wise and knowledge to the discerning."

PRAY ...

Asking the Lord to give you the faith to be distinctive from the culture around you.

Praising the Lord for the truth that He is sovereign and mighty over all the nations of the earth.

For the protection of God over your life and your family when the "lions" are all around you.

Thanking the Lord that the future is in His hands and He will be honored with whatever happens in the days ahead.

APPLY ...

In the light of Daniel, what do you:

> BELIEVE about God?
>
> REPENT of as sin?
>
> OBEY as a command from God?

SHARE ...

According to what you have learned from Daniel:

- Read the story of Daniel in the lions' den in Daniel 6 to your entire family. Talk about what happened and ask each family member what he or she thought about Daniel facing a law against praying to his God and then facing the consequences of his "disobedience" to the king. Ask each family member what he or she would have done if faced with the same situation.

- Talk to someone else about what he thinks concerning the future of the world. Ask if he believes in such things as a Judgment Day or the Second Coming of Jesus Christ. Speculation about the details of the end times is common, even among Christians, but don't lose sight of the basic Biblical teaching that in the future there will an end to the world as we know it.

Daniel:
A Man of Integrity

INTRODUCTION

Do you remember your Bible heroes from your childhood? They were men like:

- Samson – a man of strength.

- David – the slayer of giants.

- Joshua and Gideon – leaders of victorious armies.

Daniel would often be on that list of heroes. What picture do we remember about Daniel? He is sitting in a lion's den surrounded by docile beasts, at peace in a dangerous situation.

Well, that is Daniel, but there is so much more to him. Daniel, along with Joshua, is one of the few Bible characters about whom nothing negative is ever written.

Daniel was a man of integrity. He was honest, sincere, upright and complete.

THEME VERSE

Daniel's prayer in Daniel 2:20, 21:

Praise be to the name of God for ever and ever; wisdom and power are His.
He changes times and seasons; He sets up kings and deposes them.
He gives wisdom to the wise and knowledge to the discerning.

BACKGROUND

Knowing the super powers in the ancient world is important to understanding Daniel:

Nation	City	Leader
Assyria	Nineveh	Sennacherib
Babylonia	Babylon	Nebuchadnezzar
Medes & Persia	Babylon	Cyrus
Greece	Athens	Alexander the Great
Rome	Rome	Caesars

Daniel was an exilic prophet who was in Babylon with two super powers, Babylonia and the Medes and Persians.

Daniel was a servant in the court of the kings. Like Isaiah, Daniel was in a foreign country and had to win the approval of the king.

I. A MAN OF INTEGRITY (1 – 6)

Daniel's Training (1)

The Jews had been taken into captivity by Nebuchadnezzar. The cream of the crop, principally the young men, were set aside to teach them the new culture. Daniel and his three friends were in that group. Verse 1:6 gives the Jewish and Babylonian names for them:

Belteshazzar	Daniel	"God is my judge"
Shadrach	Hananiah	"The Lord shows grace"
Meshach	Mishael	"Who is what God is"
Abednego	Azariah	"The Lord helps"

Integrity begins with a mental attitude to stand on principles, even if you have to stand alone. Daniel did not want to be defiled with the royal food, so he arranged a test for him and his three friends to be on a strict vegetable-and-water diet to see if they wouldn't be healthier and better nourished than those on the royal food. They passed this test and came out stronger.

God gave to these four men "knowledge and understanding of all kinds of literature and learning. And Daniel could understand visions and dreams of all kinds" (1:17).

Daniel's Wisdom (2)

God gave Daniel special understanding for a reason: to give God the glory.

King Nebuchadnezzar was having troubling dreams. He sought wisdom from the wisest men in his court. He set up a test for their wisdom by asking them to provide the dream and the interpretation. They could not do it. The king got so angry that he ordered the execution of all the wise men of Babylon, which would have included Daniel and his three friends. Daniel called for prayer about this matter. Our theme verse comes from Daniel's prayer in 2:20-23.

Daniel then went to the king to be given the opportunity to provide the dream and the interpretation. To make a long story short, Daniel told the king his dream and interpreted it (2:24-45). The king responded to Daniel, "Surely your God is the God of gods and the Lord of kings and a revealer of mysteries, for you were able to reveal this mystery" (2:47). Daniel was promoted to a high position and given many gifts.

Daniel's Friends (3)

The king's fickleness is demonstrated in chapter 3 because, after he praised the God of Daniel as the God of gods, King Nebuchadnezzar set up an idol for worship. He declared that at a musical call, everyone was to bow down and worship this idol. In this episode, Daniel was not the center of attraction. It is his three friends, whose Babylonian names are Shadrach, Meshach and Abednego. They became the objects of a conspiracy against the Jews and, since they did not bow down when the musical call came, they were to die in the fiery furnace.

You know the story. They were brought to a furious Nebuchadnezzar. They defended themselves by simply stating that the God they served could save them from the fiery furnace. Even if he didn't, though, they would not serve other gods. Nebuchadnezzar got angrier and had the furnace stoked even hotter. As they were thrown in, however, Nebuchadnezzar saw four men walking in the fire, not three. The Lord had saved them and they came out unharmed, with not a hair of their heads singed, their robes scorched or the smell of smoke on them.

Nebuchadnezzar then praised God again and promoted Shadrach, Meshach and Abednego in his government.

Daniel's Wisdom Again (4) and Again (5)

King Nebuchadnezzar has another dream, but this time the interpretation was not good. Daniel showed courage as he still gave the negative interpretation. The king would be driven away from his people and would live among the animals. He would eat grass like the cattle. He would stay that way until he acknowledged the most high God as sovereign over all kingdoms. The fulfillment is given in 4:33:

Immediately what had been said about Nebuchadnezzar was fulfilled. He was driven away from people and ate grass like cattle. His body was drenched with the dew of heaven until his hair grew like the feathers of an eagle and his nails like the claws of a bird.

Nebuchadnezzar, however, prayed and his sanity was restored. He honored and glorified the Lord with this high praise (4:34b-35):

His dominion is an eternal dominion; His kingdom endures from generation to generation. All the peoples of the earth are regarded as nothing. He does as He pleases with the powers of heaven and the peoples of the earth. No one can hold back His hand or say to Him: "What have you done?"

This is the praise of a pagan!

The wisdom of Daniel again is shown in chapter 5. King Belshazzar, the son of Nebuchadnezzar, did not have a dream, but he did see "handwriting on the wall." He called wise men in to interpret, but none of them could help. Enter Daniel once again. The simple inscription, *mene, mene, tekel, parsin,* was interpreted as God numbering the king's days and his reign nearing its end. The king has been weighed and found wanting. The kingdom would be divided and given to the Medes and the Persians.

That very night, Belshazzar was killed, and Darius, the Mede, was made king.

Daniel's Test (6)

King Darius saw great value in Daniel, but another conspiracy arose. Because of Daniel's integrity in following God, the conspirators saw an opportunity to trap him. They influenced Darius to issue an edict that said prayer should not be given to any other god except the king. Anyone who broke this edict would be thrown to the lions. It was put into writing – into the laws of the Medes and Persians that could not be broken.

Daniel, though, was a man of integrity, so when he heard the edict he went home and prayed to the most high Lord like always. Daniel was reported to King Darius and the king, against his own wishes, sentenced Daniel to the lions' den.

Daniel survived the night in the lions' den and King Darius was the first to greet him in the morning. The king was overjoyed and had Daniel released. In retaliation, the king had Daniel's accusers thrown into the lions' den – and this time the lions did eat.

There again God received praise from a pagan king (6:26, 27):

For He is the living God and He endures forever; His kingdom will not be destroyed, His dominion will never end. He rescues and He saves; He performs signs and wonders in the heavens and on the earth. He has rescued Daniel from the power of the lions.

II. A MESSAGE OF INTEGRITY (7 – 12)

The Book of Daniel is written in two distinctive literary styles:

- Historical: The telling of the story with names, places and dates (1 – 6).

- Apocalyptic: The telling of the future. The apocalyptic style of writing is heavily symbolic, visionary and future-oriented. It is usually written during times of crisis and is designed to give hope and encouragement for the future. This section of Daniel (7 – 12) is apocalyptic, like the Book of Revelation. Apocalyptic means to "reveal."

In this section, Daniel is now the one who has the dreams and visions, and he interprets them.

Vision in Chapter 7

Daniel had a vision of four wild beasts, which symbolized the four kingdoms from Nebuchadnezzar's dream. Picturing them as beasts gives a hint of their moral character, because they represented empires that were like ferocious animals.

The first beast, representing Babylon, was like a lion with eagle's wings. Jeremiah likened Nebuchadnezzar to both a lion and an eagle (Jeremiah 49:19-22).

The second beast, representing Persia, was the bear – the cruel animal that delights to kill for the sake of killing.

The third beast, representing Greece, was the leopard or panther, a beast of prey. His four wings portrayed swiftness and symbolized the rapid conquests of Alexander the Great who, in 13 years, had conquered the world.

The fourth beast, representing the Roman Empire, was different from the rest and was described (7:7) as "dreadful and terrible, and strong exceedingly; and it had great iron teeth."

Vision in Chapter 8

The vision of the ram and the goat continue and repeat the predictions from chapter 7, especially about the Persian Empire and the Greek Empire. The Persian Empire that was a bear in the vision of chapter 7 is now a two-horned ram. The Greek Empire that was a leopard in the vision of chapter 7 is now a swift goat.

Read 8:5-8

The great horn is Alexander the Great, the leader of Greece who, in 331 B.C., conquered the Persian Empire and quickly continued conquests throughout the known world. The "four horns" refer to the division of the Greek Empire after Alexander died.

The next passage (verses 9ff) introduces the "little horn," which generally is believed to be Antiochus Epiphanes (175-164 B.C.), who was determined to stamp out the Jewish religion. He targeted Jerusalem and even sacrificed a pig on the altar in the temple to show his disdain.

This is the issue: These predictions, if you take them to be written by Daniel, were written in about 540 b.c. and tell of events that take place 200 years or more later. Could this happen? This is a raging debate in scholarly circles, and usually a dividing line is drawn between those who believe in predictive prophecy and those who don't.

Prophecy from the Old Testament had two major elements:

- Forth telling: Proclaiming the current Word of the Lord. The Old Testament prophets spoke the Word of the Lord to the people and it was usually condemning their sin, calling for repentance and warning about the judgment to come. This is like preaching today.

- Foretelling: Predicting the future Word of the Lord. The Old Testaments prophets would also speak the Word of the Lord, but there could be an element that predicted the future. Those predictions could be in three categories:

    1. Historic: These were predictions like the ones in Daniel, chapter 8, in predicting some events in history about nations and individuals.

    2. Messianic: These were predictions telling of the One to come who would be the servant and Savior of the people of God.

    3. Eschatological: These were predictions about the end of the world. They were beyond history and the Messiah and referred to the end times.

The complication with predictive prophecy is two-fold:

- Is predictive prophecy possible? Behind predictive prophecy is the sovereign God working out

His plan for His people and the whole world. Along with miracles, theophanies and supernatural occurrences, predictive prophecy is evidence that God is at work. It is described in the Bible.

- How is predictive prophecy to be interpreted? Predictive prophecy that is Messianic is the easiest because it is the primary focus of Scripture. One of the basic principles of interpretation is to interpret in the light of the Gospel, so look for Jesus. Predictive prophecy that is historic also is easier to interpret through looking into the past and seeing what has already happened. Predictive prophecy that is eschatological, however, is tricky because it can cause speculation.

In Daniel there are many elements of predictive prophecy that are eschatological. It is apocalyptic, meaning it is being revealed, but it has not yet happened. Some of those eschatological elements are the antichrist ("little horn"), the tribulation (3½ year period – "a time, times, and a half"), and other elements.

Visions in Chapters 9 – 12

Daniel ends with a series of visions that are international in scope. What this means is that they deal with all nations and even speak of kings of the north and kings of the south that are very hard to identify.

Daniel concludes with a vision of the end of the world in which images of the future are given, like "many shall run to and fro, and knowledge shall be increased" (12:4), which is seen as an apt description of our current times.

Daniel stretches us to see the panorama of God's total work in the world. God will bring all things to pass and to a conclusion … all to His glory.

Lessons From Daniel

1. God's call upon our lives is meant to be lived out, even when things are bad. Daniel was a man of integrity who knew that the Lord was his God. He was intent to live out the faith – even when there were laws against it and he would be punished for it.

2. God's call upon our lives is meant to be lived out, even when things are good. Daniel was not a fair weather follower of his God. When things were good, however, he did not forget his God either. When he was raised up to a position of leadership and prestige, he remained faithful.

3. God's call upon our lives is meant to be lived out, even when we are not sure of the future. A unique contribution of the Book of Daniel is its visionary look into the future of Israel. Within the vagueness and speculation, one thing stands out: God is going to care for His people and they were to trust that their futures were secure in His hands.

Notes

Nothing 'Minor'
About the Minor Prophets

The last section of the Old Testament is called the "Minor Prophets." It is a rapid-fire string of prophetic messages that might be as blurry in our minds as any section of the Bible.

Their message, however, is anything but "minor." They present the "major" message of how seriously God must be taken. The Minor Prophets confront issues and truths that are not touched in the rest of the Old Testament.

The Minor Prophets have been called "minor" because of the length of their books – they are simply shorter than the Major Prophets – Isaiah, Jeremiah, Ezekiel and Daniel.

In this study, two Minor Prophets at a time will be considered.

CHAPTER TWENTY-FOUR: HOSEA AND JOEL

Assignment

READ ...

Hosea, Chapters 1-14, and Joel 1-3, or selected chapters from Hosea and Joel (one a day for a week) as follows:

Hosea 1	–	Hosea's call.
Hosea 3	–	Hosea's love for his wife.
Hosea 8	–	God's judgment upon Israel.
Hosea 11	–	God's love for Israel.
Hosea 14	–	A call to repentance.
Joel 1	–	The plague of locusts.
Joel 2	–	The day of the Lord.

MEMORIZE ...

Hosea 6:1 – "Come, let us return to the Lord. He has torn us to pieces but He will heal us; He has injured us but He will bind up our wounds;"

and/or

Joel 2:28, 29 – "I will pour out my Spirit on all people. Your sons and daughters will prophesy, your old men will dream dreams, your young men will see visions. Even on my servants, both men and women, I will pour out my Spirit in those days."

PRAY ...

Asking the Lord for His blessing on your marriage and your family. Thank Him for your family, no matter the struggles or problems.

Thanking the Lord for His great love for you, even in the light of your unfaithfulness and sins.

Thanking the Lord for the work of the Holy Spirit in your life. Ask the Holy Spirit to fill you and sanctify you to make you more like Christ.

Seeking the Lord while it is still the day of mercy. Rejoice that when the day of His judgment comes you will be secure in the Lord.

APPLY ...

In the light of Hosea and Joel, what do you:

> BELIEVE about God?
>
> REPENT of as sin?
>
> OBEY as a command from God?

SHARE ...

According to what you have learned from Hosea and Joel:

- Have a candid conversation in your family about times when the family has been tested because of tough situations or the bad behavior of a family member. Then remember the grace of God in the midst of those bad times. Reflect on the lessons you learned that you would not have learned any other time, even when everything was going well.

- Have a conversation with someone you know and admire who has had some terrible trials in life – death, disease, divorce, health problems, family problems, etc. Share with him how much you admire how he has gone through such times, and ask him what secrets he could share with you, for when you have to go through similar times.

Hosea:
A Scandal for the Prophet

INTRODUCTION

Preachers do make the headlines, but usually it is for scandalous reasons: They have an affair, they live a second life or they get caught with their hands in the offering plate. Most of those headlines have been deserved and probably more headlines could have been written, but the complete stories never got told.

Such outrageous and disturbing headlines, however, could never be blamed on God. They came about because of the weaknesses and iniquities of the preacher. Or did they?

Hosea is the story of a prophet who made the headlines with a scandal that the Lord commanded. The Lord asked Hosea to do something that He never asked any other prophet to do – marry a "loose" woman who was unfaithful and receive her back into faithfulness.

What is going on here?

THEME VERSE

They sow the wind and reap the whirlwind.
Hosea 8:7a

TITLE

Hosea means "salvation." His name comes from the same root word for Joshua and Jesus, which means "Yahweh is salvation."

BACKGROUND

Hosea was a prophet to Israel, the Northern Kingdom. Israel was also called Ephraim, which was the largest of the 10 tribes in the north, and Samaria, which was the capital city.

Hosea was a native of the Northern Kingdom. His heart was with his homeland that never had a godly king.

I. HOSEA'S HOME LIFE (1 – 3)

Hosea's Wife

God called Hosea to do something scandalous:

Go, take to yourself an adulterous wife and children of unfaithfulness … (1:2a).

Hosea's wife was named Gomer. There is debate about Gomer's disposition when Hosea was told by God to marry her. Was she already a harlot? Was she just a loose woman? Or did she have a "tendency" toward unfaithfulness? It is probably the latter because Leviticus 21:7 prohibits one to marry a harlot.

Whatever the situation, a good prophet was told to marry a bad woman.

We must not, however, miss the reason for the command:

Go, take to yourself an adulterous wife and children of unfaithfulness, because the land is guilty of the vilest adultery in departing from the Lord" (1:2b).

The reason behind the command was to illustrate (accentuate) God's faithfulness and Israel's unfaithfulness.

Hosea's Children (1:4-8)

Naming children is usually one of the joyous privileges that parents have. It's because the dynamics are so positive in choosing a family name, passing on your name, choosing a name with meaning or one that you just like.

With Hosea, though, the Lord named his children – and they were not happy names, even though they were filled with meaning:

- Jezreel – "God scatters."

- Lo-ruhamah – "not loved."

- Lo-ammi – "not my people."

Hosea's children were named for the judgment that the Lord would bring on Israel.

Israel's Unfaithfulness (2)

Chapter 2 makes you wonder if Gomer or Israel is being described, they are so closely linked with the terrible aftereffects of unfaithfulness. The primary message, though, is that Israel will suffer because of her unfaithfulness – her spiritual adultery.

Hosea's Redemption (3)

Gomer had become a victim of her unfaithfulness. She was now a slave. God commanded Hosea to buy Gomer back. Thirty pieces of silver was the cost of a slave gored by a bull. It was the cost of a defective slave. Interesting, isn't it, that 30 pieces of silver was the price Judas got for betraying Jesus. Hosea, though, only paid half that price for Gomer, which is probably evidence that she was damaged goods.

Why would God have Hosea do this?

The Lord was modeling a message: God is faithful in spite of the people's unfaithfulness. We never must forget that God's grace is greater than all our sins. God has demonstrated His love for us in that while we were yet sinners, Christ died for the ungodly.

II. HOSEA'S PROPHETIC MESSAGES (4 – 14)

The remainder of Hosea is a series of messages with no logical arrangement and is rather disjointed. It is like the prophet is crying out to God and sobbing in his soul. The struggle of the prophet in the midst of this scandal is evident.

There are three basic messages:

"You are sinful, but God is holy" (4 – 7).

What is really interesting is that all Ten Commandments are being broken by Israel. The people are described this way: "There is no faithfulness, no love, no acknowledgment of God in the land" (4:1b). The priests also were at fault: "Like people, like priests. I will punish both of them for their ways" (4:8).

Israel's repentance is shallow and insincere. This is quite convicting to us. We can presume too much in our spiritual lives. It is one thing to say something – it is quite another to do it.

"You deserve judgment and God is just" (8 – 10).

Idolatry is portrayed as the worst of all sins. It is spiritual adultery. There are more than 75 references to idolatry in Hosea.

The Divine principle of judgment is stated (our theme verse): "They sow the wind and reap the whirlwind" (8:7). Sin has consequences (Galatians 6:7-10).

"You are rebellious, but God still loves you" (11 – 14).

The heart of God is demonstrated and His compassion is aroused.

It never is too late to repent. Even though we must be aware of shallow repentance, we never must forget the power of true repentance (14:1-3).

The Book of Hosea ends with the hope that the nation will return to God and have their sins forgiven. The tragic example of Israel, however, is that they did not.

Joel:
The Eleventh Hour Alarm

INTRODUCTION

When a disaster happens, how does it affect your relationship with God?

- A personal tragedy.

- A natural disaster.

- An accident.

- A disease.

- A death.

Face it! Things like this happen, and they happen to all of us. If they have not happened to you yet, they will. So, how will your faith be affected? Where is God in the middle of these disasters?

Disasters run throughout the Book of Joel:

- Locust plagues.

- Famine.

- Raging fire.

- Invading armies.

- Universal upheaval.

What does it all mean?

THEME VERSE

Alas for that day! For the day of the Lord is near;
it will come like destruction from the Almighty.
Joel 1:15

Joel means "The Lord is God."

BACKGROUND

There are 12 Joels in the Old Testament. This prophet is only mentioned in his book and in the Book of Acts when his prophecy is quoted. Joel was a prophet to Judah, the Southern Kingdom. He acts like a member of the media as he gives a commentary on a natural disaster (a locust plague) that strikes Judah.

Basically, Joel says, "See the Lord in the locust plague."

I. THE DAY OF THE LOCUSTS (1)

Details of the Devastation (1:1-12)

Total devastation happens and the prophet tells the people not to forget what they have seen. This isn't just bad luck or misfortune. They must struggle together over what has happened. They must talk about it to their children. There was a horizontal struggle with the locust plague.

Duty After the Devastation (1:13-20)

There was, however, a vertical struggle as well. The people must turn to God, not away from Him. They must repent of sin, not say that they didn't deserve the disaster. They must come together, not avoid one another. They must worship, fast and pray.

II. THE DAY OF THE LORD (2:1-17)

The Day of Judgment (2:1-11)

Joel then examines the immediate impact of the disaster in order to consider its ultimate impact. Basically, Joel says, "If you think this is bad, you ain't seen nothing yet!"

The Day of Opportunity (2:12-17)

Joel also tells the people, "It's not too late."

The Old Testament Gospel is given in 2:13b: "… the Lord is gracious and compassionate, slow to anger and abounding in love. …"

This Gospel has been a refrain throughout the Old Testament:

- Exodus 34:6 – to Moses.

- Numbers 14:18 – Moses pleads with God.

- Nehemiah 9:17 – the basis for God's continued forgiveness.

- II Chronicles 30:9 – Hezekiah.

- Psalm 86:5 – David.

- Psalm 86:15 – David.

And, we will see it one more time in the Minor Prophets in Jonah 4:2.

This is an echo throughout, and is in every section of the Old Testament – history, the Law, the writings and the prophets.

So, in the aftermath of a disaster, when everything is dark, what is God like? He is like He is all the time: He is gracious and compassionate, slow to anger and abounding in love.

III. THE DAY OF DELIVERANCE (2:18 – 3:21)

Israel will be delivered as a land and as a nation.

God, though, is about a bigger plan than just Israel (2:28-29). The work of the Holy Spirit is described here as a promise for all the people of God:

- Numbers 11:29 – a wish of Moses.

- Joel 2:28, 29 – a prophecy.

- Acts 2:16-21 – a reality.

Peter, on the day of Pentecost, described this passage from Joel as being fulfilled when the Spirit was poured out into the Church, and the work and presence of the Holy Spirit entered a new dimension in the lives of believers.

The Book of Joel ends in chapter 3 with the nations being judged and the hope of God's people being secure.

Lessons From Hosea and Joel

- God wants us to see Him in our unfaithfulness. This is the message of Hosea. When we sin and turn from our God, we often wonder if we can ever come back. We know we cannot do it on our own, so there is a need for God to do something for us that we never could do for ourselves. It is while we were sinners that God loved us in Jesus Christ. He did not wait for us to get better.

- God wants us to see Him in our problems. This is the message of Joel. When terrible things happen, we often wonder if God is even aware, much less concerned, with our condition. We know that something has happened that is much bigger than we are and that we need help that is beyond ourselves. It is in the midst of the trials and tribulations, however, that the Lord reveals Himself as our heavenly Father. He meets us in our problems

NOTES

CHAPTER TWENTY-FIVE: AMOS AND OBADIAH

Assignment

READ ...

Amos, Chapters 1-9, and Obadiah 1, or selected chapters from Amos and Obadiah (one a day for a week) as follows:

Amos 1	–	Amos' message.
Amos 3	–	Witnesses against Israel.
Amos 5	–	A call to repentance.
Amos 7	–	Amos and Amaziah.
Amos 8	–	The vision of a basket of ripe fruit.
Amos 9	–	The hope of restoration.
Obadiah 1	–	All of Obadiah.

MEMORIZE ...

Amos 5:6a – "Seek the LORD and live …;"

and/or

Amos 9:11 – "In that day I will restore David's fallen tent. I will repair its broken places, restore its ruins, and build it as it used to be …;"

and/or

Obadiah 3a – "The pride of your heart has deceived you. …"

PRAY ...

Confessing to the Lord the sin in your life that is keeping you from being faithful to Him.

Seeking the Lord in every area of your life. Do not be like the society that Amos preached to, which was so empty and hypocritical in its worship.

Hoping in the Lord that the Church will not stay the way it is now. Whatever the local congregation or national denomination, the Lord has promised to restore and return when there is repentance.

Turning from the pride in your life. Do not let your selfishness and arrogance cloud your heart and mind as you walk in integrity with the Lord.

APPLY ...

In the light of Amos and Obadiah, what do you:

> BELIEVE about God?
>
> REPENT of as sin?
>
> OBEY as a command from God?

SHARE ...

According to what you have learned from Amos and Obadiah:

- Have a conversation in your family about selfishness, self-centeredness and pride. See first if everyone understands what pride is, then have everyone share a time in which they believe they were thinking only of themselves rather than others.

- Share with a friend about how bad things are in our society. Just reference the news from the last week to highlight the terrible, hurtful things going on around each of you. Then ask your friend what needs to be done in our society in light of such bad news. Use this sharing as an opportunity to tell your friend that things have been bad in other times and in other places. Try to share the good news of God's love in Christ in the midst of the bad news.

Amos:
A Country Preacher

INTRODUCTION

Amos was a "country" preacher. He was a shepherd from Tekoa, which was a country village six miles south of Bethlehem in Judah. He did not have the royal blood of an Isaiah or the pathos of a Jeremiah. He was, however, called of the Lord to carry a message – a difficult message – to Israel. Without sophistication and without fear, Amos proclaimed the message of judgment and grace.

It would be a mistake, though, to think of Amos, the country preacher, as illiterate or ignorant. He demonstrates a variety of styles and messages that show a knowledge of Israel's inconsistency and the nation's immorality. His straightforwardness is like a slap in the face for a nation spiritually going to sleep.

By his own words, Amos describes himself this way:

I was neither a prophet nor the son of a prophet. I was a shepherd, and I also took care
of sycamore fig trees. But the LORD took me from tending the flock and said to me,
"Go, prophesy to my people Israel" (7:14, 15).

Amos was called to leave the countryside and go to Bethel, which was the center of the worship and wealth of Israel, the Northern Kingdom.

THEME VERSE

Therefore this is what I will do to you, Israel, and because
I will do this to you, prepare to meet your God, O Israel.
Amos 4:12

Amos is a book of judgment. It contains a higher percentage of judgment versus hope than any other prophetic book. That is hard to believe with judgment so prominent in most of the prophets, but Amos is at the head of the judgment class.

BACKGROUND

Amos ministered during the reign of Jeroboam II of Israel (782-753 B.C.). This meant that Amos might have been one of the earliest of all the writing prophets, prophesying for more than 30 years before Israel fell to Assyria in 722 B.C.

It was a time of peace and prosperity for Israel, but this time of blessing led to a period of rebellion. The people of Israel did not repent of their unfaithfulness and the Lord wanted them to know that judgment was near. So, Amos was sent. Amos means "burden bearer."

EIGHT ORACLES (1, 2)

An oracle is a statement of judgment. These eight oracles are all against Israel and her neighbors and they all begin with the statement: "For three transgressions ... and for four."

This was a way of saying, "Enough is enough. That's the last straw. Your time is up. Get ready for judgment."

The flow of Amos' oracles is intriguing. He begins with the enemies of Israel, and you can almost hear the people cheer. He continues to talk about the neighbors of Israel, and you almost can hear murmuring. Then he concludes with Israel, and there is shock.

It is like hearing a preacher preaching about the judgment of God on Iraq, Osama Bin Laden and the terrorists of the world. We would cheer and say, "Amen." He then would say, however, that the judgment of God was coming to England and Scotland, and we would not be as enthusiastic. The preacher then would declare that the judgment of God was about to fall on America, and we would be in shock and unbelief, saying, "This can't be so." This was the way Amos presented his oracles.

THREE SERMONS (3 – 6)

Each sermon begins with the words, "Hear this word ..." (3:1; 4:1; 5:1), which had the effect of a ship's captain declaring, "Now hear this."

1. Sermon About Israel's Privilege and Responsibility (3)

You only have I chosen of all the families of the earth; therefore I will punish you for all your sins (3:2)

Since Israel was known by God, she would not get away with anything. It is the same for the Church today. The greatest statements of judgment in the Bible, especially from the lips of Jesus, are directed toward religious people.

2. Sermon About God's Chastening and Desire for Israel to Return (4)

This is a unique judgment, because the women are singled out as the object of judgment. Amos called them "the cows of Bashan." Bashan was an area east of the Jordan River where the pasture land was lush and the cattle prospered and grew fat.

Amos applies this judgment to all of Judah, using a refrain that occurs five times in this sermon: "... yet you have not returned to me" (4:6, 8, 9, 10, 11).

Then he declares our theme verse: "Prepare to meet your God."

3. Sermon on the Sins of Israel and the Call of God to Seek Him (5, 6)

Israel's sin is described as having no regard for God or fellowmen:

You who turn justice into bitterness and cast righteousness to the ground (5:7).

Then Amos upholds the ideal:

But let justice roll on like a river, righteousness like a never-failing stream! (5:24).

FIVE VISIONS OF JUDGMENT (7 – 9:10)

Each vision is introduced with, "This is what the LORD showed me."

1.   Locusts (7:1-3).

2.   Devouring fire (7:4-6).

3.   Plumbline (7:7-9).

4.   Basket of summer fruit (8:1-14).

5.   Smitten sanctuary (9:1-10).

      All five visions, in different ways, speak of the sure judgment from God.

THREE PROMISES (9:11-15)

      The Lord says, "I will …"

1.   Reinstate the Davidic line (9:11,12).

2.   Renew the land (9:13).

3.   Restore the people (9:14, 15).

      This is the only section of hope in all of Amos.

Obadiah:
What God Hates

INTRODUCTION

It sounds strange to ask, "What does God hate?" doesn't it? We feel most comfortable talking about "What does God love?" We hope that we are at the top of His "love list."

If we are honest with the Bible, though, we will understand that there are some things that the "God of love" hates. If we want to take God seriously, we had better come to grips with what He hates.

Obadiah might be called the "most minor" of the Minor Prophets. Obadiah is the shortest book in the Old Testament – so short, in fact, that it only has one chapter comprised of 21 verses.

Yet, Obadiah deals with one of the most "major" messages in the Bible – what God hates.

Let's first take a look at the prophet.

I. OBADIAH THE PROPHET

A. 'Servant of the LORD.'

"Obadiah" means "servant of the LORD," and that is all we know about him. There are 11 other Obadiah's in the Old Testament, and none of them are major characters.

What we do know about Obadiah is that God gave him a vision about a country called Edom, and it was not a happy vision. It was more of a nightmare.

But what in the world is Edom? Good question!

B. The Pride of Edom

Edom was a country southwest of Judah known for its military prowess and its intellectual accomplishments. The people of Edom were strong and smart. They thought they were better than the people in the other nations around them.

It went deeper, however, in the relationship between Israel and Edom – and goes back to twin boys: Jacob and Esau. Go back to Genesis, chapters 25-36, to get the full account. The nation of Edom and the nation of Israel were distant relatives … and they never got along.

What had happened during the time of Obadiah was that the Southern Kingdom, Judah, had fallen to the Babylonians in 587 B.C. Not only did the Edomites not help them, they gloated over the fact that Judah had fallen.

Obadiah confronted them with their pride:

You should not look down on your brother in the day of his misfortune, nor rejoice over the
people of Judah in the day of their destruction, nor boast so much in the day of their trouble"
(12).

Judah had been devastated, the temple desecrated and the people taken into captivity. The people of Edom, secure in her mountain fortresses, were glad.

II. PRIDE: WHAT GOD HATES

The heart of the problem was the "heart of Edom" – it was prideful. Proverbs 6:16, 17:

> *"There are six things the LORD hates, seven that are detestable to him:*
> *haughty eyes,*
> *a lying tongue,*
> *hands that shed innocent blood,*
> *a heart that devises wicked schemes,*
> *feet that are quick to rush into evil,*
> *a false witness who pours out lies,*
> *and a man who stirs up dissension among brothers."*

Heading that list of seven things that the Lord hates is "haughty eyes" – in other words, a "prideful heart."

The Pride of Heart

The message of Obadiah makes this clear:

> *The pride of your heart has deceived you, you who live in the clefts of the rocks and make your home on the heights, you who say to yourself, "Who can bring me down to the ground!" (3).*

The people of Edom thought they were like eagles soaring in the sky. No one could touch them. What is interesting is that one city in Edom was Petra, an ancient wonder. Petra means "rock" and it was actually cut out of a mountain near the southern end of the Dead Sea. The Edomites were safe there. They thought no one could overtake them there, so they thought themselves secure from every enemy, like an eagle's nest in the heights. They were not safe, however, from the Lord of Judah.

God's Judgment on Pride

The judgment of the Lord is plainly stated in verse 4:

> *"Though you soar like the eagle and make your nest among the stars, from there I will bring you down," declares the LORD.*

If there is one thing that is plain in Scripture, it is this: The Lord is against the proud. One verse in Proverbs 3:34 is repeated twice in the New Testament: "God opposes the proud but gives grace to the humble." (James 4:6; I Peter 5:5)

Please listen: Edom is not the only one with the problem of pride. Many of us have this sin as possibly the main spiritual barrier in our lives. We think we don't need God. We can handle any problem ourselves. We are better than anyone else. We can do it ourselves!

All of this shows the pride of our hearts.

What God hates is pride.

What God honors is humility.

Lessons From Amos and Obadiah

1. God loves for His people to see their sin, repent and be restored. This is the message of Amos. Even though we are not told of the success of this message by Amos, that did not keep God from confronting Israel with her sin and calling her people to prepare to meet their God. God is always ready to receive us back.

2.   God hates for His people to see only themselves and be proud. This is the message of Obadiah. Even though Obadiah's prophecy was for Israel's neighboring country, Edom, there is a lesson for all of us. God is against the proud and He draws near to the humble.

NOTES

CHAPTER TWENTY-SIX: JONAH AND MICAH

Assignment

READ ...

Jonah, Chapters 1-4, and Micah 1-7, or selected chapters from Jonah and Micah (one a day for a week) as follows:

Jonah 1   –   Jonah's first call.

Jonah 2   –   Jonah's prayer.

Jonah 3   –   Jonah's second call.

Jonah 4   –   Jonah's problem with God.

Micah 1   –   Micah's message of judgment.

Micah 4   –   The mountain of the Lord.

Micah 6   –   What the Lord requires.

MEMORIZE ...

Jonah 4:2b: "I knew that you are a gracious and compassionate God, slow to anger and abounding in love, a God who relents from sending calamity."

and/or

Micah 6:8: "He has showed you, O man, what is good. And what does the LORD require of you? To act justly and to love mercy and to walk humbly with your God."

PRAY ...

Responding to the call of God upon your life.

Repenting of how you have not responded to the Lord's call on your life in the past.

Asking for the courage and faith to do what you know is right and good. We do not always like what God wants us to do, but He always provides the grace to do what pleases Him.

Seeking the wisdom of the Lord about showing justice, mercy and humility in your walk with God.

APPLY ...

In the light of Jonah and Micah, what do you:

      BELIEVE about God?

      REPENT of as sin?

      OBEY as a command from God?

SHARE ...

According to what you have learned from Jonah and Micah:

- Share with your family Micah 6:8 and ask everyone what they think it means to "act justly, and to love mercy, and to walk humbly with your God." Encourage one another to demonstrate lives that follow this requirement from God.

- Think of where the Lord is sending you, like He did Jonah. It may not be pleasant and it may not be what you want, but it is where you will find God working. Go to that person or persons that the Lord has put on your heart, and let them know you love them and God does, too.

Jonah:
The Sending God

INTRODUCTION

The Book of Jonah is a delight to read. If you have not liked Hosea, Joel, Amos or Obadiah, you will love Jonah. The best part about Jonah is that it tells a story, and its story is somewhat familiar.

Jonah means "dove."

He was a prophet from Israel who served during the reign of Jeroboam II. There is a reference to Jonah the prophet in II Kings 14:25. Beyond the message of the Book of Jonah itself, we do not know much more about him.

The story of Jonah is familiar, or at least parts of the story are familiar, like the "whale," or what more accurately is known as the "great fish."

The Book of Jonah is unique among the prophets because it is autobiographical. It tells a story rather than preaches a sermon.

Jesus upheld the historicity of Jonah. In Matthew 12:40, Jesus related His death, burial and Resurrection with Jonah's three days and three nights in the belly of the great fish. He then made the point that something greater than Jonah was about to happen.

It is a crucial question: How can a man stay in the belly of a fish for three days and survive? Well, he can't – no more than a dead man is buried, and three days later rises again. In other words, Jesus saw the survival of Jonah as a miracle, not some natural event.

I. RUNNING AWAY FROM GOD (1)

A. God's Call (The Sending God)

Go to the great city of Nineveh and preach against it, because its wickedness has come up before me (2).

This call was for Jonah, a native of Israel, to go to Nineveh, the capital city of Assyria, the enemy of Israel. It was the equivalent of God calling someone in America during World War II to go to Berlin as a missionary or during the Cold War to go to Moscow.

The only message that Jonah was to bring was judgment. You would think that Jonah would have liked that, but he had another response.

B. Jonah's Response

But Jonah ran away from the LORD and headed for Tarshish (3).

Jonah's response was to run away from God, which was disobedience.

Instead of going 500 miles northeast to Nineveh, he heads 2,000 miles due west to Tarshish in southern Spain. Tarshish for Jonah would be like Tahiti to us. The text makes it clear that the main reason for Jonah going in such an opposite direction was to flee from the Lord.

The rest of chapter 1 happens in rapid-fire fashion:

- Jonah gets on the boat.

- There is a storm at sea.

- Jonah is asleep.

- Jonah is awakened to pray for safety.

- Jonah confesses he is the culprit (he had guilt).

- The men (pagans) throw Jonah overboard.

- The Lord provides (prepares) a "great fish."

- The "great fish" swallows Jonah.

- Jonah is in the belly of the "great fish" for three days and three nights.

II. RUNNING TO GOD (2)

In this chapter, Jonah reveals his true heart. This very often happens when we are in distress and in a terrible situation.

From the inside of the fish Jonah prayed to the LORD his God. He said, "In my distress I called to the LORD, and He answered me" (1,2).

There is no disobedience that can separate God from us as long as we cry out to Him. Even in our rebellion, the Lord deals with us.

III. RUNNING WITH GOD (3)

The persistent, patient and gracious God calls Jonah a second time to go to Nineveh. Notice that the sending God will continue to send and give the command to go. Disobedience and distress will not keep God from being the sending God.

The sending God is continuing to tell His people to go:

Go and make disciples of all nations, baptizing them in the name of the Father and the Son and the Holy Ghost, teaching them to observe all that I have commanded you, and, lo, I am with you even to the end of the age (Matthew 28:19, 20).

So, the sending God tells Jonah to go a second time – and this time, Jonah goes.

Nineveh was under the verdict of God as a wicked city, and Assyria as a wicked nation. History tells us that the Assyrians were as cruel as the people of any nation have ever been. They would put hooks in the noses of their captives and lead them to Nineveh. When they conquered a land, they would cut off the heads of many of the captives and pile them up as a reminder to others.

Nineveh was a large city. Verse 3:3b says that "a visit required three days." What that probably meant was that it took three days to walk across the diameter of the city of Nineveh, probably about 60 miles. That's about the size of Atlanta inside Interstate 285.

Jonah preached a simple message of eight words: "Forty more days and Nineveh will be overturned." In Hebrew, this sermon was even shorter – five words. It was a simple message of apparently unavoidable judgment. One author speculates that Jonah made a spectacular deliverer of this message because he could have been bleached and marred by the three days in the fish. The story about the messenger and the "great fish," therefore, became known by all.

Nineveh repented. Some say that this might have been the most pervasive revival of all time. A difference was made from the king down to every beast.

God responded. Verse 10 in the King James Version can be misleading because it says:

God repented of the evil, that He had said that He would do unto them; and He did it not.

What makes this misleading is the popular understanding of evil, which is something that is sinful, wicked or even demonic. In the English of the King James Version, evil also could refer to what we would call a calamity, or distress, or a natural disaster, or judgment. In other words, in the time of King James, something evil definitely was unpleasant.

The New International Version of verse 10 more properly conveys God's gracious response to true repentance, without any hint of judgment being evil:

When God saw what they did and how they turned from their evil ways, He had compassion and did not bring upon them the destruction He had threatened.

God is not capricious or fickle in His plans. He is not evil or wrong in His judgments. This passage shows that God is compassionate. His grace will overcome His anger.

We, however, must repent! The choice gets down to repent and experience God's grace or do not repent and experience God's wrath.

IV. RUNNING AHEAD OF GOD (4)

Jonah tried to second-guess God in verse 2:

He prayed to the LORD, "O LORD, is this not what I said when I was still at home? That is why I was so quick to flee to Tarshish. I knew that you are a gracious and compassionate God, slow to anger and abounding in love, a God who relents from sending calamity."

Jonah thought he knew what was best and right. He also knew that God was gracious and compassionate and that He might forgive Nineveh. Jonah did not like what God did, but God confronted Jonah with his limitations (4:4).

Have you any right to be angry?

God gave Jonah the lesson of the vine:

- The comfort of the shade.

- The work of the worm.

- The discomfort of the sun.

- Jonah wanted to die.

God then asked the same question in another way:

Have you any right to be angry because the vine died? (4:9).

Verses 4:10, 11: God teaches Jonah that God will be merciful on whom He wishes to show mercy. God will be God! Jonah was to be merciful even as God had been merciful.

The Book of Jonah ends with a rhetorical question that vindicates God. "Should I not be concerned about that great city?"

This sending God has the first word, and He will have the last word – and each word demonstrates the Lord to be gracious, compassionate and merciful.

Micah:
What Does God Require?

INTRODUCTION

Micah doesn't start from the standpoint of a religion, a ritual or a spiritual routine, but from the standpoint of God – true spiritual reality. Micah's name, which really is a rhetorical question, says it all: "Who is like God?" The answer clearly is, "No one."

Micah's prophecy is punctuated with the commands "Hear" and "Listen." Those commands only made sense in the light of a God who is above us and sovereign over us, yet He desires to communicate with us. He is not a God separated from us, but a God who longs to be intimate with us.

I. GOD'S REQUIREMENTS

It is easy, however, to confuse religious and spiritual matters. One either gets so simple that he settles for some sentimental religion, or he gets so complex that he creates a strident, confusing faith.

God, though, speaks with clarity:

He has shown you, O man, what is good. And what does the LORD require of you? To act justly
and to love mercy and to walk humbly with your God.
Micah 6:8

Micah 6:8 is one of the classic summary statements in all of Scripture. The Bible is a big book, and our tendency is to elaborate and complicate the teaching of Scripture. Scripture, though, often gives us insights to simplify things:

Hear, O Israel, the LORD our God the LORD is One. Love the LORD your God will all your heart,
with all your soul, and with all your strength.
Deuteronomy 6:4, 5

Jesus gives the "greatest commandment:"

Love the Lord your God with all your heart and with all your soul and with all your mind. This
is the first and greatest commandment. And the second is like it. Love your neighbor as yourself.
All the Law and the Prophets hang on these two commandments.
Matthew 22:37-40

So in everything, do to others what you would have them do to you, for this sums up the Law
and the Prophets.
Matthew 7:12

Religion that God our Father accepts as pure and faultless is this: to look after orphans and widows in their distress and to keep oneself from being polluted by the world.
James 1:27

And then comes Micah 6:8:

And what does the Lᴏʀᴅ require of you? To act justly and to love mercy and to walk humbly with your God.

II. Oᴜʀ Fᴀɪʟᴜʀᴇ

How, though, does one measure up with God's requirements "to act justly, to love mercy, and to walk humbly with your God?"

That is the message of Micah as well. He constantly confronts Israel with her sin and shortcomings.

All this is because of Jacob's transgression, because of the sins of the house of Israel (1:5).

Listen, you leaders of Jacob, you rulers of the house of Israel. Should you not know justice, you who hate good and love evil (3:1, 2).

Woe to those who plan iniquity, to those who plot evil on their beds! At morning's light they carry it out because it is in their power to do it (2:1).

The requirements of God are given so that we might live beneficial lives, but we never must forget another reason: The requirements of God are given so that sinners might know their need of grace.

III. Gᴏᴅ's Gɪꜰᴛ

The requirements of God are proclaimed and sinners are confronted with their failures. That, however, is not the end of the story.

Sin is no surprise to God. He knows sinners better than they know themselves – and He still loves them. Even more than that, He does something that sinners never could do for themselves – He gives a gift.

Micah proclaims a unique insight into God's gift in chapter 5:2, 4:

But you, Bethlehem Ephrathah, though you are small among the clans of Judah, out of you will come for me one who will be ruler over Israel, whose origins are from of old, from ancient times. … He will stand and shepherd His flock in the strength of the Lᴏʀᴅ , in the majesty of the name of the Lᴏʀᴅ His God. And they will live securely, for them His greatness will reach to the ends of the earth. And He will be their peace.

A ruler would come from Bethlehem, and He will shepherd sinners and give them peace.
It is Jesus! The Savior. The Lord. The Ruler. God's gift to sinners.

Lessons From Jonah and Micah

1. God sends us into the world to share His message. This is the message of Jonah. Jonah did not like it and resisted the Lord, but the Lord eventually had His way. Jonah discovered many things about his God and also many things about himself.

2. God sends us into the world to live His life. This is the message of Micah. The life of one who follows God is to be distinctive. It is to be marked by such things as justice, love and humility. The lives we live are to demonstrate that we are living for Him and not for ourselves.

NOTES

CHAPTER TWENTY-SEVEN: NAHUM AND HABAKKUK

Assignment

READ ...

Nahum, Chapters 1-3, and Habakkuk 1-3, or selected chapters from Nahum and Habakkuk (one a day for a week) as follows:

Nahum 1   –   The Lord's anger against Nineveh.

Habakkuk 1   –   Habakkuk's complaint against the Lord.

Habakkuk 2   –   The Lord's answer to Habakkuk's complaint.

Habakkuk 3   –   Habakkuk's prayer.

MEMORIZE ...

Nahum 1:3: "The LORD is slow to anger and great in power; the LORD will not leave the guilty unpunished."

   and/or

Habakkuk 2:20: "But the LORD is in His holy temple; let all the earth be silent before Him."

   and/or

Habakkuk 3:18: "Yet I will rejoice in the LORD, I will be joyful in God my Savior."

PRAY ...

Meditating on the nature of God as "slow to anger" and "not leaving the guilty unpunished."

Bringing to God the main complaint you have about what He has done in your life or in the world.

Being silent in the Lord's presence, knowing that He is in His holy Temple.

Rejoicing in the Lord for who He is and what He has done for you.

APPLY ...

In the light of Nahum and Habakkuk, what do you:

> BELIEVE about God?
>
> REPENT of as sin?
>
> OBEY as a command from God?

SHARE ...

According to what you have learned from Nahum and Habakkuk:

- Have a conversation with a friend or a family member about the troubling truth that God "will not leave the guilty unpunished." How does that make you feel and how does that truth inform your faith?

- Spend some time with a friend who is un-churched or who is struggling with his or her faith. Ask what they would say if God asked what their main complaint was about how God was doing at being God. Honest exchanges are good, but the Book of Habakkuk helps us in getting the right perspective.

Nahum:
The Wrath of God

INTRODUCTION

Talking about the wrath of God is never comfortable. Talking about the love of God, the goodness of God and the grace of God always feels better. It is possible, however, to talk about such things in a sentimental and shallow way. The depth of God's love and grace can only be understood when one of the most unpleasant and significant truths of Scripture – the wrath of God – is confronted.

I. NAHUM AND HIS MESSAGE

The wrath of God is where Nahum is helpful.

Nahum and Jonah

There is an interesting connection between Jonah and Nahum. God called Jonah to go to Nineveh and, after a little diversion, he went where God was sending him. The people of Nineveh repented of their sin and God did not judge them.

Nahum wrote about Nineveh 100 years after Jonah's mission there. Nineveh had returned to her old ways, so Nahum prophesied that Nineveh was to be judged by God, and this time it would come true.

Nineveh

Nineveh was one of the marvels of the ancient world. It was a mighty city with impregnable walls that could stand against any enemy. Nineveh was one of the greatest of the ancient cities.

The greatness of Nineveh and the Assyrian empire, however, was lost in their cruelty to others. Nahum prophesied:

Woe to the city of blood, full of lies, full of plunder, never without victims! The crack of ships, the clatter of wheels, galloping horses and jolting chariots! Charging cavalry, flashing swords and glittering spears! Many casualties, piles of dead, bodies without number, people stumbling over the corpses. …

Then Nahum writes: "I am against you, declares the LORD Almighty." (3:1-3)

Nahum's Message

Nahum's basic message is not the revenge of one nation against another or the desire of an occupied nation to be freed from a tyrannical enemy. It is a look into the character of God when evil seems to be victorious, and we see how God responds.

Are you ever disturbed about the evil in the world? Do you ever wonder where God is and if He ever will do something? If we are honest, we all have struggled with evil in the world and where God fits into the equation.

Nahum, though, tells us plainly: "The LORD is a jealous and avenging God; the LORD takes vengeance and is filled with wrath."

II. THE WRATH OF GOD

Nahum 1:1-8 contains almost every Hebrew word relating to judgment and wrath – jealous, zealous, avenging, vengeance, wrath, power, indignation, fierce anger, fire, trouble, etc.

Every one of these words directly describes the Lord. He is jealous. He is avenging. He has vengeance and wrath. He has fierce anger. He sends fire and trouble.

This gets to the heart of the matter of sin and how God looks at sin. Sinners are prone to downplay their situation before a holy God and naturally will think that anything called wrath toward sin is extreme, harsh or overkill.

III. THE WRATH OF GOD IN THE OLD TESTAMENT

The wrath of God permeates the Old Testament in more than 600 passages connected with every theme, epoch and major character. It must be understood, however, that wrath should not be compartmentalized to the Old Testament. The New Testament is full of the wrath of God, and Jesus spoke more about judgment and hell than anyone else in the New Testament.

The clearest statement about wrath in the New Testament, though, is from Paul in Romans 1:18:

"For the wrath of God is revealed from heaven against all ungodliness and wickedness of men who by their wickedness suppress the truth."

IV. THE COMFORT OF GOD

Wrath, though, is not the whole story.

Nahum makes a unique contribution to balance the teaching about the wrath of God. The most striking is the meaning of Nahum's name. It means "comfort" or "consolation." The prophet that majored in the wrath and judgment of God is named "Comfort."

Nahum was consistent with his name, as he sought to be truthful about the wrath of God and the comfort of God. He comforted with these words:

The LORD is good, a refuge in times of trouble. He cares for those who trust in Him (1:7).

The LORD is slow to anger and great in power (1:3).

To draw the conclusion that God is wrathful and, therefore, mean, unfair, cruel and unloving misses the mark. As a matter of fact, it might be more of an evidence of idolatry rather than a correct observation about God.

The truth is that the justice of God, where "the LORD will not leave the guilty unpunished," gives the most comfort as one struggles with the presence of evil in the world.

Habakkuk:
Wrestling With God

INTRODUCTION

Habakkuk makes a unique contribution to the prophetic section of the Bible because it is the only prophecy where there is a one-on-one between the prophet and God. The usual pattern of the prophets is that God calls a prophet to preach to the people, calling them to repentance. The prophet tells the people that judgment will come from the Lord unless they change.

With Habakkuk, however, there is a dialogue exclusively between the prophet and God, and the prophet is not a "happy camper." We need to know that sometimes we will look to God and struggle with Him – we wrestle with God.

What do you think of wrestling? Some men love it. I heard someone say one time that wrestling is the man's version of soap operas. Well, I don't know about that, but I do know that wrestling, as we know it on television, is fake. It is scripted. It is smoke and mirrors. It is hype and hoopla.

There is a real kind of wrestling, however, where there is a one-on-one struggle to see who comes out on top. It is as gritty as it gets. It is nose-to-nose and body-to-body. It calls for every ounce of energy, skill and muscle that a person has.

Well, the Book of Habakkuk is about a prophet wrestling with God.

It is interesting that the name of Habakkuk means "to embrace" or "to cling." Isn't that exactly what a wrestler does with his opponent? There is a lot of body contact and grabbing, embracing and clinging.

Wrestling (struggling) with God is one of the most righteous things we can do:

- Abraham did it in interceding for Sodom and Gomorrah.

- Moses did it when God was about to wipe out Israel in the desert.

- Jacob did it in wrestling with the angel.

- Job did it in the midst of his suffering.

- Jesus did it in the Garden of Gethsemane.

- Thomas did it in his doubting.

- Habakkuk does it.

THE PROPHET

We don't know much about Habakkuk, outside of this prophecy. He was a contemporary of Jeremiah's and well aware of the domestic and foreign problems of his day.

Domestically, Judah had just had a spiritual reformation during the kingship of Josiah, but he had been replaced by Jehoiakim, who was one of the most wicked kings Judah ever had. So, Habakkuk was very upset over Judah and the spiritual deterioration of the people.

Militarily, Judah was surrounded by powerful and aggressive enemies. They were caught in the middle of two nations that were fighting one another: Egypt and Babylon. Babylon, though, was the most powerful and was hated by Judah.

I. HABAKKUK'S COMPLAINTS

The prophecy of Habakkuk begins with a dialogue between Habakkuk and the Lord.

A. Frustration With God

It all begins with Habakkuk's first complaint.

This may sound heretical to you, but expressing our complaints to God is a sign of a confident relationship with Him. I am not talking about being a "complainer" – that's someone who complains about the sun rising. No, I am speaking of someone so upset about something that they must bring it to the most important person in their lives – God.

Habakkuk's complaint to the Lord went like this:

How long, O LORD, must I call for help, but you do not listen. Or cry out to you, "Violence!" but you do not save?

From Habakkuk's perspective, God was not working. He was allowing evil to run rampant and things were getting worse. Habakkuk was frustrated with God.

The Lord answers that He is going to do something, and He tells Habakkuk that "you won't believe it" (5). He is going to use Babylon, wicked Babylon, to punish Judah.

B. Disagreement With God

This leads to Habakkuk's second complaint, which is of a different nature than his initial one. At first, Habakkuk was frustrated. Here, he disagrees with God. God's method of using a wicked nation to punish Judah just did not sound right to Habakkuk. It is like our thinking during World War II that God would use Germany and Japan to invade the United States to punish us. Would any of us have been pleased with that?

So, Habakkuk tells God what he is thinking and then says, "Now, I'll sit down and wait for the LORD to answer me."

Habakkuk is so wise here. He wrestles with God, registers his complaint, then he sits down and waits upon the Lord. This matter of waiting on the Lord is what is missing from so many of us in our "instant," "vending machine," "name it and claim it" mentality of experiencing God. Habakkuk's waiting upon the Lord was a demonstration of his faith in the Lord and submission to Him.

II. GOD'S ANSWERS

A. God's Sovereignty

The flow of the dialogue between Habakkuk and God went something like this:
Habakkuk: "God, what is your game plan?"
God: "Habakkuk, you wouldn't believe me if I told you" (1:5b).
Habakkuk: "Try me."
God: "All right. I am raising up the Babylonians to punish Judah."
Habakkuk: "I don't believe it!" (1:12).

The Lord answers Habakkuk's two complaints with the same answer – "I'm in control."

"Habakkuk, you wonder how long before I work? Real soon. Just wait."

"Habakkuk, you don't like what I'm doing? You don't see the whole picture like I do. Trust me."

The Lord wanted Habakkuk to know that He was in control, and He emphasizes that with these words at the end of chapter 2, verse 20:

... the LORD is in His holy temple; let all the earth be silent before Him.

B. Our Faith

The key lesson for God's people in Habakkuk is found in 2:4:

... the righteous will live by his faith.

This verse in Habakkuk is in seed form, which blossoms into full flower in the New Testament – the just will live by faith:

I am not ashamed of the gospel, because it is the power of God for the salvation of everyone who believes: first for the Jew, then for the Gentile. For in the gospel a righteousness from God is revealed, a righteousness that is by faith from first to last, just as it is written: "The righteous will live by faith" (Romans 1:16, 17).

Clearly no one is justified before God by the law, because, "The righteous will live by faith" (Galatians 3:11).

This means that the way we live is not by feelings or trends, the influence of others or our culture, but by faith.

III. HABAKKUK'S PRAYER (3)

The third chapter of Habakkuk reads like one of the Psalms. It is a combination of praising God and praying to God. The chapter begins and ends with some musical instruction, meaning that it was for the purpose of public worship. There is the periodic occurrence of Selah, which is very common in the Psalms and probably is a liturgical term that suggests a brief musical interlude or congregational meditation.

There are two features of Habakkuk's prayer:

A. Praise of God

After Habakkuk expresses his complaints and hears the Lord's response, Habakkuk praises the Lord:

LORD, I have heard of your fame; I stand in awe of your deeds, O LORD. Renew them in our day, in our time make them known, in wrath remember mercy. (3:2)

Verses 3-15 continue with a description of God and His power that is demonstrated in nature – the earth, sunshine, the mountains, the hills, rivers, streams, sea, water, waves and lightning.

This praise of God is in the context of military power and victory over an enemy. God is talked about in terms of an army, chariots, the bow, arrows, spears, warriors and the defeat of the enemy.

What are your reasons to praise God this morning? What if I pointed at you right now and asked you to stand up and share something for which to praise God. Would you have anything?

B. Submission to God

The most striking part of Habakkuk's prayer is seen in verses 17-18 as he struggles with and then submits to the Lord:

Though the fig tree does not bud and there are no grapes on the vines, though the olive crop fails and the fields produce no food, though there are no sheep in the pen and no cattle in the stalls (notice all of these things are not pleasant occurrences), yet I will rejoice in the LORD. I will be joyful in God my Savior.

Then, in verse 19:

The Sovereign LORD is my strength; He makes my feet like the feet of a deer, He enables me to go on the heights.

Lessons From Nahum and Habakkuk

1. We will not always like the way God works in His wrath. This is the message of Nahum. God being angry with the wicked every day is not a pleasant thought for us. We would rather count on and recount the love of God. When we are most honest, however, we will admit that we do not fear God as much as we ought. An understanding of the God of wrath will restore some of that fear and respect.

2. We will not always like the way God wrestles with us. This is the message of Habakkuk. A comfortable walk with God will not last forever. The day will come when we do not like what has happened or how it happened. The blows of life will cause us to see God as against, rather than for, us. So, we will wrestle with Him – and we will learn.

NOTES

CHAPTER TWENTY-EIGHT: ZEPHANIAH AND HAGGAI

Assignment

READ ...

Zephaniah, Chapters 1-3, and Haggai 1-2, or selected chapters from Zephaniah and Haggai (one a day for a week) as follows:

      Zephaniah 1   – A warning of judgment.

      Zephaniah 3   – The future of Jerusalem.

      Haggai 1   – A call to rebuild the Temple.

MEMORIZE ...

Zephaniah 1:14: "The great day of the Lord is near – near and coming quickly. ..."

   and/or

Haggai 2:8: "'The silver is mine and the gold is mine,' declares the Lord Almighty."

PRAY ...

Rejoicing in the Lord for who He is and what He has done for you.

Asking the Lord to lead you to where you are to rebuild, renew or reform. The Lord always is calling us to be salt and light in the world.

Committing your possessions to the Lord, knowing that it all is His anyway.

APPLY ...

In the light of Zephaniah and Haggai, what do you:

      BELIEVE about God?

      REPENT of as sin?

      OBEY as a command from God?

SHARE ...

According to what you have learned from Zephaniah and Haggai:

- Talk to a family member or a friend about what the day of the Lord will look like. Know that the day of the Lord most often is seen as a reference to the Second Coming of Christ, but also know that the day of the Lord can be some special visitation of the Lord into our personal lives, the Church or a nation.

- Talk to an unchurched friend about what needs to change in the Church and in the nation. Be honest about things not being what they should be, then share with the friend about how God is about the rebuilding and the reforming of His people and His world. Give hope in the light of things not being what they should be.

Zephaniah:
The Day of the Lord

INTRODUCTION

Zephaniah means "he whom Jehovah has hidden or protected."

Zephaniah is one of the few prophets with a pedigree (1:1) – the only prophet to come from royal blood. He was the great-great-grandson of good King Hezekiah.

This makes two observations possible:

1. Zephaniah was very bold in his judgment of royalty (1:8).

2. Zephaniah had access to the royal court of King Josiah. He was where the action was and, possibly, Zephaniah was to Josiah what Nathan was to David.

Zephaniah prophesied during "the reign of Josiah:"

- Josiah reigned from 639-608 B.C.

- He became king of Judah at the age of eight.

- He succeeded his father, Amon, and grandfather, Manasseh, who both were evil kings who led Judah through 55 years of idolatry and immorality.

- At the age of 16, Josiah began to turn to God.

- At the age of 20, he instituted his first reform by tearing down all the altars of Baal.

- At the age of 26, he started a second reform when Hilkiah, the priest, found the Book of the Law in the Temple.

Zephaniah probably prophesied just before the second reform (625 B.C.).

THEME

The theme of Zephaniah is the coming of the day of the Lord. Zephaniah 1:14, 15
What other minor prophet had the theme of the day of the Lord? Joel.
Zephaniah referred to "the day of the Lord" 23 times:

- Verse 1:2, 3: It will fall on all creation.

- Verse 1:14: It is imminent.

- Verse 1:15, 17: It is a day of terror and judgment on sin.

- Verse 2:4-15: It will involve all nations.

- Verse 3:9-13: A remnant will return on that day.

- Verse 3:14-20: It will bring a great blessing.

Jesus alludes to Zephaniah twice, in Matthew 13:41 and 24:29. Both allusions are associated with Christ's second coming.

I. DAY OF THE LORD: JUDGMENT (1:1 – 3:7)

This is the ninth minor prophet and the ninth verse of the same song – God will judge idolatry and immorality.

Zephaniah moves from the general to the specific:

- From universal judgment (1:1-3) to judgment upon Judah (1:4 – 2:3).

- From judgment on the surrounding nations (2:4-15) to judgment upon Jerusalem (3:1-7).

When he prophesies against the nations, he looks in all four directions and then at the center, Jerusalem:

- Assyria in the north.

- Philistia in the west.

- Moab and Ammon in the east.

- Ethiopia in the south.

- Jerusalem in the center.

II. DELIVERANCE OF THE LORD: JOY (3:8-20)

A change in tone takes place … the day of the Lord will be a source of judgment for those who remain in their sin and a source of joy for those who trust God (3:12-17).

Zephaniah opens with idolatry, wrath and judgment, but then closes with true worship, rejoicing and blessing.

Haggai:
God's Work God's Way

THE POST-EXILIC PROPHETS

Most of the prophets had a ministry of pronouncing judgment either upon Israel or Judah if they did not repent. As the centuries passed, however, both Israel and Judah dramatically were judged by being conquered and devastated by invading armies:

- 722 B.C. – Israel, the Northern Kingdom, was conquered and scattered by Assyria.

- 586 B.C. – Judah, the Southern Kingdom, was conquered, the city walls leveled, the Temple destroyed and the people taken into exile by Babylon.

This small group of prophets (Haggai, Zechariah and Malachi) are called post-exilic prophets because their ministry was after the time of exile in Babylon, as the people returned to Judah, specifically Jerusalem, to rebuild the walls, the Temple and to reform the faith.

This is the setting of Haggai. It's the story of returning Jews who are seeking again to do the work of God in the land that the Lord had given them. The work of God that they were doing was the rebuilding of the Temple (you can read this fascinating story in Ezra 4-6).

Cyrus, the king of Persia, who had conquered Babylon, issued a decree allowing the Jews to return to Jerusalem to rebuild the Temple. The first wave of returnees, about 50,000, was led by Zerubbabel and, after two years of labor, they had laid the foundation of the Temple. They then faced stiff opposition from the Samaritans, however, and work on the Temple was halted for several years.

Then Haggai and Zechariah entered. They both began to preach to encourage the people to be about the work of God in rebuilding the Temple.

Haggai, meaning "festal," or a shortened form of "festival, of the Lord," was an older prophet who might have had a faint memory of the glory of Solomon's Temple. He prophesies using questions and repetition to make his point.

CHARACTERS IN HAGGAI

One of the unique features of the Book of Haggai is the naming of names and the giving of dates. The exact date of each address delivered over a four-month period by Haggai is provided. The naming of names gives a contemporary relevance and impact to the prophecy:

- Darius was the king of Persia.

- Zerubbabel was the governor.

- Joshua was the high priest.

The focus in Haggai, however, is on the people. We would say the people sitting in the pews. They were the ones who needed to be doing God's work, so Haggai made several points clear to them.

I. Put God's Work First (1:1-15)

First, the returning Jews had placed themselves above God's work. In typical fashion, Haggai made his point by asking a question (1:4):

Is it a time for you yourselves to be living in your paneled houses, while this house remains in ruin?

It may not sound like it, but the description of their homes being "paneled houses" is like our referring to our homes as "mansions." Paneled houses for the Jews at this time were unheard of. They normally lived in stone and mortar homes with dirt floors. Paneled houses only demonstrated that they were caring for themselves first.

So, Haggai drew a comparison between them living in their paneled houses and the house of God that was in ruin.

Haggai went on to point out that, even while they were putting themselves first in all they did, they still were not blessed:

Give careful thought to your ways (Haggai uses this phrase five times in this short book. He's saying, "Think about it."). You have planted much, but have harvested little. You eat, but never have enough. You drink, but never have your fill. You put on clothes, but are not warm. You earn wages, only to put them in a purse with holes in it.

Haggai was making the point that, when we put ourselves first, we naturally think that everything will be all right – but it is not! There is no blessing, no peace, no purpose, no meaning, no significance.

Haggai tells them to get to work: "Know that the Lord is with you and get to work on the house of God."

The people respond positively (1:14b): "They came and began to work on the house of the Lord Almighty, their God. …"

This older prophet (probably close to 80 years old) is proclaiming that true happiness and fulfillment come as the building of God's house and Kingdom is done.

II. God's Work Is Greater Than It Appears (2:1-9)

It is easy to get lost in the "way it used to be" or the "way it should be" and miss the blessing of seeing the "way things are by God's grace right now."

The returning Jews did that with the Temple. They remembered Solomon's Temple, with all of its gold and silver, and they looked at what they were building. It looked a disgrace to them in comparison. They were discouraged.

Haggai asks another question (2:3):

Who of you is left who saw the house in its former glory? How does it look to you now? Does it not seem to you like nothing?

What is lost when you look at the past or speculate into the future and compare it with the present work of God is the truth of the greatness of God's work right now.

All of those things might be true to some degree, but what is lost in the passion for the past or the idealism of the future is the ability to see and enjoy the blessings of God's work now.

What really is missing in the work of God often is encouragement: the encouragement to see the hand of God now; the encouragement to listen and hear the voice of God now; the encouragement to be a part, even a small part, of what God is doing in this world.

Haggai was such an encourager. And he did it with the basic promises of God. Notice (in 2:4, 5) the words of the Lord to the people:

"Be strong"

"I am with you."

"I covenanted with you."

"My Spirit remains among you."

"Do not fear."

Haggai's encouragement? Believe that God's work is greater than it looks.

III. GOD'S BLESSING ON HIS WORK (2:10-23)

Verse 2:19: "… from this day on I will bless you."

Blessings on Doing God's Work

Therefore, my dear brothers, stand firm. Let nothing move you. Always give yourselves fully to the work of the Lord, because you know that your labor in the Lord is not in vain.
I Corinthians 15:58

This verse occurs at the end of a chapter that elaborated on the Resurrection. In other words, because Christ is alive, the work "in the Lord" never is useless or vain. God Himself is committed to bless it – in His own time and in His own way.

Blessing on Zerubbabel

Haggai ends in a strange manner, because it closes with a unique blessing on Zerubbabel. We might wonder about this, because we don't hear much about Zerubbabel. What is being given to us here, though, is the blessing of God – yes, on the work right now being done for Him, but also the blessing of God in the future in the coming Messiah.

What is impressive is that Zerubbabel is in the line of the Messiah, both in Joseph's lineage (Matthew 1) and in Mary's (Luke 3).

Haggai closes with the reminder of the greatest blessing of all – the Messiah. Today, for us, it is the Savior and Lord … Jesus Christ.

Lessons From Zephaniah and Haggai

1. The day of the Lord can be a day of judgment. This is the message of Zephaniah. The visitation of the Lord can be terrible, with a reminder that our sins will be punished and there are consequences to our wickedness.

2. The day of the Lord can be a day of blessing. This is the message of Haggai. The visitation of the Lord can be terrific, with the fulfillment of promises and the restoration of what has been destroyed.

Notes

Assignment

READ ...

Zechariah, Chapters 1-14, and Malachi 1-4, or selected chapters from Zechariah and Malachi (one a day for a week) as follows:

Zechariah 4   –   The vision of the gold lamp stand.

Zechariah 10   –   The care of the Lord.

Zechariah 14   –   The day of the Lord.

Malachi 1   –   The confrontation of sin.

Malachi 2   –   The priests and Judah as unfaithful.

Malachi 4   –   The day of the Lord.

MEMORIZE ...

Zechariah 4:6: "This is the word of the Lord to Zerubbabel: 'Not by might nor by power, but by my Spirit,' says the Lord Almighty."

and/or

Malachi 2:16: "'I hate divorce,' says the Lord God of Israel."

and/or

Malachi 3:10: "'Bring the whole tithe into the storehouse, that there may be food in my house. Test me in this,' says the Lord Almighty, 'and see if I will not throw open the floodgates of heaven and pour out so much blessing that you will not have room enough for it.'"

PRAY ...

Depending on doing the Lord's work by the Spirit of God. Ask the Lord to give you wisdom and strength from on high.

Committing your marriage to the Lord, recognizing that the Lord's standard is for husbands and wives to stay together.

Seeking to be faithful in the giving in your life, especially in your giving of the tithe.

APPLY ...

In the light of Zechariah and Malachi, what do you:

BELIEVE about God?

REPENT of as sin?

OBEY as a command from God?

SHARE ...

According to what you have learned from Zechariah and Malachi:

- Talk with your family about what needs to be rebuilt, renewed or reformed in your personal lives, your family, your church or your nation. These Minor Prophets were called by God to be about the work of renewal. This is God's call on our lives all the time.

- Ask an unchurched friend about his or her complaints about the established Church. Find out where he or she thinks that the Church is wrong, and really listen to the complaints. Try not to be defensive. In fact, agree with him or her where you can about the problems in the Church. The reality is that the Church is always in a state of needing renewal and reformation.

Zechariah:
The Way God Works

Verse 4:6: "Not by might nor by power, but by my Spirit, says the Lord Almighty."

The following paragraph from "The Paradox of Our Age," by Dr. Bob Moorehead, former pastor of Seattle's Overlake Christian Church, makes it clear that we not always are in tune with the way God works:

The paradox of our time in history is that we have taller buildings but shorter tempers; wider freeways, but narrower viewpoints. We spend more, but have less; we buy more, but enjoy less. We have bigger houses and smaller families; more conveniences, but less time. We have more degrees but less sense; more knowledge, but less judgment; more experts, yet more problems; more medicine, but less wellness. We drink too much, smoke too much, spend too recklessly, laugh too little, drive too fast, get too angry, stay up too late, get up too tired, read too little, watch TV too much, and pray too seldom. We have multiplied our possessions, but reduced our values. We talk too much, love too seldom, and hate too often. We've learned how to make a living, but not a life. We've added years to life not life to years. We've been all the way to the moon and back, but have trouble crossing the street to meet a new neighbor. We conquered outer space but not inner space. We've done larger things, but not better things. We've cleaned up the air, but polluted the soul. We've conquered the atom, but not our prejudice. We write more, but learn less. We plan more, but accomplish less. We've learned to rush, but not to wait. We build more computers to hold more information, to produce more copies than ever, but we communicate less and less. These are the times of fast foods and slow digestion; big men and small character; steep profits and shallow relationships. These are the days of two incomes but more divorce; fancier houses but broken homes. These are days of quick trips, disposable diapers, throwaway morality, one night stands, overweight bodies, and pills that do everything from cheer, to quiet, to kill. It is a time when there is much in the showroom window and nothing in the stockroom. A time when technology can bring this letter to you, and a time when you can choose either to share this insight, or to just hit delete. ...

People are living life according to human "might and power" – "taller buildings;" "bigger houses;" "more degrees;" "more knowledge;" "multiplied possessions;" "too much talk;" "living longer;" "scientific advancement;" "more medicine;" "higher incomes;" "taller men;" "steep profits;" "two incomes;" etc.; ... and are lesser people accomplishing fewer meaningful deeds and experiencing diminishing pleasure.

The problem is that lives can be lived depending on our own human efforts, resources, wisdom and power. This, though, is not the way God works. God works "not by human might nor by human power, but by His Spirit."

Zechariah provides this important truth about how God works.

The context of Zechariah is the same as that of Haggai. The Jews were returning to Jerusalem from exile in Babylon and they found a discouraging and devastating situation.

So, how do you respond to such a situation? Haggai was encouraging, but Zechariah was of a different temperament and texture. He was a visionary. Some have called the Book of Zechariah the "Book of Revelation of the Old Testament" because it is so full of visions and symbols.

With all of his visions, though, Zechariah had one message: Encourage the people to be about God's work God's way. This was more encouragement than conviction. Zechariah did not necessarily point the finger as much as he put his arm around the shoulder of his hearers.

The way he encouraged them in our passage was to remind them of something from the old Tabernacle and Temple – the menorah, the seven-branched golden lamp stand that was to be kept burning all the time by the priests to symbolize the presence of God (Exodus 25:31-40; 37:17-24).

In Zechariah's vision, however, he sees other details that went beyond the menorah. There was a bowl on top with channels running to the seven lights, and there were two olive trees on either side that continually provided oil. The elements of the vision can be interpreted this way:

• The lampstand itself is the people of God – Israel then and the Church today. So, the lampstand is us.

• The two olive trees are Joshua, the high priest, and Zerubbabel, the governor (4:14), who are types of Christ, the Messiah, who would be both the great high Priest and the King in the line of David.

• The oil is the Holy Spirit.

So, the vision teaches us that Christ sends His Holy Spirit to us, the Church, so that we might shine in this dark world.

Thus, there is the message: "Not by might nor by power, but by my Spirit, says the Lord Almighty."

The people were defeated and discouraged. They were not feeling "mighty" or "powerful." It was the absence here of human might and power that was more the problem than the presence of human might and power. The people were feeling a poverty, rather than a pride, about doing the work of God.

In that context, through Zechariah, God tells them in a comforting and encouraging way, "That's OK. I know you are weak. I know that you do not think you can do it. I am very aware of your limitations. But you need to hear – it is not by might nor power, but by my Spirit."

Malachi:
God Does Not Change

INTRODUCTION

It is an axiom in today's culture that change is a way of life. Change is what politicians promise and preachers preach. The desire for change is behind the fashion industry, Madison Avenue and the entertainment business.

The need for change bolsters the sale of diet books, self-improvement tapes and exercise programs. The recording of change is found in history, science and religion. The experience of change is acute, even intense, in transportation, communications and computers.

There is, however, a need to hear something loud and clear: In a time of change, there is a constant. There is something – or, to be more exact, someone – who does not change:

I the LORD do not change. (3:6)

I. A GREAT TRUTH

The Context of Malachi

Malachi is the last book of the Old Testament. Malachi was a prophet to the returning exiles from captivity in Babylon. When he prophesied, the Temple had been built, sacrifices had restarted, the walls around Jerusalem had been constructed and life was returning to normal.

Normal, though, not always is good.

The message of Malachi is that the people had changed, but God had not:

- The people doubted that God loved them, but the love of God had not changed.

- The people offered blemished sacrifices, but the holiness of God remained the same.

- The priests were not faithful to the covenant, but God was staying faithful even in the light of their unfaithfulness.

- The people had confused evil and good, but God always had pure and true justice.

- The people had broken faith with their families, but the heart of God never wavered from the message: "'I hate divorce' says the Lord God."

- The people had taken back control of their goods, but the ownership of God stood firm as He confronted the people: "You have robbed me in tithes and offerings."

Change is a part of our lives, but too often our change is for the worse, not the better. God, in eternal holiness and purity, does not change. As James put it in James 1:17:

"Every good and perfect gift is from above coming down from the Father of the heavenly lights, who does not change like shifting shadows."

Did you hear the adjective "unchangeable?" It describes the very nature and work of God. He is wise, but He never changes to be less wise. He is powerful, but He never changes to become weak. He is holy, but He never will evolve to be anything below holiness. He is just, but there is not a chance of any fluctuations toward injustice. He is good, and you always can count on Him to be good. He is truth, and that will never mutate into untruth.

II. A GREAT COMFORT

The text goes on to tell us something phenomenal regarding the truth that God does not change. It is true that, in His nature, He remains the same for all of eternity, but a consequence of God not changing is this:

... So you, O descendants of Jacob, are not destroyed (3:6).

Here, the great truth that the Lord does not change gives great comfort.

The comfort is for the people of God, described here as the descendants of Jacob, but it applies to us as the people of God today. This means that, if "God is for us, then God is for us!" He does not change. He remains our Father. He stays as our Savior. He permanently resides as our counselor. If God is your Lord today, He will remain your Lord tomorrow. He is more committed to us than we are to Him. Our affections, knowledge and commitments can wax and wane, but His remain constant. We may run away from God, but we – His children – always find Him ready to receive us back.

The plans and purposes of God for us and our good are secure and safe because He does not change:

The Lord of hosts has sworn: "As I have planned, so shall it be,
and as I have purposed, so shall it stand."
Isaiah 14:24

My counsel shall stand, and I will accomplish all my purpose.
Isaiah 46:10

Many are the plans in the mind of a man,
but it is the purpose of the Lord that will be established.
Proverbs 19:21

Jesus Christ is the same yesterday and today and forever.
Hebrews 13:8

Lessons From Zechariah and Malachi

1. God's way is not our way, but that is OK. We are getting in the way most of the time. We think we know how to do the work of God in God's way, but often it is using our own human resources and efforts. God is about bringing His Kingdom by His Spirit. That is not our way.

2. God's way doesn't change, but that is OK. God is the same throughout the ages. His nature and His will stay the same, while we and the world around us constantly change. God provides the stability needed to live a life of righteousness and blessing. Our trusting Him is the call upon our lives.

NOTES

CHAPTER THIRTY

Lessons From Our Journey Through the Old Testament

THE NATURE OF GOD

"The Lord is gracious and compassionate ..." yet His grace and compassion do not negate His justice and wrath.

The Old Testament is so full of thunder and lightning (judgment and discipline) that it is easy to think that is the full nature of God. It is true, God is holy, just and "will punish sin." This only accentuates, however, the fuller nature of God that is loving and gracious. Behind all the warnings of judgment to come and behind all the events when judgment fell, there is one main message: "It's not too late." Judgment does not have to have the final word. Our God is doing something bigger than punishment. He is drawing His people.

The Old Testament Gospel: "The Lord is gracious and compassionate, slow to anger and abounding in love." This is an echo throughout the Old Testament, and it is in every section – the history, the Law, the writings and the prophets:

- Exodus 34:6: To Moses.

- Numbers 14:18: Moses pleads with God.

- Nehemiah 9:17: The basis for God's continued forgiveness.

- II Chronicles 30:9: Hezekiah.

- Psalm 86:5: David.

- Psalm 86:15: David.

- Joel 2:13: The truth about God in the midst of a disaster.

- Jonah 4:2: The trait of God that Jonah did not like.

In the light of a disaster, when everything is dark, what is God like? He is like Himself all the time – gracious and compassionate, slow to anger and abounding in love.

THE NATURE OF THE COVENANT

"I am your God and you shall be my people."

The people of God are not real impressive in the Old Testament. There are the highlights of Abraham, Joseph, Moses, Joshua, Caleb, David, Solomon, Elijah, Elisha, King Hezekiah and King Josiah, Isaiah and Jeremiah. With almost every one of them, though, their feet of clay begin to crumble. The nation of Israel was always on the edge of idolatry and immorality, and rebellion was often manifested.

This, however, never turned away God. Those times of rebellion did turn on His wrath and judgment, but they also were expressions of the covenant that included blessings and curses.

The covenant is God's commitment to His people, where He takes the initiative, demands the conditions, executes blessings and curses, and is always faithful to His promises.

THE NATURE OF THE MESSIAH

The covenant is primarily fulfilled in God's promise to send the Messiah.

Jesus is the key to the Old Testament. He is not known by name there, but He is known by work and promise. The Messiah is the promise that runs throughout the Old Testament and comes to fruition in the New Testament.

The Old Testament contains more than 300 references to the Messiah that are fulfilled in Jesus. A major part of the New Testament, especially the Gospels, is comprised of quotes from the Old Testament that are fulfilled in Jesus.

Jesus is all over the place in the Old Testament:

- The seed of the woman (Genesis 3:15).
- Born of a virgin (Isaiah 7:14).
- The Son of God (Psalms 2:7).
- The seed of Abraham (Genesis 22:18).
- The lion of the tribe of Judah (Genesis 49:10).
- A shoot out of Jesse (Isaiah 11:1).
- From the house of David (Jeremiah 23:5).
- The suffering servant (Isaiah 53).
- Born in Bethlehem (Micah 5:2).
- Herod's killing of the children (Jeremiah 31:15).
- He shall be called Lord (Psalms 110:1).
- He shall be Immanuel (Isaiah 7:14).
- He shall be a prophet like Moses (Deuteronomy 18:18).
- He shall be a priest after the order of Melchizedek (Psalms 110:4).
- He shall be a king (Psalms 2:5).
- He shall have a special anointment of the Holy Spirit (Isaiah 11:2).
- He will have a messenger to precede Him (Isaiah 40:3).

- He will be a worker of miracles (Isaiah 35:5, 6).

- He will be a teacher of parables (Psalms 78:2).

- He will be a "stone of stumbling" for the Jews (Psalms 118:22).

- He will be the "light" for the Gentiles (Isaiah 60:3).

- He will be betrayed by a friend (Psalms 41:19).

- He will be sold for 30 pieces of silver (Zechariah 11:12).

- He will be forsaken by His disciples (Zechariah 13).

- He will be accused by false witnesses (Psalms 35:11).

- He will be spit upon, mocked and crucified with thieves (Isaiah 53).

- His hands will be pierced (Psalms 22:16).

- He will pray for His persecutors and be rejected by His people (Isaiah 53).

- His garments will be parted and gambled for (Psalms 22:18).

- He will suffer thirst (Psalms 69:21).

- He will give a forsaken cry (Psalms 22:1).

- His bones will not be broken (Psalms 34:20).

- His side will be pierced (Zechariah 12:10).

- Darkness will come over the land (Amos 8:9).

- He will be buried in a rich man's tomb (Isaiah 53:9).

- He will rise from the dead (Psalms 16:19).

- He will ascend into heaven (Psalms 68:18).

- He will be seated at the right hand of God (Psalms 110:1).

THE INTERTESTAMENTAL PERIOD

The Intertestamental Period denotes the history of Judaism between the Old Testament and the New Testament. Most people would think of the last verse of Malachi and the first verse of Matthew as the beginning and ending points of the Intertestamental Period, but that is not exactly the case. It is more exact to speak of the post-exilic period and the coming of Christ as the Intertestamental Period. Those dates would be about 400 B.C. to A.D. 1 – in other words, a period of about 400 years.

This Intertestamental Period is marked by several features:

1. The close of the Old Testament canon. It commonly was believed in Judaism that no more prophets from God were being sent, so it was recognized that the books understood to be the standard (meaning of "canon") for being Scripture were set. There were some debates about including some or excluding others. Daniel, for example, was disputed by some to be authentic but generally there was agreement.

This close of the Old Testament canon becomes clear as the oral tradition of Jewish leaders totally changed to interpretation of the Old Testament texts – in particular, the Torah, the Law (the Five Books of Moses). Those interpretations were widely used and, in many cases, would receive more attention than the sacred texts themselves. These oral traditions and interpretations would later be put in written form in the Midrash (running commentary on the law) with legal implications (Halachah) and moral implications (Haggadah). Later, they were part of the Talmud, the interpretation of the Torah (the Law).

2. The struggle with world powers. This 400-year Intertestamental Period was a significant time of shifting world powers. At the start of this period, the Persian Empire was dominant. At the end, it was the Roman Empire. Here is an overview of how this happened:

- The start of the Intertestamental Period saw the Persian Empire in control. It had taken over from the Babylonians and had allowed the intermittent return of the Jews to their homeland and the rebuilding of Jerusalem the Temple. This was around 400 B.C.

- Around 350 B.C., a new power began to emerge – Macedonia under the leadership of Phillip. Macedonia began to conquer the Greek city states and, when Phillip was murdered, his son Alexander took over at the age of 20. Alexander the Great then began an aggressive expansion of what we know as the Greek Empire and, in 333 B.C., conquered the Persian Empire.

- The expansive Greek Empire used a new strategy called hellenization to control conquered lands. Hellenization implemented the setting up of colonies of Greek soldiers and officials in conquered lands and influencing the culture, language and economy of the land. Hellenization was so successful that by the end of the Intertestamental Period, Greek was the common language of the known world. That is why the New Testament was originally written in Greek.

- After Alexander, the Greek Empire was divided into many sections under the leadership of many generals. Palestine was in between two of these sections and so was fought over several times during the Intertestamental Period. The Seleucid Empire finally gained control of Palestine and the Jews revolted. This was known as the Maccabean revolt because it was led by Judas Maccabeus. During this time, a Seleucid king named Antiochus Ephiphanes was vicious in his treatment of the Jews and showed disdain for the Jewish faith by offering a pig as a sacrifice at the Temple. All this took place around 160 B.C.

- Then a time of relative peace was enjoyed in Palestine before another empire came to power. The Roman Empire began to conquer the previous Greek Empire and, in 60 B.C. conquered Jerusalem. The Romans were different than the Greeks in their conquering of other lands because the Romans practiced a military occupation backed by cruel enforcement, governmental control and little local tolerance. Thus, by the time of Jesus, the Jewish people longed to be freed from Roman rule.

3. The development of the synagogue. The Intertestamental Period saw the development of the spiritual life of the Hebrews in a different way than before. The Temple had been the main focal point of their faith. The synagogue now came into existence as an important expression of their faith.

Synagogue means "gathering." It was first of all an informal gathering of Jews who sat at the feet of a teacher, like Ezra, to learn the Law. It later developed into a place where Jews would gather to read the Law, the Torah and worship. A synagogue could happen in any community. You did not have to be in Jerusalem or come to the Temple to worship, you could do it in your own community. One still would come to Jerusalem and the Temple for the feasts (Passover, Pentecost, Tabernacles), but the day-to-day and week-to-week worship would be focused on the local synagogue.

The Diaspora was the dispersion of Jews into other lands and countries. This had started during the time of Solomon, but later grew as Israel was conquered and the people scattered. The exile in Babylon was the most dramatic dispersion of the Jews, as many were taken away from Jerusalem. While in this dispersion, however, they formed synagogues to keep the faith. This dispersion of the Jews continued throughout this Intertestamental Period to such an extent that the New Testament depicts a synagogue in every community in the Roman Empire where Paul went. We are also told that in Jerusalem itself, there were more than 400 synagogues.

4. *The organization of distinctive Jewish groups.* During the Intertestamental Period, many distinctive leadership groups developed within Judaism. The main ones were the Pharisees, the Sadducees, the Zealots and the Essenes.

The Pharisees continued the tradition of the scribe from the Old Testament as teachers and keepers of the Law. They were meticulous in their observance of the Law, and their understanding of why Israel had been judged by God time and time again in the past was that they had not followed the Law as they should. So, their passion was to keep the Law and make sure others did as well. They would develop very legalistic regulations to judge whether or not you kept the Law. Politically, they were not supportive of a revolt against Rome. They thought that God would take care of them if they kept the Law, so military efforts would never succeed.

The Sadducees were more like a political party. They were well-to-do families who used every influence at hand to benefit themselves. They were very small in number and the common Jew did not associate with them. Most of the priests were Sadducees because they came from priestly families who usually were prominent. Theologically, they were not as literal as the Pharisees and did not hold some of the beliefs they thought were later developments in Jewish thought, like the immortality of the soul, a Resurrection, angels and demons.

The Zealots were a militant group that started during the Maccabean revolt. They were zealous for the Law to the extent that the taking up of arms against an aggressor was seen as holy and right. One of Jesus' disciples was Simon, the Zealot. During the Roman occupation, they manifested their zeal more in guerrilla-type opposition. After the destruction of Jerusalem in 70 A.D. by Rome, the Zealots continued their fighting and were destroyed in their last stronghold at Masada, where they all committed suicide.

The Essenes were another distinctive expression of the Jewish faith from the Intertestamental Period. They are not known from the New Testament, but from the writings of Josephus. The Essenes were communities of Jews who lived together separate from other Jews. They gave themselves to the simple life of agriculture and the study of the Law. They stressed ceremonial purity, held all property in common and did not associate with other Jews. They did not take part in any military or commercial endeavors outside their community. The most commonly known Essene community was the Qumran community, where the Dead Sea Scrolls were found.

5. *The writing of the Apocrypha.* The Apocrypha (which means "hidden") was written during the Intertestamental Period and has been debated throughout Church history as being or not being a part of Scripture. The Roman Catholic Church recognizes it as Scripture, but Protestant churches do not. The Apocrypha is considered by all as profitable writings to understand the history of the Intertestamental Period and may give private edification.

What is to be included in the Apocrypha is debatable, but most listings would include the following books:

- I and II Esdras.

- Tobit.

- Judith.

- Additions to Esther.

- Ecclesiasticus, or the Wisdom of Jesus the Son of Sirach.

- Baruch.

- The Letter of Jeremiah.

- The Prayer of Azariah and the Song of the Three Young Men.

- Susanna.

- Bel and the Dragon.

- The Prayer of Manasseh.

- I and II Maccabees.

Some of the reasons for not accepting the Apocrypha as part of Holy Scripture are:

1.   The Apocrypha was not recognized by the Jews to be part of Scripture.

2.   The Apocrypha was never quoted by Jesus, nor anywhere in the New Testament.

3.   The Apocrypha was never recognized by the Early Church as Scripture.

The Westminster Confession of Faith puts it this way:

The books commonly called Apocrypha, not being of divine inspiration, are no part of the canon of the Scripture; and therefore are of no authority in the Church of God, nor to be any otherwise approved, or made of us, than other human writings.
Chapter 1, paragraph 3

Comparing Old Testament and New Testament

Old Testament	New Testament
Looking forward to Messiah	Looking back on Messiah
Written in Hebrew	Written in Greek
Prophetic in nature	Fulfillment in nature
Incomplete	Complete

Do not avoid the Old Testament. Some people can have such a high view of the New Testament that they feel the Old Testament no longer is needed. The view in the Reformed tradition is expressed in the Westminster Confession:

Under the name of Holy Scripture, or the Word of God written, are now contained all the Books of the Old and New Testaments.

NOTES

The New Testament

The Synoptic Gospels: Matthew, Mark and Luke

The New Testament opens with the four Gospels, with the first three sharing a common framework and many stories. Thus, these three (Matthew, Mark and Luke) are called the Synoptic Gospels, meaning that they hold a common view of the life, death and Resurrection of Jesus Christ.

Because they are synoptic, however, it does not mean that they are the same. Each Gospel is unique in its authorship, presentation, audiences and emphases.

What is presented with the four Gospels is a comprehensive eyewitness account from four different and distinctive witnesses, who all tell the same story and give a unified picture of Jesus Christ.

Chapter Thirty-One: Matthew

Assignment

Read ...

Matthew, Chapters 1-28, or selected chapters from Matthew (one a day for a week) as follows:

Matthew 1   –   The birth of Jesus Christ.

Matthew 4   –   The temptation of Jesus.

Matthew 5-7 –   The Sermon on the Mount.

Matthew 13   –   Some parables by Jesus.

Matthew 16   –   Peter's confession.

Matthew 17   –   The Transfiguration.

Matthew 28   –   The Resurrection and the Great Commission.

Memorize ...

Matthew 1:21: "She will give birth to a son, and you are to give Him the name Jesus, because He will save His people from their sins."

and/or

Matthew 5:17: "Do not think that I have come to abolish the Law or the Prophets; I have not come to abolish them but to fulfill them."

and/or

Matthew 28:18-20: "All authority in heaven and on earth has been given to me. Therefore go and make disciples of all nations, baptizing them in the name of the Father and of the Son and of the Holy Spirit, and teaching them to obey everything I have commanded you. And surely I am with you always, to the very end of the age."

PRAY ...

Thanking God for the "good news," the Gospel of His Son Jesus Christ coming into the world to save sinners.

Submitting to the teachings of the Lord that you might be a faithful disciple.

Committing yourself to the Great Commission to go and make disciples of all nations.

APPLY ...

In the light of Matthew, what do you:

> BELIEVE about God?
>
> REPENT of as sin?
>
> OBEY as a command from God?

SHARE ...

According to what you have learned from Matthew:

- Have a conversation with your family about the life of Jesus. Ask each member of the family to relate their favorite event, their favorite parable or their favorite disciple. Then interact with one another in learning more about who Jesus was and what He did in His ministry.

- Ask unchurched friends what they think the mission of the Church is. Listen carefully to them, seek to learn what others might think of the Church and why there is a Church. Then share with your friends the Great Commission (28:18-20) and get their reaction to the words of Jesus about what the Church is to be doing.

Matthew:
Meet the King

INTRODUCTION

There are verses from Matthew that have become part of common Christian communication, but they have not always been recognized as being from Matthew. Here are some of them:

She will give birth to a son, and you are to give Him the name Jesus,
because He will save His people from their sins. (1:21)

Jesus answered, "It is written, 'Man does not live on bread alone,
but on every word that comes from the mouth of God.'" (4:4)

In the same way, let your light shine before men,
that they may see your good deeds and praise your Father in heaven. (5:16)

But seek first His kingdom and His righteousness
and all these things will be given to you as well. (6:33)

Come to me, all you who are weary and burdened, and I will give you rest.
Take my yoke upon you and learn from me, for I am gentle and humble in heart, and
you will find rest for your souls. For my yoke is easy and my burden is light. (11:28-30)

Simon Peter answered, "You are the Christ, the Son of the living God." (16:16)

All authority in heaven and on earth has been given to me. Therefore go
and make disciples of all nations, baptizing them in the name of the Father and of the Son
and of the Holy Spirit, and teaching them to obey everything I have commanded you.
And surely I am with you always, to the very end of the age. (28:18-20)

There is a unique perspective in Matthew that is distinctively Jewish, with a focus on Jesus being the King.

Matthew begins with a genealogy (the pedigree or blood line or racial purity always is important to the Jew) that starts with Abraham, but its whole purpose was to show that Jesus was the "son of David," emphasizing the promise of God that the kingship of David would never pass and that Jesus was the King. The phrase, "son of David," is used nine times in Matthew and six times in the rest of the Gospels.

Matthew is the only Gospel to give the story of the visit of the Magi to the baby Jesus. The whole thrust of that story is that they came from a Gentile land to see the "King of the Jews."

The phrase, "kingdom of heaven," is used 32 times in Matthew and nowhere else in the rest of the New Testament. Matthew definitely was focusing on the King and His Kingdom. The full implication of kingship is claimed by Jesus Himself and especially is shown in the Great Commission (28:18) when He said, "All authority in heaven and on earth has been given to me." Now, that's a king!

AUTHOR

Matthew was one of the 12 disciples called by Jesus. The Lord called him from the life of being a tax collector, which meant that he was a hated man in his own community – not only because he collected taxes, but because tax collectors then collected for Rome, and he was seen as a traitor. So, it had to be shocking for Jesus to call someone like Matthew to follow Him.

Matthew was very aware of his sinfulness, and his call to discipleship stands as a prime example of the truth that our sin does not keep God away from us. Our past never can keep us from God's purposes for our lives.

Matthew was also known as Levi. This is interesting, because Levi was the priestly tribe. This meant that Matthew might have been the son of a priest who had gone bad. In growing up in a priest's home, this explains why Matthew, even as a tax collector, knew the Old Testament Scriptures and had a burden for the Jews to see Jesus as their King.

I. THE KING'S CREDENTIALS (1 – 4)

Matthew's Gospel begins with an obvious attempt to affirm the kingly credentials of Jesus. His bloodline, which absolutely was crucial for Jewish acceptance, was delineated in generation after generation from Abraham to Mary's husband, Joseph. There was to be no doubt that this baby was from the line of David.

Matthew then gives a birth narrative that is distinctive. Joseph is given proper attention by the angel of the Lord and it was made clear to him that this baby was to be called "Jesus, because He will save His people from their sins" (1:21). The visit of the Magi uplifted the kingly, even cosmic, character of this baby, and no earthly king, especially Herod, could get close to Him in glory and holiness.

The baptism of Jesus by John authenticated the ministry of Jesus far beyond any bloodline or foreign emissaries or angelic visit. The Father from heaven spoke:

This is my Son with whom I am well pleased (2:17).

People are often known more by their enemies than their friends. This was shown when Jesus had His first experience of ministry – the temptation in the desert. Satan came to Him, and the reality of what was at stake in Jesus' ministry came to light. Jesus was confronted with another way to do things – but He chose to stand by what was written.

II. THE KING'S TEACHING (5 – 7)

The Sermon on the Mount takes 15 minutes to read, but has a lifetime of teaching in it. There is another version of the Sermon on the Mount in Luke 6, but it is not close to the content in Matthew 5 – 7.

Jesus gathered with the crowd, but was focused on His disciples. He taught them how to live and how to die. He taught them how to be in the world and how to be under the Law. He raised the bar of morality above legalism to a righteousness that demanded a personal relationship with God. He taught them how to pray, give, fast and love. He set the standard for the uncommon life that He had come to establish.

The impact of this teaching was immediate (7:28, 29):

When Jesus had finished saying these things, the crowds were amazed at His teaching, because He taught as one who had authority, and not as their teachers of the law.

And this was only the beginning. The King was more than a rabbi.

III. THE KING'S MIRACLES (8, 9)

He was also a miracle worker. A series of 10 miracles are recorded in succession. The words of Jesus are immediately followed by the works of Jesus. This has the effect of verifying His claims and credentials.

Jesus demonstrated that He was sovereign over disease, demons and disasters. He did things that the people only had read about, and the people responded – they came to Him in the thousands.

IV. THE KING'S FRIENDS AND ENEMIES (10:1 – 16:12)

Even as He was confronted with the nameless thousands, however, He concentrated on a few relationships. Jesus was about people – people who hurt, people with questions, people who hated Him, people who were kin to Him, people who were willing to follow Him.

The people in Jesus' life are presented:

- The twelve are called.

- John the Baptist is described in more detail.

- The Pharisees make several appearances, and their disdain of Jesus is obvious.

- Jesus' own family is talked about.

- Different needy people come to Jesus.

- And the multitude, the ever present multitude, always seems to be there.

V. THE KING'S DISCOURSES (16:13 – 25:24)

The teaching of Jesus was not limited to a hillside or a healing. Every situation in life became the occasion to teach and model the Kingdom of heaven. Jesus seemed to always have His disciples on His mind. He wanted them to know who He really was. The time was drawing near when Jesus would suffer and die. He knew that, but the disciples were not there yet.

"Who do people say the Son of Man is?" Jesus was not interested in His public image. He quickly got to His main concern: "But what about you? Who do you say I am?" This was a question directed to the disciples and marks a pivotal point in discipleship.

Peter spoke up, "You are the Christ, the Son of the living God." Upon that confession, the tide turned. The disciples still did not understand, but Jesus began to be clearer about what was ahead.

Some of the disciples were given a glimpse of glory as Jesus was transfigured before them, but that only became the backdrop for getting back into discipleship training. The miracles continued and the teaching intensified with more parables.

Jesus entered into Jerusalem and the opposition intensified, but the training did not. Jesus at the Temple was questioned and ridiculed, but He stood, related stories, and talked about the Kingdom of heaven that would be much more glorious than the surrounding Temple.

Jesus responded to His enemies by pronouncing a series of "woes" upon the teachers of the Law and the Pharisees. He exposed them for who they really were. Using the language of the covenant, He pronounced curses that could only make those who heard them either soften or harden in their attitudes.

Jesus wanted the disciples to see beyond the existing religious life and structure. He talked about the signs of the end of the age. It was not pleasant talk, but it was straight talk. He went on to dramatize these days of judgment with parables, making the necessity of being prepared for the Kingdom.

The talk was so plain and the impact so potent that the days ahead were almost predictable for the disciples. Something would have to give.

VI. THE KING'S FINAL DAYS (26 – 28)

The final days of the King were unimaginable to the disciples. A plot was afoot that involved one of the disciples, but Jesus only wanted to celebrate the Passover with His friends. A new day was dawning, but it still was dark. Jesus was prepping them to remember Him in this new day and to never forget what they were about to experience. He cemented this remembrance with the common meal for the Jew that became an uncommon sacrament for believers.

Jesus was betrayed, arrested, tried and condemned. Peter, Judas and Pilate all played their parts, but each in a distinctive and striking way. The end result was that Jesus carried His Cross to Golgotha and was nailed upon it.

With all that occurred while Jesus was on the Cross, the cry of being forsaken hung in the air as if amplified by the very soul of Jesus: "My God, my God, why have you forsaken me?" That question was answered by His death and burial.

The day of Resurrection, however, dawned. "He has risen from the dead" became a new truth to be shared among the disciples, no matter how unbelievable. That shared truth became the experience of many people and the disciples were commissioned to a work for which they had been prepared:

The risen Lord told them: "All authority in heaven and on earth has been given to me. Therefore go and make disciples of all nations, baptizing them in the name of the Father and of the Son and of the Holy Spirit, and teaching them to obey everything I have commanded you. And surely I am with you always, to the very end of the age."

Lessons From Matthew

1   Jesus is the King of the Kingdom of heaven. Matthew is as clear as any other Gospel writer that Jesus is in the royal line of David and is the fulfillment of all the promises of the Kingdom to David. The Kingdom of heaven is ruled by Jesus Himself, and we are to be His subjects.

2.   Jesus is the teacher of disciples. The teaching ministry of Jesus is displayed in Matthew by sermons, parables and discourses. Jesus desired His disciples to know who He was, what He came to do and what He wanted them to do.

3.   Jesus is the sender of disciples. Jesus was not just about education and knowledge; He was about work and action. The disciples were trained so that they might be about the very work that Jesus did. The disciples, from preaching to healing to reproducing themselves, were being prepared for a day when they would be doing their work like Jesus and unto Jesus.

NOTES

Chapter Thirty-Two: Mark

Assignment

Read ...

Mark, Chapters 1-16, or selected chapters from Mark (one a day for a week) as follows:

Mark 1 – John the Baptist and first disciples.

Mark 2 – The healing of the paralytic.

Mark 4 – The parable of the sower.

Mark 8 – The feeding of the five thousand.

Mark 11 – The triumphal entry.

Mark 13 – Signs of the end.

Mark 15 – The Crucifixion.

Memorize ...

Mark 1:17: "'Come, follow me,' Jesus said, 'and I will make you fishers of men.'"

and/or

Mark 12:30-31: "'Love the Lord your God with all your heart and with all your soul and with all your mind and with all your strength.' The second is this: 'Love your neighbor as yourself.'"

and/or

Mark 16:15: "He said to them, 'Go into all the world and preach the good news to all creation.'"

Pray ...

Thanking God for the "good news," the Gospel of His Son Jesus Christ coming into the world to save sinners.

That you might be a disciple responding to the call of Jesus to be "fishers of men."

Marveling over what Jesus did on the Cross. Read the account of His death on the Cross and know that it was done for you.

APPLY ...

In the light of Mark, what do you:

BELIEVE about God?

REPENT of as sin?

OBEY as a command from God?

SHARE ...

According to what you have learned from Mark:

- The Gospel of Mark is a fast-paced account of the life, death and Resurrection of Jesus. Ask members of your family about one of the events in Jesus' life (the feeding of the five thousand or Jesus calming the storm), then read the story and imagine what it would have been like if you had been there. Let the imagination flow.

- Talk to someone who isn't regular in church attendance and ask them what they think of Jesus. Let it be clear that you are not asking them to express what they think about the Church or the Bible or anything else. Just see what they think about Jesus. Use this as an opportunity to share what Jesus means to you. Be clear. Be honest. Be humble. Be faithful.

Mark:
The 'Go' Gospel

INTRODUCTION

The commentary by Manford George Gutzke on Mark is titled, *The GO Gospel*. He calls it that because action is a characteristic of Mark. Events happen quickly. Things occur immediately. The story moves swiftly along. The word "immediately" (or "straightaway" in the King James Version) is Mark's favorite word. Mark is the shortest and the simplest of all the Gospels, but it is as fast-paced as any book in the Bible.

Jesus is portrayed as the servant who constantly is ministering to others and it ultimately leads to His death. Forty percent of Mark is devoted to the last seven days of Jesus' life.

Only 18 out of Christ's 70 parables are found in Mark, yet he describes more than half of Christ's 35 miracles – the largest proportion of any Gospel writer. This is evidence of the "not time to talk, let's go" portrayal of Jesus in Mark.

AUTHOR

Who is this Mark? He was not one of the twelve and he was not prominent in Acts, yet he is there:

- Mark 14:51, 52: A singular account found only in this Gospel and the man referred to was probably Mark.

- Acts 12:2: Mark's home was probably a meeting place for early Christians and maybe was a large home, suggesting prominence and wealth. It also was a place of prayer. It was perhaps the location of the Upper Room, where the Last Supper took place and where the disciples gathered to choose a replacement for Judas (Acts 2:13).

- Acts 13: Mark (or John or John Mark) became the center of a controversy:

  Verse 5:   He was with Paul and Barnabas on their first missionary journey.

  Verse 13:   Mark, for some reason, left Paul and returned home. We do not know the reasons. Some people say things got tough, and he wanted to go home to be with his mother.

- Acts 15:36-41: Mark caused a "sharp disagreement" between Paul and Barnabas.

- Colossians 4:14: Mark was Barnabas' cousin, so that may account for his patience with and loyalty to Mark.

That, however, is not the whole story – Paul did soften and Mark did mature:

• Colossians 4:10, 11: Mark is mentioned as a fellow worker with Paul and an encouragement to him.

• II Timothy 4:9-11: Lists some of those who deserted Paul, like Mark did earlier, but now Mark is listed as among those who prove useful in Paul's ministry.

It is believed that the apostolic authority behind Mark's Gospel was Peter. The Gospel of Mark was recognized as such by the Early Church fathers and was known as the "Memories of Peter" and also "The Gospel of St. Peter."

Mark was probably the earliest Gospel, written around A.D. 60. The other Gospel writers, therefore, probably had it before them as they wrote their own Gospels – hence, the similar outline followed by the three Synoptic Gospels.

I. SERVANT TO THE MULTITUDES (1 – 7)

Without a genealogy or birth narrative, Mark opens with the public ministry of Jesus. John the Baptist flashes onto the scene, and the ministry of Jesus is launched. In Jesus' ministry in these early chapters of Mark, there is a blend of His words and works, message and miracles.

Jesus is portrayed as doing all those things that are central to His ministry:

• Calling disciples.

• Casting out demons.

• Healing the sick.

• Praying.

• Teaching.

• Preaching.

As a result, the multitude – the crowds – quickly came to Him and for a while dominated His ministry.

One miracle that is recorded in all four Gospel records, but first occurred in Mark (6:30-44), was the feeding of the five thousand. This episode, maybe more than any other, demonstrated the compassion of Jesus for the multitudes. Mark's account gives the vivid detail of the people sitting down in groups on "green grass."

II. SERVANT TO THE DISCIPLES (8 – 10)

Jesus had all along been calling and training His disciples (4), but a time came when their training intensified.

Jesus knew that the time had come to be clear about what would happen to Him in the future. The disciples were not prepared for the shock of such a prediction.

He then began to teach them that the Son of Man must suffer many things; be rejected by the elders, chief priests and the teachers of the Law; and that He must be killed and, after three days, rise again. He spoke plainly about this. Peter took Him aside and began to rebuke Him (8:31, 32), but Jesus tells them again (10:33, 34):

We are going up to Jerusalem and the Son of Man will be betrayed to the chief priests and
teachers of the law. They will condemn Him to death and will hand Him over to the Gentiles,
who will mock Him and spit on Him, flog Him and kill Him. Three days later He will rise.

III. Sacrifice for the World (11 – 16)

Mark gives over a third of his narrative to the last week of Jesus' life. With all of the service rendered to the multitudes and the disciples, there was another service He had to perform. It was a sacrifice. His teaching, calling and miracle-working only were preliminary to the suffering, death and Resurrection for the sins of others.

Within the turmoil of that week, Jesus' debates with the teachers of the Law before His suffering and death stand out. One of the teachers asked an apparently genuine question: "Of all the commandments, which is the most important?"

Jesus chose to see this as a question that needed a direct answer, not an ambiguous one (12:29-31):

The most important one is this: "Hear, O Israel, the Lord our God, the Lord is one. Love the Lord your god with all your heart and with all your soul and with all your mind and with all your strength." The second is this: "Love your neighbor as yourself." There is no commandment greater than these.

The time of Jesus' suffering and death, however, had come. The Lord's Supper, Gethsemane, the betrayal, the arrest and the trials all occur and, right in the middle of them all is the disowning of Jesus by Peter. This detail has immense impact if Peter really is the apostolic source behind the Gospel of Mark. This meant that Peter gave a first-hand account to Mark of what had to have been a terrible memory.

The Crucifixion and burial of Jesus are simply and clearly recorded. The Resurrection was undeniable in its reality and truthfulness.

The last verses of chapter 16, however, are a disputed section of this Gospel. The most reliable early manuscripts do not contain Mark 16:9-20, but one part of this ending that corresponds to the ending of all the other Gospels is the Great Commission from Jesus to the disciples:

Go into all the world and preach the good news to all creation.

Lessons From Mark

1. Jesus came to be a servant. His selfless and loving actions toward the diseased, demon-possessed and the deprived demonstrated a compassion that marked His ministry. He called His disciples to follow in His footsteps in serving one another.

2. Jesus came to be a sacrifice. Supremely, Jesus came to die. He was to give His life as a ransom for many. This was Jesus' call and it was fulfilled in every way.

Notes

CHAPTER THIRTY-THREE: LUKE

Assignment

READ ...

Luke, Chapters 1-24, or selected chapters from Luke (one a day for a week) as follows:

Luke 2 – The birth of Jesus.

Luke 5 – Calling disciples and working miracles.

Luke 10 – Sending out the disciples and the parable of the Good Samaritan.

Luke 11 – Jesus' teaching on prayer.

Luke 15 – Parables about the lost.

Luke 23 – The Crucifixion.

Luke 24 – The Resurrection.

MEMORIZE ...

Luke 9:23: "If anyone would come after me, he must deny himself and take up his cross daily and follow me."

and/or

Luke 10:2: "He told them, 'The harvest is plentiful, but the workers are few. Ask the Lord of the harvest, therefore, to send out workers into His harvest field.'"

and/or

Luke 24:46, 47: "He told them, 'This is what is written: The Christ will suffer and rise from the dead on the third day, and repentance and forgiveness of sins will be preached in His name to all nations, beginning at Jerusalem.'"

PRAY ...

Thanking God for the "good news," the Gospel of His Son Jesus Christ coming into the world to save sinners.

Asking the Lord to give you a fuller understanding of Jesus' birth as it is detailed in the Gospel of Luke.

Desiring to be a modern-day disciple, sent by Jesus into a harvest field ready to be picked.

For the wisdom and strength to share the good news of Jesus Christ with anyone and everyone.

APPLY ...

In the light of Luke, what do you:

> BELIEVE about God?
>
> REPENT of as sin?
>
> OBEY as a command from God?

SHARE ...

According to what you have learned from Luke:

- Read Luke 1-2 with your family. It may not be Christmas, but talk about the birth of Jesus and the truth of that story for your lives today. In a season other than Christmas, think about the radical truth of God becoming man and how history thereby was changed forever.

- Share with someone the story of the Good Samaritan in Luke 10:25-37. See if your friend can see the shocking truth of Jesus using a story about someone who wasn't a Jew in order to teach a Jew about being right with God. Confess to your friend how people in the Church do not always have it together, and we always have things to learn to be more pleasing to the Lord.

Luke:
The Beloved Physician

INTRODUCTION

If you can say that you are one who loves God, then the Gospel of Luke is for you. Luke wrote the Gospel account, as well as the Book of Acts, for a man named Theophilus, which is Greek for "the one who loves God."

Therefore, since I myself have carefully investigated everything from the beginning, it seemed good also to me to write an orderly account for you, most excellent Theophilus, so that you may know the certainty of the things you have been taught. (1:3, 4)

More than likely, Theophilus was a real man, possibly a Roman official, who was Luke's patron and a convert to Christianity. If you are a generic "Theophilus," though, you will find the Gospel of Luke a special help in your relationship with the God you love.

AUTHOR

Who was Luke?

Luke was a Gentile and the only Gentile author in the New Testament. A well-educated Greek and a Roman citizen, he may have studied in the schools of Tarsus, like Paul and Apollos. Maybe they even knew each other in school.

Luke was a companion of Paul's. In Colossians 4:14, Paul called Luke "the beloved physician." In II Timothy 4:11, when Paul was in prison, Luke was the only one loyal enough to Paul to stay with him. There are sections of Acts (also written by Luke) that are "we" sections, which means the author (Luke) included himself as traveling with Paul (Acts 16:10-17; 20:5 – 21:18; 27:1 – 28:16).

Luke was a scholar. He wrote what is thought to be the best Greek in the New Testament. He investigated and researched in writing his Gospel. He was not an eyewitness, so he depended on testimony. It is thought that he had to have interviewed Mary, the mother of Jesus, to get the details in Luke 2.

CHARACTERISTICS OF LUKE

Luke presents Jesus as a true man. His favorite reference to Jesus is the "Son of Man." Jesus is portrayed as a man with compassion and feelings. The description of His birth is given the most attention in any Gospel and His ancestry goes back to Adam.

Luke is very person-oriented. Luke's Gospel contains 30 parables, stories and events not found anywhere else in the Gospels. The parables of the rich man and Lazarus (16:19-31), the persistent widow (18:1-8) and the Pharisee and the tax collector (18:9-14) are found only in Luke and each one focuses on individuals and their walk with God. Luke 15 provides the most unique material, with the parables of the lost sheep, the coin and the son. The prodigal son story lives on as one of the most poignant studies in human depravity and human forgiveness. It is also from Luke that we learn of Zacchaeus (19:1-10). The common thread in all these unique aspects of Luke is the individual story of someone seeking God and finding Him.

Luke gives us the deepest insight into Jesus' prayer life. All of the Gospels give us a glimpse into the private world of Jesus' prayer life, but none of them do it like Luke. In 3:21; 5:16; 6:12; 9:18, 28, there are insights into Jesus' relationship with His heavenly Father that are natural and instructive. The one passage that is most unique to Luke and Jesus' prayer life, however, is found in Luke 11. Here, the disciples asked Jesus to teach them to pray the way He prayed and Jesus gave us The Lord's Prayer.

I. ADVENT (1:1 – 4:13)

Luke provides the most detailed and insightful account of the birth of Jesus. There is, though, so much more here than just the birth narrative. It includes the visit by the angel, Elizabeth's pregnancy with John the Baptist, Mary's song, Zechariah's song and the participation of the shepherds. In it all, however, the grandeur of the birth is not lost (2:13, 14):

> *Suddenly a great company of the heavenly host appeared with the angel, praising God and saying, "Glory to God in the highest, and on earth peace to men on whom His favor rests."*

The early years of Jesus are uniquely covered in Luke, wherein we read about His presentation in the Temple at the age of 12 and the contribution of the unknown saints, Simeon and Anna. A summary statement of His boyhood is given in 2:52:

> *And Jesus grew in wisdom and stature, and in favor with God and men.*

Just after Jesus' baptism by John, a distinctive genealogy is given. It complements the one given by Matthew, as it gives the line of Mary, rather than Joseph, and goes all the way back to Adam, rather than Abraham. Jesus is portrayed as being born of a woman and for all mankind.

II. ACTIVITIES (4:14 – 9:50)

The early years of Jesus' ministry are filled with activities showing His authority over every realm – demons, disease, nature, tradition and sin.

These activities, though, were not meant to be done by Jesus alone. He calls disciples, then selects 12 apostles and sends them out with these instructions (9:3-5):

> *Take nothing for the journey – no staff, no bag, no bread, no money, no extra tunic. Whatever house you enter, stay there until you leave that town. If people do not welcome you, shake the dust off your feet when you leave their town, as a testimony against them.*

III. ANTAGONISM AND ADMONITIONS (9:15 – 19:27)

Antagonism (9:15; 11)

The level of opposition intensifies and Jesus is accused of being a demon: "By Beelzebub, the prince of demons, He is driving out demons." Jesus responded:

> *Any kingdom divided against itself will be ruined, and a house divided against itself will fall. If Satan is divided against himself, how can his kingdom stand? ... But if I drive out demons by the finger of God, then the kingdom of God has come to you (11:15, 17, 20).*

The antagonism only increased against Jesus. Some people openly opposed Him. Many doubted. All were amazed.

Jesus pronounces six woes on the Pharisees and the teachers of the Law, but the intensity of their opposition only increased (11:53, 54):

When Jesus left there, the Pharisees and the teachers of the law began to oppose Him fiercely and to besiege Him with questions, waiting to catch Him in something He might say.

Admonitions (12:1 – 19:27)

In the midst of all the opposition and unbelief, however, Jesus never forgot His disciples. He instructed them on a number of practical matters like prayer, faithfulness, repentance, humility, discipleship, money, forgiveness, service, thankfulness, the second coming and salvation.

The main lesson taught in this section that is unique to Luke is the cost of discipleship. In Luke 14, Jesus was as plain and blunt as he could be (25-27):

Large crowds were traveling with Jesus, and turning to them He said: "If anyone comes to me and does not hate his father and mother, his wife and children, his brothers and sisters – yes, even his own life – he cannot be my disciple. And anyone who does not carry his cross and follow me cannot be my disciple."

The self-consciousness of the disciples was central in the mind of Jesus. They must understand themselves as being committed to Him, first and foremost, with no exceptions. Close behind self-consciousness, though, was service-consciousness. Jesus wanted the disciples to know that they were to associate with "sinners." The disciples were to have the same service orientation as their Master in seeking the lost.

Luke 15 is a classic chapter that emphasizes seeking the lost. Jesus told three consecutive parables to make one point (15:7):

I tell you that in the same way there is more rejoicing in heaven over one sinner who repents than over ninety-nine righteous persons who do not need to repent.

Self-consciousness and service-consciousness then come together in the story of Zacchaeus, the tax collector (19:1-10). This man, who had thought only of himself, wanted to see Jesus more than anything. Awaiting him, however, was a new life marked by salvation and a new experience of self and service. He came to see that Jesus had come to seek and to save what was lost.

IV. AFFLICTION (19:28 – 23:56)

The last week in the life of Jesus was marked by different levels of affliction. Jesus, from the fickle crowds at His coming into Jerusalem to the ferocious Roman soldiers at the Cross, suffered grief, pain, ridicule and torture.

Everything came down to His final moments upon the Cross (23:44-46):

It was now about the sixth hour, and darkness came over the whole land until the ninth hour, for the sun stopped shining. And the curtain of the temple was torn in two. Jesus called out with a loud voice, "Father, into your hands I commit my spirit." When He had said this, He breathed His last.

V. AUTHENTICATION (24)

The account of the Resurrection in Luke corresponds with the other Gospels, but a remarkable story that Luke shares, no doubt found by his meticulous investigations, adds so much drama and depth to the reality of the risen Lord.

It happened on the road to Emmaus. Two unnamed disciples who had left Jerusalem were talking about the extraordinary events surrounding Jesus. Jesus Himself then came up and walked along with them –

unrecognized and unappreciated – for awhile. They walked and talked about the happenings and the Scriptures. The unbelievable was being discussed and the evidence was walking with the two disciples.

They spent more time together, shared a meal and then it happened. The disciples' eyes were opened and they recognized Him – and then He was gone. The impact was obvious to both of them (24:32):

Were not our hearts burning within us while He talked with us on the road and opened the Scriptures to us?

Jesus again gave the commission to the disciples (24:46, 47):

This is what is written: The Christ will suffer and rise from the dead on the third day, and repentance and forgiveness of sins will be preached in His name to all nations, beginning at Jerusalem.

Lessons From Luke

1. Jesus came as a baby who would be the Savior. The first two chapters of Luke are so clear about the nature and work of this baby born to Mary. The one born was the Savior of the world and all of heaven and earth were full of praise.

2. Jesus came to seek and save the lost. The teaching of seeking that which was lost and the practice of seeking the lost is as clear in Luke as in any of the Gospels. The finding of that which was lost again caused rejoicing in heaven.

3. Jesus sent the disciples to do the same. The rejoicing, though, was not to end with Jesus' life on earth. The disciples were called to carry on the task of seeking the lost. The work of the Savior who died and rose again was to continue. The rejoicing in heaven would continue.

NOTES

CHAPTER THIRTY-FOUR: JOHN

Assignment

READ ...

John, Chapters 1-21, or selected chapters from John (one a day for a week) as follows:

John 1   –   The Word.

John 3   –   Nicodemus.

John 4   –   The woman at the well.

John 10 –   The Good Shepherd.

John 11 –   The death of Lazarus.

John 13 –   The washing the disciples' feet.

John 15 –   The vine and the branches.

MEMORIZE ...

John 1:14: "The Word became flesh and made His dwelling among us. We have seen His glory, the glory of the one and only, who came from the Father, full of grace and truth."

and/or

John 10:14: "I am the good shepherd; I know my sheep and my sheep know me."

and/or

John 14:6: "I am the way and the truth and the life. No one comes to the Father except through me."

PRAY ...

Praising God for who Jesus really is. He is the Word; the light of the world; the bread of life; the Resurrection and the life; the good shepherd; the door; the way, the truth and the life.

Asking the Lord to teach you about being a disciple. Commit yourself to walk with the Lord like the disciples of old.

Longing to see Jesus in His fullness.

Asking the Lord what it means for you to "feed His sheep." What is it that the Lord wants you to do to strengthen the people of God?

APPLY ...

In the light of John, what do you:

> BELIEVE about God?
>
> REPENT of as sin?
>
> OBEY as a command from God?

SHARE ...

According to what you have learned from John:

- Talk within your family about all the descriptions you can think of about Jesus. There are many in the Gospel of John, but there are many more in the New Testament. See how many different names, titles and descriptions you can come up with about Jesus.

- Have a conversation with a friend about what Jesus meant when He said, "I am the way, the truth and the life." Respect what your friend says, but share with him or her about the central place Jesus plays in our getting to know God. Try to steer the conversation away from the Church, the nation, morals or such things as the sins of Christians in order to focus on Jesus in all of His glory and grace.

John:
The 'Believe' Book

THEME VERSE

*Jesus did many other miraculous signs in the presence of His disciples,
which are not recorded in this book. But these are written that you may believe that Jesus
is the Christ, the Son of God, and that by believing you may have life in His name.*
John 20:30, 31

Martin Luther has written about John: "Never in my life have I read a book written in simpler words than this, yet the words are inexpressible."

Some simple words in John:

- Truth.

- Light.

- Darkness.

- Word.

- Knowledge.

- Abide.

- Love.

- World.

- Witness.

- Judgment.

- Life.

- Believe.

Yet, these simple words describe the indescribable!

The key word in John is "believe." The word and its derivatives occur 98 times in this Gospel. John makes it clear that to believe in Jesus is to "receive" Him, while not believing is to "not receive" Him:

He came to that which was His own, but His own did not receive Him. Yet to all who received Him, to those who believed in His name, He gave the right to become children of God.
John 1:11, 12

AUTHOR

The author of the Gospel of John is not John the Baptist. It is John, the brother of James, one of the "sons of thunder," the son of Zebedee and Salome. He was one of the twelve, which makes him an eyewitness to the life of Jesus, like Matthew and unlike Mark and Luke.

John was in the inner circle of the disciples with Peter and James. He refers to himself in his Gospel as "the beloved disciple" or "the disciple whom Jesus loved" (13:23; 19:26; 20:2; 21:7, 20).

UNIQUE CHARACTERISTIC

Jesus is presented as the "Son of God" (John's favorite title for Jesus), meaning that Jesus was God the Son. Jesus was the "only begotten of the Father full of grace and truth" (1:14). The "I am ..." statements of John all point to His divinity:

- "I am the bread of life" (6:35, 48).

- "I am the light of the world" (8:12; 9:5).

- "I am the door" (10:7, 9).

- "I am the good shepherd" (10:11, 14).

- "I am the resurrection and the life" (11:25).

- "I am the way, the truth and the life" (14:6).

- "I am the true vine" (15:1, 2).

The "I am ..." statements culminate in Jesus equating Himself with the Old Testament "I AM" or Yahweh from the burning bush: "I tell you the truth, before Abraham was born, I am!" (8:58). Time and again, throughout the Gospel of John, Jesus reveals Himself to someone and that person comes to the same conclusion – Jesus is the Son of God.

I. PUBLIC MINISTRY (1 – 12)

The prologue to the Gospel of John is known as one of the most profound theological statements ever written. The Word of God spans eternity and makes it clear that Jesus was more than just a man. John 1:14: "The Word became flesh and dwelt among us." The message is that "the Word became flesh and blood and moved into the neighborhood."

The next few chapters introduce several individuals who Jesus personally and directly confronts. They are a mixture of people, which shows how Jesus came to reach all people:

- John the Baptist (1).

- Philip and Nathaniel (2).

- Nicodemus (3).

- The Samaritan woman at the well (4).

John records seven miracles that uniquely portray Jesus as Divine. Some of them were told by the other gospels, some of them are unique to John and some of them are accompanied with "I am ..." teachings by Jesus:

- Transforming water to wine (2:1-11); unique to John.

- The healing of the nobleman's son (4:46-54); unique to John.

- The healing of the paralytic (5:1-18); unique to John.

- The feeding of the multitude (6:1-13); in all the other Gospels, but in John it is accompanied by "I am ..." teachings by Jesus.

- The walking on water (6:16-21); also recorded in Matthew and Mark.

- Restoring sight to man born blind (9:1-7); unique to John and accompanied by "I am ..." teachings by Jesus.

- The raising of Lazarus from the dead (11:1-44); unique to John and accompanied by "I am ..." teaching by Jesus.

II. PRIVATE MINISTRY (13 – 17)

This section is a very unique and special part of the Gospel of John. Look at it in a "Red Letter" edition of the Bible and the text is almost entirely in red, meaning that they are words Jesus personally spoke to the disciples in the Upper Room. This section sometimes is called the "Upper Room Discourse."

In this section, Jesus is alone with His disciples on the night before He is crucified. The Lord is focused on the disciples in order to comfort and teach them. In these, His last words to the twelve, Jesus tells them about many things:

- Servanthood (13:1-17).

- The betrayer (13:18-32).

- Loving one another (13:33-38).

- Comfort (14:1-4).

- The relationship with the Father (14:5-14).

- Prayer (14:13, 14).

- Obedience (14:15-31).

- Abiding in the vine (15:1-17).

- The opposition of the world (15:18 – 16:4).

- The Holy Spirit (16:5-16).

- Joy (16:17-33).

All of this is followed in chapter 17 with a prayer by Jesus. This is the true "Lord's prayer" because it is His unique prayer for the disciples (17:1-26).

III. PASSION MINISTRY (18 – 21)

The passion (sufferings) of the Lord is especially poignant in John, mainly because he was the lone disciple who was there. The account of Mary, the mother of Jesus, being taken care of by Jesus from the Cross is one that John never would forget (19:25-27):

Near the cross of Jesus stood His mother, His mother's sister, Mary the wife of Clopas, and Mary of Magdala. When Jesus saw His mother there, and the disciple whom He loved standing nearby, He said to His mother, 'Dear woman, here is your son,' and to the disciple, "Here is your mother." From that time on, this disciple took her into his home.

There are some Resurrection appearances unique in John. One was when Jesus appeared to Thomas, who had sworn:

Unless I see the nail marks in His hands and put my finger where the nails were, and put my hand into His side, I will not believe it (20:25).

The Lord graciously appeared and directly spoke to Thomas (20:27, 28):

"Put your finger here; see my hands. Reach out your hand and put it into my side. Stop doubting and believe." Thomas said to Him, "My Lord and my God!"

Another Resurrection appearance described in John was to Peter. Peter had returned to his fishing and Jesus came to him. The Lord called Peter a second time to discipleship with a miracle, a meal and with a simple message: "Feed my sheep."

Lessons From John

1. Jesus is God.

2. The "I am …" statements in John make this point better than any other part of the New Testament.

3. Our basic response to Jesus is to believe.

4. John was written so that we might believe.

5. Jesus is primarily concerned with our growth as disciples.

6. John was not meant to be the only "beloved disciple."

NOTES

CHAPTER THIRTY-FIVE: ACTS

Assignment

READ ...

Acts, Chapters 1-28, or selected chapters from Acts (one a day for a week) as follows:

    Acts 1 – The Ascension.

    Acts 2 – Pentecost.

    Acts 4 – A look at the Early Church.

    Acts 6 – The start of deacons.

    Acts 9 – Saul's conversion.

    Acts 10 – Peter's vision.

    Acts 18 – Paul in Corinth.

MEMORIZE ...

Acts 1:8: "But you will receive power when the Holy Spirit comes on you; and you will be my witnesses in Jerusalem, and in all Judea and Samaria, and to the ends of the earth."

and/or

Acts 2:38, 39: "Peter replied, 'Repent and be baptized, every one of you, in the name of Jesus Christ for the forgiveness of your sins. And you will receive the gift of the Holy Spirit. The promise is for you and your children and for all who are far off – for all whom the Lord our God will call.'"

and/or

Acts 16:30, 31: "'Sirs, what must I do to be saved?' They replied, 'Believe in the Lord Jesus, and you will be saved – you and your household.'"

PRAY ...

Asking the Holy Spirit to fill you and make you a bold witness for Jesus Christ toward those near you, as well as opening up ways to bear witness far beyond you.

For the Church, that it might be like the Church in Acts to which the Lord daily added those who were being saved.

That the Lord would send out of your congregation missionaries and ministers to serve Him anywhere in the world.

For the missionaries who are supported by local congregations, asking the Lord's blessing on them.

APPLY ...

In the light of Acts, what do you:

> BELIEVE about God?
>
> REPENT of as sin?
>
> OBEY as a command from God?

SHARE ...

According to what you have learned from Acts:

- Have a conversation with a friend who is a Christian about what you read in Acts. What are some things you see in Acts that you also see in the Church and what are some things you see in Acts that you do not see in the Church? Encourage one another in this conversation.

- Have a conversation with a friend who is not a Christian. Share with him or her what you learned about the Church in Acts and how the Church today not always is what it should be. Be humble in admitting to your unchurched friend the inadequacies of the Church. See how he or she responds, and go with the conversation in whatever direction it takes you.

Acts:
The Spreading Flame

INTRODUCTION

F.F. Bruce, an excellent Church historian and Biblical scholar, has written a book on Early Church history titled *The Spreading Flame*. There could not be a better description of the story of Acts. The flame symbolizes the Holy Spirit, outpouring and active in Acts, what was happening to the Early Church in Acts – spreading from Jerusalem to the outermost parts of the earth.

THEME VERSE

But you will receive power when the Holy Spirit comes on you; and you will be my witnesses in Jerusalem, and in all Judea and Samaria, and to the ends of the earth.
Acts 1:8

These are the very last words of Jesus Christ upon earth. They provide the primary themes of Acts:

- The Holy Spirit.

- Witnessing.

They also provide the outline of Acts:

- Jerusalem (1 – 7).

- Judea and Samaria (8 – 12).

- The outermost parts of the world (12 – 28).

AUTHOR

Luke, the physician, wrote the Gospel of Luke and Acts. Acts was produced as an accompanying story to the Gospel. Initially, the two books were in one volume, but in the second century they were separated into two books.

Luke was an eyewitness to much of the occurrences in Acts. The "we sections" of Acts show the author participating in the action when he used the first person plural pronoun in several places when he was traveling with Paul.

Luke was an exact historian. He gives more than 80 geographical references, records more than 100 different people by name, and is precise in giving exact titles and locations.

A prominent feature of Acts is the amount of space devoted to sermons and speeches – 24 of them in 28 chapters. This is a presentation of primary sources unparalleled in the New Testament.

UNIQUE CHARACTERISTIC

Acts is a book of transitions:

- The presence of Jesus to the presence of the Holy Spirit.

- The Gospels to the Epistles.

- Judaism to Christianity.

- The twelve apostles to a growing Church.

- Jerusalem to the world.

- Peter to Paul as leaders of the Church.

There is dramatic and definite movement and growth of the Church all the way through Acts. Nothing could stop it. Through all that was occurring – the sin of Ananias and Sapphira; the divisions between Hebrew and Hellenistic Jews; disagreements among the apostles; persecution by the Jews; and controversy over how the Gentiles could become Christians – the Church, filled with the Holy Spirit, continued to grow. Acts is testimony to the truth of what Jesus said:

I will build my church, and the gates of Hell will not overcome it.

I. IN JERUSALEM (1 – 7) (TWO YEARS)

The first chapter of Acts gives the account of the Ascension. The Ascension is more of a foundational doctrine than usually is realized. It is reaffirmed in the Apostles' Creed:

… He ascended into heaven and sitteth on the right of the Father. …

One aspect of its truth is that Jesus had to leave earth for the Church to enter into its next stage, but the fullest understanding of the Ascension sees Jesus being exalted and ascending to the place where He now reigns as Lord and King.

Chapter 1 ends with the election of Matthias, the replacement for Judas.

Acts 2 might be one of the most significant chapters in the entire New Testament. It gives us Pentecost (an annual feast – the Feast of Weeks) celebrated by the Jews seven weeks after Passover. At this feast, the Holy Spirit is poured out upon the Church. The disciples are enabled to preach the wonders of God in other languages and everyone was amazed to hear the wonders of God in their own language. Peter stands up, preaches and explains what is happening as the fulfillment of the prophecy from Joel 2 and he proclaims the Resurrection of Jesus. The people ask what they must do, and Peter instructs them to "repent and believe."

The ministries of Peter and John are highlighted in chapters 3 and 4. There is healing, preaching, teaching, testifying before the Sandedrin (the Jewish leadership council) and suffering for the sake of the Gospel.

We can have an idealistic view of the Early Church in Acts, but chapters 5-7 show the Church filled with problems – the sin of members, persecution from outsiders, complaints within the Church and martyrdom.

The sin was the sin of Ananias and Sapphira (5:1-11) who, in keeping back part of what they had promised to the Lord, dropped down dead. Listen to the impact of this "discipline" (5:11): "Great fear seized the whole church and all who heard about these events."

The ministry of the apostles grew with signs and wonders, but persecution was not far behind. The response of the apostles to this persecution was remarkable (5:41):

The apostles left the Sanhedrin, rejoicing because they had been counted worthy of suffering disgrace for the name.

A practical problem arose in the distribution of food to the needy, so the office of deacon came into existence and the Church kept growing (6:7):

So the word of God spread. The number of disciples in Jerusalem increased rapidly, and a large number of priests became obedient to the faith.

The martyrdom of Stephen occurred, and chapter 7 provides the remarkable speech of Stephen before his death. As he was being stoned to death, Luke 8:1 reveals: "And Saul was there, giving approval to his death." This is the Saul who will appear a little later in Acts as the Apostle Paul.

II. IN JUDEA AND SAMARIA (8 – 12) (12 YEARS)

In chapter 8, the persecution continues, but it is more intense than the others, and the Church became scattered. It had to leave Jerusalem. In other words, it was persecution that led to the next expansion of the Church into Judea and Samaria. God will use anything to grow His Church.

Philip, another deacon like Stephen, becomes an evangelist and is instrumental in taking the Gospel north of Jerusalem into Samaria and south of Jerusalem into Gaza.

Chapter 9 then introduces the man who will be one of the most influential men in the Early Church for the rest of the New Testament – Paul. Here in chapter 9, though, he still is Saul persecuting the Church. He was dramatically converted on the road to Damascus, a testimony he gives several times in the rest of Acts. He then begins to preach but, understandably, the Church and the apostles had a hard time believing it was true. Chuck Swindoll comments, "This is like Madeline Murray O'Hare being in charge of the Presidential Prayer Breakfast or John McEnroe leading a seminar on keeping your cool under stress." Barnabas, though, takes Saul under his wing and encourages him.

From the end of chapter 9 to the middle of chapter 11, the scene changes back to Peter. Peter undergoes a "second conversion," this one being converted to mission. Peter was called to the house of a Gentile, Cornelius. Peter had to receive a vision from the Lord to teach him that what the Lord declares to be clean is clean. Peter goes to visit Cornelius and preaches – and a "second Pentecost" occurred (10:44):

While Peter was still speaking these words, the Holy Spirit came on all who heard the message. The circumcised believers who had come with Peter were astonished that the gift of the Holy Spirit had been poured out even on the Gentiles.

God was growing His Church.

The Church in Antioch is described in the latter part of chapter 11. It was obvious that God was doing a new thing and the Church in Antioch was evidence of it. It was a very diverse Church and it was alive in the Lord. Barnabas was sent to investigate the Church and found it to be true to the faith. Barnabas gets Saul to come and help at the Church in Antioch, and it was in Antioch that the disciples first were called Christians.

Chapter 12 is Peter's swan song in Acts. He miraculously is released from prison and the believers were in awe of what God had done.

III. TO THE OUTERMOST PARTS OF THE WORLD (13 – 28) (15 YEARS)

Paul's first missionary journey (13:1 – 15:35) started in Antioch when Barnabas and Saul were set apart for the work of taking the Gospel to other places. Notice that Barnabas is listed first, when Saul was Saul, but when Paul is used as his name, the order changes to Paul and Barnabas. The cities this missionary team went to are given in rapid-fire succession – Cyprus, Pisidian Antioch, Iconium, Lystra, Derbe and then to Jerusalem.

In chapter 15, the Council at Jerusalem confronts the controversial issue of taking the Gospel to the Gentiles. We cannot underestimate how radical this was for these Jewish Christians to know that God was spreading this Gospel among the Gentiles. The end result of the council was the development of some regulations to follow, but it generally was acknowledged that the Gentiles were turning to God in Jesus Christ.

Paul's second missionary journey (15:36 – 18:22) starts with a sharp disagreement between Paul and Barnabas over John Mark. After this, Paul and Silas traveled together and Barnabas took John Mark. Paul and Silas revisited the Church in Antioch from his first journey and added Philippi, Thessalonica, Berea, Athens and Corinth.

Paul's third missionary journey (18:23 – 21:26) also has Paul revisiting churches to strengthen them. In Corinth, Paul was joined in the missionary endeavor by a couple, Priscilla and Aquila, and a man named Apollos. Paul then goes to Ephesus and, from there into Macedonia and Greece. He then turns around to go back to Ephesus, ending up in Jerusalem.

In Jerusalem, Paul is arrested (21:27-36) and accused of bringing Gentiles into the Temple. Paul testifies to the crowd and the Sanhedrin. There is a plot to kill him, so he was transferred to Caesarea.

Paul undergoes a series of trials (24 – 26) in Caesarea before several officials: first, Felix, the governor of Caesarea; then Festus, where he appeals to Caesar as a privilege of a Roman citizen; and then before King Agrippa. In every opportunity, Paul gave his testimony of how God had changed his life and that Jesus Christ had risen from the dead. Agrippa found no fault in him and was of a mind to let him go, but since Paul had appealed to Caesar, he was sent on to Rome.

Paul's trip to Rome (27, 28) is filled with high adventure on the seas. Acts ends with Paul in Rome, seen as the outermost part of the world at that time. There then is an abrupt end to Acts.

Lessons From Acts

1. The Holy Spirit is the one who acts. The work of the Holy Spirit is the major emphasis in the Book of Acts as He "comes upon," is "poured out," "baptizes" and "fills" believers. In each case, when the Holy Spirit acts, people are saved, the Church grows and the Church goes to the ends of the earth.

2. Believers are the ones who act. The Holy Spirit was to come upon the believers and they were to be witnesses. Peter, James, Stephen, Philip and Paul are major characters who do extraordinary deeds of ministry and sacrifice as they go forth in the power of the Holy Spirit.

NOTES

CHAPTER THIRTY-SIX: ROMANS

Assignment

READ ...

Romans, Chapters 1-16, or selected chapters from Romans (one a day for a week) as follows:

Romans 1   –   The need for the Gospel.

Romans 3   –   We all are sinners.

Romans 5   –   Justification by faith.

Romans 7   –   Our struggle with sin.

Romans 8   –   Our life in the Spirit.

Romans 12   –   Our life as living sacrifices.

Romans 13   –   Submission to authorities.

MEMORIZE ...

Romans 3:23: "For all have sinned and fall short of the glory of God."

and/or

Romans 5:8: "But God demonstrates His own love for us in this: While we were still sinners, Christ died for us."

and/or

Romans 6:23: "For the wages of sin is death, but the gift of God is eternal life in Christ Jesus our Lord."

and/or

Romans 8:28: "And we know that in all things God works for the good of those who love Him, who have been called according to His purpose."

PRAY ...

Agreeing with the truth that you are a sinner who falls short of the glory of God.

Trusting once again in what Christ has done for you and you receive by faith. Knowing that you are justified before God by faith in Christ.

Asking the Lord to give you the eyes to see Him in all the events in your life, even in those that hurt and don't make any sense.

Submitting to the sovereignty of God and presenting yourself as a living sacrifice to Him.

APPLY ...

In the light of Romans, what do you:

>   BELIEVE about God?

>   REPENT of as sin?

>   OBEY as a command from God?

SHARE ...

According to what you have learned from Romans:

- Talk with your family about the essentials of the Gospel found in Romans: that we all are sinners (3); that we are saved by faith (5); that we still struggle with sin (7); that we are secure in the faith (8); and that we are to live for God (12). Make sure that the basics of the faith are understood by your family in order to face whatever might come your way.

- Share the "Roman Road" with someone who is not a Christian. The Roman Road is:

>   Romans 3:23   –   All have sinned;

>   Romans 5:8   –   While we were sinners, Christ died for us;

>   Romans 6:23   –   The gift of God is eternal life in Christ Jesus;

>   Romans 10:13 –   Call on the name of the Lord and you will be saved.

Romans:
Theology That Is Alive

INTRODUCTION

The Epistle to the Romans has been a landmark book in the history of the Church. Martin Luther was confronted with the reformational truth of justification by faith from Romans. John Wesley had his heart "strangely warmed" after hearing a message from Romans. Karl Barth confronted the European liberalism of his day primarily by his exposition of Romans.

These things happened because Romans presents a theology that is alive. No dead legalism here. No evil antinomianism here. No empty Gospel here.

The heart and soul of Romans is salvation by grace through faith in Christ that results in changed lives. This epistle teaches how the Christian is to live now and forever.

THEME VERSE

I am not ashamed of the gospel, because it is the power of God for the salvation of everyone
who believes: first for the Jew, then for the Gentile. For in the gospel a righteousness
from God is revealed, a righteousness that is by faith from first to last,
just as it is written: "The righteous will live by faith."
Romans 1:16, 17

AUTHOR

The Apostle Paul's story is given in Acts. Paul emerged as the Early Church's missionary to the Gentiles and his call took him to the outermost part of the earth, which, for the Palestinian Jew, was Rome. The Book of Acts ends with Paul's arrival in Rome.

Romans is the first of 13 epistles written by Paul. From what we know, he wrote Romans in A.D. 57 at the end of his third missionary journey in Corinth. What is unique about Romans is that Paul wrote it before he visited Rome. In his other epistles, he wrote after visiting, indeed after starting, the Church he addressed. The Church in Rome was not planted by Paul, but Paul had heard about it and knew many in it. "Paul, a servant of Christ Jesus, called to be an apostle and set apart for the gospel of God. ..." (1:1)

This was the pattern of first-century letter writing – the first words of the letter (epistle) identify the author. This is different than the contemporary practice of signing at the end of the letter. Paul calls himself a servant (a bond servant) in regard to Jesus, an apostle in regard to the Church and set apart for the Gospel.

What is interesting is that Paul did not pen the original letter himself. He had a secretary, an amanuensis (16:22):

I, Tertius, who wrote down this letter greet you in the Lord.

Paul's pattern in epistle writing was to be very personal and pastoral. Romans has some of this in it, but primarily it is theological and formal. It is more like a treatise or tract than a personal letter.

I. WHY WE NEED RIGHTEOUSNESS – SIN (1:1 – 3:20)

After all of the opening formalities, Paul states his desire to come to the Church in Rome so that he could minister to them and they could minister to him. He commends them for their faith, which was well-known throughout the "whole world."

Paul then plunges into the meat of his message. He gives the verses (1:16, 17) that we have identified as our theme verses for Romans:

I am not ashamed of the gospel, because it is the power of God for the salvation of everyone who believes: first for the Jew, then for the Gentile. For in the gospel a righteousness from God is revealed, a righteousness that is by faith from first to last, just as it is written: "The righteous will live by faith."

These verses give three of the most central concepts of Romans – salvation, faith and righteousness. In Romans 1:18, Paul also gives one of the most fearsome statements in the whole New Testament:

The wrath of God is being revealed from heaven against all the godlessness and wickedness of men who suppressed the truth by their wickedness. ...

Paul, in regard to the universal theological principle of God's wrath against all sin, launches into his teaching like an Old Testament prophet:

- All Gentiles are sinners (1:18-32). The knowledge of God is generally known through nature, which leaves all Gentiles without excuse for their behavior.

- All Jews are sinners (2:2 – 3:8). Here, he hits closer to home. The Jew is without any excuse either, and especially so because Jews have the very Law of God given to them.

- The Divine verdict, therefore, is on everyone (3:9-20). He quotes from four Old Testament passages (Psalm 5:9; Psalm 10:7; Isaiah 59:7, 8; and Psalm 36:1) that back up his charge that "there is no one righteous, not even one."

III. HOW WE GET RIGHTEOUSNESS – FAITH (3:21 – 5:21)

After building his argument about the pervasive nature of sin in all people and the total futility of anyone making themselves righteous, Paul, in Romans 3:21, 22 presents the heart of the matter: How one can get righteous?

But now a righteousness from God, apart from law, has been made known. ... This righteousness from God comes through faith in Jesus Christ to all who believe.

That is as simple as it gets. If there are none who are righteous, not one, then righteousness cannot come from man. There must be a "righteousness from God" if there is any hope. That righteousness only comes "through faith in Jesus Christ to all who believe."

Paul isn't satisfied with a simple statement. He is, remember, presenting a case, an argument, a theology. So, he spends the next two chapters elaborating about this righteousness, which is received in what is called justification. Justification is an important word in Romans and in our faith, but we don't often use it. Justification is an act of God's grace whereby He treats us as if we had never sinned. It is a law court term for declaring a guilty person innocent. That only can happen if he or she is "justified," when something is done outside of the person.

Paul makes three crucial points about justification:

- Justification is by grace (3:21-24). This means that the source of justification is from God, and it is undeserved. "We are freely justified by His grace."

- Justification is by blood (3:25, 26). This means that a sacrifice had to be made in our place. This sacrifice was the death of Jesus Christ. "God presented Christ as a sacrifice of atonement, through faith in His blood."

- Justification is by faith (3:27-31). This justification must be received, and the only way to receive it was by faith. "For we maintain that a man is justified by faith apart from observing the law."

In chapter 4, Paul goes on to illustrate this justification by faith with the life and example of Abraham. Abraham, even though he lived before Christ, was made righteous by faith, just like everyone after Christ. The faith principle was as true in the Old Testament as it was in the New Testament.

This justification restores the relationship between God and man, and a new day dawns in one's relationship with God.

> *Therefore, [a very important word in Romans] since we have been justified through faith,*
> *we have peace with God through our Lord Jesus Christ, through whom we have gained access*
> *by faith into this grace in which we now stand. And we rejoice in the hope of the glory of God.*
> *(5:1, 2)*

Paul then presents the principle of headship to make it clear about the work of Christ as being for everyone. He speaks of the disobedient first Adam, through whom all sinned, and that Christ was the obedient second Adam. It is through Him and only Him that all can be saved.

III. WHAT WE GET WITH RIGHTEOUSNESS – SANCTIFICATION AND GLORIFICATION (6:6 – 8:39)

The panorama of the practical life of the believer is covered in chapters 6-8, from beginning with belief, to struggling with sin, to growing by the Spirit, to being in glory forever.

Chapter 6 presents the radical change that takes place in the life of the believer. Those who have been baptized have died to sin and are alive in Christ. All this takes place because of union with Christ.

Shall we sin so that grace may abound? By no means (6:15).

Absolutely not. No. The calling now is to be slaves to righteousness.

For the wages of sin is death, but the gift of God is eternal life in Christ Jesus our Lord (6:23).

Chapter 7 is honest and frank regarding the present struggle with sin that believers have. Paul described it this way: "I do what I don't want to do and don't do what I want to do." Paul admits that even as a believer is dead to sin, he or she still is struggling.

Chapter 8, though, emphasizes that a believer in this struggle is not without God. His Holy Spirit has been given to all believers so that He might live in them and through them (8:16):

The Spirit Himself testifies with our spirit that we are God's children.

Paul ends chapter 8 with some of the greatest affirmations of the faith:

- All things work together for good.

- Those God foreknew, he also predestined.

- If God is for us, who can be against us?

- We are more than conquerers in Christ Jesus.

- Nothing can separate us from the love of God in Christ Jesus our Lord.

IV. WHY WE STRUGGLE WITH RIGHTEOUSNESS – SOVEREIGNTY OF GOD AND RESPONSIBILITY OF MAN (9 – 11)

The next three chapters struggle with one of the most puzzling tensions in the believer's life: the working together of the sovereignty of God and the responsibility of man. Chapter 9 maintains that God is sovereign, chapter 10 affirms that man is responsible and chapter 11 admits that the whole thing is baffling. It only leads to an awe of, and praise to, God. Some of the strongest language in all of Scripture upholding the sovereign election of God is given in chapter 9.

> *"Jacob I loved, but Esau I hated." What then shall we say? Is God unjust? Not at all! For He*
> *says to Moses, "I will have mercy on whom I have mercy, and I will have compassion on whom*
> *I have compassion."*
> *Romans 9:13-15*

> *Does not the potter have the right to make out of the same lump of clay some pottery for noble*
> *purposes and some for common use?*
> *Romans 9:21*

In chapter 10, salvation and how we are to respond is made very clear: "If you confess with your mouth, 'Jesus is Lord,' and believe in your heart that God raised Him from the dead, you will be saved" (9) and "Whoever calls on the name of the Lord will be saved" (13).

As Paul runs through his mind the mysteries of God's sovereignty and the marvel of the simplicity of the Gospel, he cannot help but think of the future of his own people, Israel. In the early part of chapter 11, you can feel his heart as he, the apostle to the Gentiles, still has a burden for Israel. The Gentiles have been ingrafted into the people of God, but what will happen to Israel?

> *I do not want you to be ignorant of this mystery, brothers, so that you may not be conceited.*
> *Israel has experienced a hardening in part until the full number of the Gentiles has come in.*
> *And so all Israel will be saved.*
> *Romans 11:25, 26*

Paul then ends chapter 11 with one of the most glorious doxologies in the whole of Scripture.

It almost feels like the end of Romans, and it could have been, but on the basis of all the truth about righteousness, Paul then moves on to the practical outworking of being right with God.

V. HOW WE LIVE OUT RIGHTEOUSNESS – PRACTICE (12 – 16)

In a pattern Paul has shown in several of his epistles, he moves from belief to behavior, from theology to practice, from what is to be believed to what is to be done.

Chapter 12 gives the encouragement to make a basic commitment based on all that God has done in mercy:

> *Therefore, I urge you, brothers, in view of God's mercy, to offer your bodies as living sacrifices,*
> *holy and pleasing to God – this is your spiritual act of worship.*
> *Romans 12:1*

He calls for the use of gifts in ministry and the demonstration of love in the fellowship.

Chapter 13 tackles what must have been a very burning issue for the Christians in Rome: How does one live in a state that is persecuting them? It must have been almost a slap in the face to read Paul's words:

Everyone must submit himself to the governing authorities, for there is no authority except that which God has established (13:1).

He goes on to again apply the call of love in living with one another and in the culture. No matter what might be going on around us, the calling is the same – love one another, repent of sin, be like Jesus Christ.

Chapters 14, 15 present Paul's understanding of Christian liberty in dealing with matters that not always are black and white. He recognizes that there are weak Christians and strong Christians, and everything must be done by faith and with the desire to help one another.

Let us therefore make every effort to do what leads to peace and to mutual edification. Do not destroy the work of God for the sake of food. All food is clean, but it is wrong for a man to eat anything that causes someone else to stumble.
Romans 12:19, 20

At the end of chapter 15 and in all of chapter 16, Paul gets personal. He expresses his desire to come to Rome and gives a personal greeting to a long list (the longest list in all his letters) of people to greet. Even though Paul had never been to Rome, he knew a lot of people there from his earlier travels and by contact with others.

Lessons From Romans

1. Our justification is by grace through faith. Getting right with God is the most crucial issue in anyone's life. Romans is clear that we get right with God – not on our own, but by the grace of God in Jesus Christ, whom we receive by faith. It is not by works or the Law, but it is by trusting in what God has already done in His Son.

2. Our sanctification is by grace through faith. Staying right with God is the next most crucial issue in one's life. We are to live like those who are right with God. We are dead to sin and alive to God in Christ Jesus. This living for God is not a matter of effort and discipline alone. God's grace again is absolutely necessary in the presence and power of the Holy Spirit, and we are to trust Him as He leads, gifts and fills us.

NOTES

CHAPTER THIRTY-SEVEN: I CORINTHIANS

Assignment

READ ...

I Corinthians, Chapters 1-16, or selected chapters from I Corinthians (one a day for a week) as follows:

    I Corinthians 1   –   Divisions in the Church.

    I Corinthians 7   –   On marriage.

    I Corinthians 11 –   Worship and the Lord's Supper.

    I Corinthians 12 –   Spiritual gifts.

    I Corinthians 13 –   A chapter on love.

    I Corinthians 14 –   Speaking in tongues and prophecy.

    I Corinthians 15 –   The Resurrection.

MEMORIZE ...

I Corinthians 12:12: "The body is a unit, though it is made up of many parts; and though all its parts are many, they form one body. So it is with Christ."

and/or

I Corinthians 13:13: "And now these three remain: faith, hope and love. But the greatest of these is love."

and/or

I Corinthians 15:58: "Therefore, my dear brothers, stand firm. Let nothing move you. Always give yourselves fully to the work of the Lord, because you know that your labor in the Lord is not in vain."

PRAY ...

Asking for the wisdom of God to handle the problems in your own life, as well as grace for the Church to handle its problems.

That the Body of Christ, with its many members, will know its gifts and that the whole Church will be edified.

That love will be known and shown in every part of your life and the lives of others in the Church.

That the truth of the Resurrection of Jesus Christ might add life to your Christian walk and witness.

APPLY ...

In the light of I Corinthians, what do you:

> BELIEVE about God?
>
> REPENT of as sin?
>
> OBEY as a command from God?

SHARE ...

According to what you have learned from I Corinthians:

- Read I Corinthians 13 with your family. Get everyone to reflect on how love is important to them and how they understand they are doing when it comes to loving others in the way they should. Pray with one another so that love would be more real in your lives.

- Do you really want a lively conversation with someone in or out of the Church? Then ask them about speaking in tongues. Don't look for a fight, but read I Corinthians 12-14 and simply share what you read.

I Corinthians:
Conflicts in the Church

INTRODUCTION

Here is a true and false test:

- First-century churches were free of conflict, quarrels and cliques.

- No church founded by Paul ever struggled with man worship, immorality or marital problems.

- Sound Biblical teaching and the exercise of spiritual gifts are sufficient to keep a church free from being worldly.

- Affluence guarantees generosity. A wealthy church is always a giving church.

All four propositions are false and the proof is the Church in Corinth. All of these topics are covered in I Corinthians. Churches, even early churches, had conflicts, immorality, divisions, spiritual extremes, worldliness and false teaching in them.

BACKGROUND

The background for I Corinthians is Paul's second missionary journey, which is covered in Acts 15:39 – 18:22. God led Paul into Macedonia (Europe) and a whole new world was opened up for the Gospel.

Paul ministered in Macedonia (in places like Philippi, Thessalonica and Berea), then he traveled alone to Athens (Acts 17) and confronted the philosophical preoccupation of that city, where he was somewhat discouraged. He then left Athens and went to Corinth. Even though Athens and Corinth were 50 miles apart, they were as different as two cities could be. They were two totally different cultures:

- Athens was like a university community, where intellectual and philosophical pursuits were primary.

- Corinth was a commerce center that was a place of materialism, debauchery and idolatry.

In Corinth, Paul met Aquila and Priscilla (Acts 18:1ff), who were fellow tentmakers, and they become a missionary team. Later on, they are joined by Apollos.

Corinth was a commerce center because of its location on an isthmus between the Aegean Sea and the Adriatic Sea. Crossing the isthmus saved a dangerous 200-mile trip around the southern horn of Greece. Corinth became a place of luxury visited by people from all of the civilized world. It was the New York City or the Los Angeles of that time. If you could name it, you could get it in Corinth.

Corinth was also a religious center. The city was filled with shrines and temples, but the most prominent was the temple of Aphrodite. The religion of the people was connected with sexual immorality.

Corinth became so notorious for its immorality that the term "Corinthian" became a synonym for debauchery and prostitution.

Paul's going into Corinth with the Gospel pitted him head-to-head against the greatest materialism and immorality in the ancient world. Paul found out that even as a Church could go into a culture, that culture could begin to go into the Church. It is not surprising, therefore, that the Church in Corinth struggled.

I. REBUKES OF SINFUL BEHAVIOR (1 – 6)

Rebuke for Divisions (1 – 4)

Divisions in the Church

First of all, Paul gave a rebuke for divisions in the Church in Corinth. In verse 1:13, he confronted the fact of the divisions that were connected with some personality cults in the Church: "One of you says, 'I follow Paul;' another, 'I follow Apollos;' another, 'I follow Cephas;' still another, 'I follow Christ.'" Then he confronts them with the absurdity of these cliques: "Is Christ divided?"

People are important in the Church in their varied and gifted functions. Paul recognizes this in I Corinthians 3:6: "I (Paul) planted the seed, Apollos watered it, but God made it grow." People, however, can become divisive if they form groups, cliques or factions in the Church. There must be a balance of good, gifted leadership and a dependence on God so that He is the only one who gets the glory.

Causes of the Divisions

Paul looked at these divisions a little closer and saw that there were some causes for them that were a little deeper than personalities. Some were caused by human wisdom vs. God's wisdom. In 1:26, 27, Paul wrote:

> *Brothers, think of what you were when you were called. Not many of you were wise by human standards; not many were influential; not many were of noble birth. But God chose the foolish things of the world to shame the wise; God chose the weak things of the world to shame the strong.*

Paul also saw a cause of division in the different understandings of things. Are they understood worldly or spiritually?

> *We have not received the spirit of the world but the Spirit who is from God, that we may understand what God has freely given us (2:12).*

Finally, Paul saw a cause of their divisions as being the level of their spiritual maturity. The Church in Corinth was not very mature in the faith. Verses 3:1, 2 read:

> *Brothers, I could not address you as spiritual but as worldly – mere infants in Christ. I gave you milk, not solid food, for you were not yet ready for it. Indeed, you are still not ready.*

Godly Leadership

Paul then calls the Church in Corinth to submit to godly leadership – in particular the apostles, who are servants of Christ and have been entrusted with the secret things of God (4:1). Paul encourages the Church to imitate him in his life and teachings, while also promising to send Timothy to them in the future to provide more godly leadership.

Paul also promises to some day personally return to them, and he makes an interesting comment that sounds like a combined threat and encouragement:

> *What do you prefer? Shall I come to you with a whip, or in love and with a gentle spirit? (4:21).*

Rebukes for Immorality (5 – 6)

A specific instance of sexual immorality is confronted in the first verse of chapter 5:

It is actually reported that there is sexual immorality among you, and of a kind that does not occur even among pagans: A man has his father's wife.

This is an instance of a member of the Church having sex with his stepmother, a situation that is common knowledge and regarding which the Church has not done anything. Paul calls for the man to be put out of the Church, with the hope that he will be restored. Paul confronts the Church with the pride and apathy it had in confronting this issue.

In chapter 6, Paul exhorts the Corinthian Christians not to take one another to court. He said it was a poor testimony if believers could not handle their own problems in a Christian manner and, instead, go before non-Christian judges.

In 6:9-20, Paul then generally exhorts them about sexual immorality, specifically in verses 18-20:

Flee from sexual immorality. All other sins a man commits are outside his body, but he who sins sexually sins against this own body. Do you not know that your body is a temple of the Holy Spirit, who is in you, whom you have received from God? You are not your own; you were bought at a price. Therefore honor God with your body.

II. REPLIES TO SPECIFIC QUESTIONS (7 – 16)

Paul then deals with the thorny questions sent to him by the Corinthians. Each answer begins with, "Now, concerning. …"

Marriage (7)

I Corinthians 7 is one of the major passages in the Bible concerning marriage. In it, Paul touches on celibacy, marriage, sex, divorce and remarriage. He speaks to different situations in which people find themselves – single, widowed, divorced, a believer, a non-believer, virgins, a slave, an uncircumcised Gentile, a circumcised Jew, an unmarried man and a married man. Paul's primary pastoral advice is included in verse 17:

Nevertheless, each one should retain the place in life that the Lord assigned to him and to which God has called him. This is the rule I lay down in all the churches.

What he means here is that in whatever marital status you find yourself, start right there and be faithful to God.

Meat Sacrificed to Idols (8 – 10)

Paul also confronted a moral dilemma for Christians living in that pagan society. Should a Christian eat meat that had been sacrificed to idols? Paul goes back and forth in his argument: Those idols are not real gods, so the meat sacrificed to them is no affront to the living God but, then again, there were some Christians who used to worship those idols and for them it was a matter of conscience not to eat it. Paul's final advice is clear:

Be careful, however, that the exercise of our freedom does not become a stumbling block to the weak (8:9).

In chapter 9, Paul continues to talk about freedom, but it was the freedom and the rights of an apostle. He speaks of how he sees his apostleship as freedom, but he is willing to be a slave to anyone in order to win them to the Gospel, as he says in 9:19:

Though I am free and belong to no man, I make myself a slave to everyone, to win as many as possible.

Chapter 10 shows the history of Israel, which should serve as models and examples for us to follow. As Christians, we are free and our freedom only should strengthen our impact on others:

Nobody should seek his own good, but the good of others (Romans 10:24).

Public Worship (11 – 14)

Paul then turns to matters of importance and controversy regarding worship in the Church in Corinth – women in worship, improper behavior at the Lord's Table and controversy over spiritual gifts.

Chapters 12-14 are as comprehensive regarding spiritual gifts as any part of the New Testament. Chapter 12 positively presents spiritual gifts as an expression of many members with different gifts, but in one body. Chapter 13 upholds the supremacy of love over all the gifts. Chapter 14 does a comparison with the gifts of prophecy and tongues and provides guidelines on how worship is to be edifying for all, meaningful even for the unbeliever, and orderly.

The Resurrection (15)

The Corinthians had a problem with the Resurrection because the idea of a resurrected body was disdainful to Greek thought. The Greeks thought the body was evil, so Paul had to do some theological instruction with them in order to affirm the reality of Jesus' bodily resurrection and the prospect of our bodily resurrection in the future.

Conclusion (16)

Paul ends this first epistle to the Corinthians with an exhortation about offerings, personal requests and greetings.

Lessons From I Corinthians

1   The Church is always in danger of divisions. Paul confronts the fellowship in Corinth as being drawn in different directions by personalities and persuasions. Even in the light of divisive talk and commitments, the nature of the Church as the Body of Christ with many members must be recognized and honored. The Church is made up of many distinctive parts, but it must never lead to division.

2.   The Church is always in danger of sexual immorality. Sexual sin was in the Church in Corinth. Paul called for discipline. Paul called for discipleship. The seriousness of sexual immorality and its impact on marriage is uppermost but, supremely, sexual sin is a sin against one's own body. As Christians, our bodies do not belong to us. We have been bought with a price, and we are not our own. We are to honor God with our bodies.

3.   The Church is always in danger of immaturity. Paul knew that at the heart of many of the struggles in the Corinthian Church (spiritual gifts, immorality, false teaching, etc.), there was an immaturity like that of little children. The Church needed to grow more in the faith and stand on pure doctrine, right behavior and loving commitment.

NOTES

CHAPTER THIRTY-EIGHT: II CORINTHIANS

Assignment

READ ...

II Corinthians, Chapters 1-13, or selected chapters from II Corinthians (one a day for a week) as follows:

    II Corinthians 1 – The God of all comfort.

    II Corinthians 4 – Treasures in jars of clay.

    II Corinthians 5 – The ministry of reconciliation.

    II Corinthians 8 – Christian generosity.

    II Corinthians 9 – Christian generosity again.

    II Corinthians 11 – Paul's hardships.

    II Corinthians 12 – Paul's thorn in the flesh.

MEMORIZE ...

II Corinthians 5:17: "Therefore, if anyone is in Christ, He is a new creation; the old has gone, but the new has come!"

and/or

II Corinthians 5:21: "God made Him who had no sin to be sin for us, so that in Him we might become the righteousness of God."

and/or

II Corinthians 12:9: "My grace is sufficient for you, for my power is made perfect in weakness."

PRAY ...

Asking for the wisdom to see ourselves as having a "building from God, an eternal house in heaven, not built by human hands" (5:1). Thank God for your heavenly home.

That the Lord might make you generous, even as He has been generous to you.

Committing yourself to the ministry of reconciliation in your life and in your circles. Go in the name of Jesus.

That even if your "thorn in the side" is not removed, you will find strength from the Lord in the time of your weakness.

Apply ...

In the light of II Corinthians, what do you:

> BELIEVE about God?
>
> REPENT of as sin?
>
> OBEY as a command from God?

Share ...

According to what you have learned from II Corinthians:

- Have a conversation with your family about the giving habits of the family. Reflect on the teaching in II Corinthians 8-9 and get the family to share how you might become a family known for its generosity. Let the children know how you give and what the blessings of giving are.

- Share with an unchurched friend about the struggles of being a Christian. Paul was honest and open in II Corinthians about all the pains and problems he had because he was a Christian. Let your friend know that in being a Christian, there are struggles, but the grace of God is always sufficient (12:9).

II Corinthians:
An Apostle Gets Personal

THEME VERSE

For we do not preach ourselves, but Jesus Christ as Lord,
and ourselves as your servants for Jesus' sake.
II Corinthians 4:5

The Apostle Paul gives more of his personal history in II Corinthians that in any other of his epistles. He reveals some details of his life not found anywhere else:

- His escape from Damascus in a basket (11:32, 33).

- His experience of being caught up into the third heaven (12:1-4).

- His thorn in the flesh (12:7).

- His unusual suffering (11:23-27).

Paul, though, reveals all this personal history in the context of defending his apostleship.

BACKGROUND

After Paul in I Corinthians confronted the Church in Corinth with some of their sins, and answered many of their questions, how did they respond? Paul heard that some people had received his letter in the proper spirit, but there were others who doubted Paul's motive and questioned his apostleship.

Judaizers were false teachers in the Early Church who had Jewish backgrounds, yet sought to shape the Christian Church into a Jewish sect. They would often come to a church and raise doubts about some of the basic teachings – primarily the teaching that in order to be a Christian you only had to believe in Jesus and be baptized. Judaizers taught that you needed to become Jewish before you could become a Christian, so they emphasized circumcision, following the Mosaic Law and observing the Jewish feasts.

Well, the Judaizers attacked Paul. They had infiltrated the Corinthian Church and raised doubts about him. They claimed Paul was fickle (1:17, 18, 23); proud and boastful (3:1; 5:12); fleshly (10:2); unimpressive in appearance (10:10); unimpressive in speech (11:6); unstable in thought (5:13; 11:16-19); not qualified to be an apostle (11:5; 12:11, 12); and dishonest (12:16-19). Paul wrote II Corinthians to defend himself. What is interesting is that it is the most disjointed and rambling letter that Paul wrote.

I. Paul's Conduct and Character (1 – 7)

The opening section of this epistle focuses on the theme of comfort. The word "comfort" occurs nine times! Paul was hurting and needing comfort, but he also wanted to share comfort with those in the Church who might be hurting like he was:

> *Praise be to the God and Father of our Lord Jesus Christ, the Father of compassion and the*
> *God of all comfort, who comforts us in all our troubles, so that we can comfort those in any*
> *trouble with the comfort we ourselves have received from God.*
> *II Corinthians 1:3, 4*

Toward the end of chapter 1, Paul begins to explain himself. He encourages forgiveness for the one whom he urged to be disciplined in I Corinthians (2:5-11). The man apparently repented, and Paul rejoiced in the goal of discipline in the Church – which is ultimate restoration, not simply punishment.

In 2:12 – 6:10, Paul speaks of his ministry, giving several different explanations:

- He calls himself the aroma of Christ (2:15, 16).

- He says he is a minister of a new covenant (3:6).

- He preaches Jesus Christ (4:5).

- He has an eternal home (5:1).

- He has had hardships (6:3-10).

After Paul describes his ministry in many distinctive ways, he gives the admonition to the Church in Corinth that they are to separate themselves from the wickedness of the world around them:

> *Come out and be ye separate, says the Lord. Touch no unclean thing … (6:17).*

In chapter 7, Paul – in very personal words – expresses his joy and blessing in being associated in ministry with the Church in Corinth. He obviously is pleased with the vast majority of the members of the Church and their faithfulness, and he encourages them to remain faithful.

II. Paul's Collection (8 – 9)

This is the longest passage of Scripture on giving. Paul is not addressing the regular offerings for the Church, but a special offering for famine relief in Jerusalem. He uses the example of the poorer churches in Macedonia that had already given generously – and even sacrificially – to this cause.

Paul is very practical about how to give:

- Give out of what you have, even if it is poverty (8:2).

- Give generously (8:3).

- Give yourself first to the Lord (8:5).

- Give proportionately (8:12-14).

- Give willingly (9:7).

- Give cheerfully (9:7).

- Give bountifully (9:6).

- Give because you have received (9:14, 15).

All of this encouragement to give was based on the principle of blessing those who were generous in their giving:

Remember this: Whoever sows sparingly will also reap sparingly, and whoever sows generously will also reap generously. Each man should give what he has decided in his heart to give, not reluctantly or under compulsion, for God loves a cheerful giver. (9:6, 7)

III. PAUL'S CREDENTIALS (10 – 13)

Paul presents a defense of his apostleship by presenting his credentials. He struggles between boasting and meekness as he seeks to be blunt and true about the call of God on his life. His bottom line is found in verse 10:18: "For it is not the one who commends himself who is approved, but the one whom the Lord commends." The call of God was upon his life.

Chapters 11-12 are unique as Paul "boasts" of what is true in his life that points to the call of God: his knowledge (11:6); integrity (11:9); his blood line (11:22); his sufferings (11:23-28); his weakness (11:30); his visions (12:1-4); and miracles (12:12). He gives the account of the "thorn in his side" (12:7-10) that was a great lesson in humility and God's sufficiency. He learned from the Lord (12:9):

My grace is sufficient for you, for my power is made perfect in weakness.

Paul went on to very personally apply this to his own life (12:10):

For when I am weak, then I am strong.

Paul comes to the end of II Corinthians by making known his plans to visit Corinth, exhorting the people to repent of their sins and continually examine themselves. The last section of the letter is Paul's final greetings and a powerful benediction:

May the grace of the Lord Jesus Christ, and the love of God, and the fellowship of the Holy Spirit be with you all.

Lessons From II Corinthians

1. The Christian life is a life of reconciliation. Paul knew first-hand what it was like to be God's enemy and someone else's enemy. Therefore, reconciliation was important to him. Because we have been reconciled to God, we are to be reconciled to one another.

2. The Christian life is a life of giving. Paul could not get over the generosity of the poor Macedonian churches. Sacrificial giving was demonstrated there and Paul called for the Christians in Corinth to have the same generosity. God loves a cheerful giver.

3. The Christian life is a life of hardship. Paul knew hardship. His call to apostleship had a unique hardness to it, but Paul also knew that there was something in the nature of life itself that called for times of trouble and pain. In the midst of that hardship, Paul learned one of the most valuable lessons of the Christian life – God grace's was sufficient.

NOTES

Chapter Thirty-Nine: Galatians

Assignment

READ ...

Galatians, Chapters 1-6, or one chapter a day from Galatians for a week.

MEMORIZE ...

Galatians 2:20: "I have been crucified with Christ and I no longer live, but Christ lives in me. The life I live in the body, I live by faith in the Son of God, who loved me and gave Himself for me."

and/or

Galatians 4:4: "But when the time had fully come, God sent His Son, born of a woman, born under law, to redeem those under law, that we might receive the full rights of sons."

and/or

Galatians 6:2: "Carry each other's burdens, and in this way you will fulfill the law of Christ."

and/or

Galatians 5:22, 23: "But the fruit of the Spirit is love, joy, peace, patience, kindness, goodness, faithfulness, gentleness and self-control. Against such things there is no law."

PRAY ...

Examining your life to see if you believe in a distortion of the Gospel or not. Believing the Gospel is as basic a belief as we have.

For any you know of who might be in the Church, but not faithful to the Gospel. This can be those in the Church who do not uphold the Gospel or those who are hypocritical in their faith.

Thanking the Lord that He has done all that is necessary for you to become a child of God.

That the fruit of the Spirit would be evident in your life.

APPLY ...

In the light of Galatians, what do you:

> BELIEVE about God?
>
> REPENT of as sin?
>
> OBEY as a command from God?

SHARE ...

According to what you have learned from Galatians:

- Read Galatians 5:16-26 with your family. Have a discussion about the works of the flesh and the fruit of the Spirit. Focus on the fruit of the Spirit and talk about each of the fruits, about what they are and how they are evident in your lives and the lives of others.

- Talk to someone who is not a member of your congregation about hypocrites in the Church. You may want to mention this to someone who does not go to Church. You will probably find that one of the objections someone not in the Church might have is the number of hypocrites in the Church. Tell them the story of Galatians 2:11-21, about how Paul confronted Peter with his hypocrisy. Admit that there are hypocrites in the Church, but recognize that this is not the ideal.

Galatians:
The Christian's
Declaration of Independence

THEME VERSE

It was for freedom that Christ set us free; therefore keep
standing firm and do not be subject again to a yoke of slavery.
Galatians 5:1

CHRISTIAN FREEDOM

Christian freedom is a topic that Paul often wrote about. Many times it is thought that freedom is an American concept backed up by documents like "The Declaration of Independence." It is shallow and wrong, however, to think that freedom is an American invention.

Clarity about freedom is needed. When Paul wrote, he was not writing about democracy. In other words, he was not writing about politics and government – he was writing about the Christian life.

When he applies "freedom" to the Christian life, he talks about it in two ways:

- Freedom in being a Christian. He refers to this freedom in I Corinthians 8:9: "Be careful, however, that the exercise of your freedom does not become a stumbling block to the weak." Here, freedom is discussed in dealing with the issue of eating meat sacrificed to idols. Some Christians who had come out of worshipping those idols just could not eat it. It made them feel guilty. Other Christians, though, felt free to eat it, since it was just meat, and those idols were not gods. Paul's advice was that they were free to eat the meat, except when it was a stumbling block to another Christian. In other words, a Christian limited his own freedom for the sake of someone else. Passages that refer to this freedom in being a Christian are in Romans 14, I Corinthians 8 and I Corinthians 10:23-33.

- Freedom in becoming a Christian. This freedom is the freedom Paul refers to in Galatians. It is the freedom from bondage to sin through faith in Jesus Christ and to a new life. It is the freedom Jesus referred to when He said, "I tell you the truth, everyone who sins is a slave to sin. Now a slave has no permanent place in the family, but a son belongs to it forever. So if the Son set you free, you will be free indeed" (John 8:34-36). Paul put it this way:

But thanks be to God that, though you used to be slaves to sin, you wholeheartedly obeyed the
form of teaching to which you were entrusted. You have been set free from sin and have become
slaves to righteousness.
Romans 6:17, 18

It is this "freedom in becoming a Christian" that Paul defends in Galatians – and I do mean defends. In Galatians, you will hear an angry apostle. He is upset with the Galatians because they were listening to another "gospel" that went against the freedom in being a Christian that they had heard from Paul. This epistle to the Galatians is the only one in which Paul does not express thankfulness or ask for their prayers. He is upset with them and disappointed in them.

BACKGROUND

Galatia is a region, rather than a city. Most of the letters of Paul were written to churches in cities (Rome, Ephesus, Philippi, Thessalonica, Corinth), but Galatia was a region where Paul had established many churches on his first missionary journey, such as in:

- Derbe.

- Iconium.

- Lystra.

- Antioch of Pisidia.

What was going on in these churches was the infiltration of a new teaching. This new teaching was by a group called Judaizers. Judaizers were a sect of Jewish Christians who taught that you had to become a Jew before you could become a Christian. They taught that in order for a Gentile to become a Christian, he must be circumcised, obey the Mosaic Law and observe the Jewish feasts. They said that one was saved – not by faith in Christ alone – but by obeying the Law and faith in Christ.

LAW AND GRACE

Galatians has been a central book in a longstanding debate within the Church – the debate about Law and grace. It is so easy to get out of balance within this tension. Two extremes to avoid are:

- Legalism: This is a dominance of the Law, where grace is belittled and not needed.

- Antinomianism: This is a dominance of grace, where the Law is belittled and not needed.

This is the debate in Galatians, and it is very crucial in determining how one is saved and how one is to live.

I. BIOGRAPHICAL ARGUMENT (1 – 2)

Paul was as personally invested and agitated in the Epistle to the Galatians as he was in any of his epistles. He considered the stakes high and the danger intense. He was not so much defending himself in this epistle, as he did in II Corinthians, as he is defending the Gospel. What was at risk in the churches of Galatia was the good news of Jesus Christ. This called for Paul's personal, passionate, pastoral and persuasive involvement.

He began the letter affirming his apostleship and the Gospel's power to rescue, then he attacked:

I am astonished that you are so quickly deserting the one who called you by the grace of Christ
and are turning to a different gospel (1:6).

Paul was incredulous. He couldn't believe they were deserting the Gospel. He couldn't believe how quickly they were doing it. He couldn't believe that they were turning to another gospel, even though he had made it clear that there was no other Gospel. Paul pronounced the most intense judgment he could on those who preached "another gospel" by saying "let him be 'eternally condemned'" (New International Version), "accursed" (King James Version), "anathema" (Greek).

Paul proceeded to uphold his call to preach the Gospel, saying that this Gospel was not from him, but from God: "I did not receive it from any man, nor was I taught it; rather, I received it by revelation from Jesus Christ" (1:12). Then, in verses 2:13-24, he gave a personal testimony of what God had done in his life.

In chapter 2:11ff, there is a striking passage. Paul relates an episode in which he confronted Peter with his hypocrisy. Think of it! Paul confronting Peter. What Paul opposed to Peter's face was his inconsistent behavior. He would associate with his Jewish friends and then with Gentile brothers in the faith, but when Jewish friends came around, Peter separated himself from the Gentiles because he was afraid. Peter was hypocritical and Paul confronted him.

Paul then gave the most powerful personal statement of faith in the whole New Testament (2:20):

I have been crucified with Christ and I no longer live, but Christ lives in me. The life I live in the body, I live by faith in the Son of God, who loved me and gave Himself for me.

Paul used the first person singular pronoun seven times to nail down the truth that this Gospel of Jesus Christ was something he knew was true, and he was not about to see such good news distorted.

II. THEOLOGICAL ARGUMENT (3 – 4)

Paul then launched into a theological argument in which he used eight lines of reasoning to defend justification by faith alone as the heart of the Gospel:

- You begin by faith and you continue by faith (3:1-5).

- Abraham was justified by faith (3:6-9).

- The law cannot justify you. It only curses you (3:10-14).

- The promise of God still stands (3:15-18).

- The Law is to lead to faith (3:19-22).

- Believers are adopted into the family of God (3:23 – 4:7).

- You, Galatians, are to go back to the original freedom of faith (4:8-20).

- Abraham's two wives (Hagar and Sarah) represent two distinctive ways in which God has worked and only one produced the true son of promise – Isaac (4:21-31).

III. MORAL ARGUMENT (5 – 6)

Paul then moved to an argument that was direct, practical and moral:

It is for freedom that Christ has set you free. Stand firm, then, and do not let yourselves be burdened again by a yoke of slavery (5:1).

Paul understood this issue to be one of life and death or, put another way, a matter of freedom and slavery.

Paul complimented the Galatians on how they had been doing – "you were running a good race" (5:7) – but, in their legalistic leanings, they were beginning to turn on one another (5:14, 15):

Love your neighbor as yourself. If you keep on biting and devouring each other, watch out or you will be destroyed by each other.

Paul then gave one of the most referred to and inspirational passages in all of his letters. It was his teaching on life by the Spirit and his list of the fruit of the Spirit. He wanted to make it clear that they either will live by the flesh, which he said the Galatians were doing in the Law, or they will live by the Spirit, where there is freedom and fruitfulness.

Paul drew as clear a distinction between the Christian living in the flesh and the Christian living by the Spirit as there is in the whole of the New Testament. The list of the "works of the flesh" is chilling:

- Sexual immorality.

- Impurity.

- Debauchery.

- Idolatry.

- Witchcraft.

- Hatred.

- Discord.

- Jealousy.

- Fits of rage.

- Selfish ambition.

- Dissension.

- Factions.

- Envy.

- Drunkenness.

- Orgies.

- And the like.

It is the "fruit of the Spirit," however, that is revolutionary. Notice the singular "fruit." It was not the "fruits" of the Spirit, meaning that one could pick and choose which ones they wanted. No, there is a unity about them, since they come from one Spirit.

The "fruit of the Spirit" can be categorized in three units for the nine graces:

- Fruit toward God – love, joy, peace.

- Fruit toward others – patience, gentleness, goodness.

- Fruit toward yourself – faith, meekness, self-control.

Lessons From Galatians

1. The Christian is called to a life of freedom. Bondage is the order of the day for those without Jesus Christ. The bondage is to self and sin and is unbreakable by human efforts and religious practices. The freedom that comes in following Jesus Christ is the freedom to be all that God wants us to be.

2. The Christian is called to a life of fruit-bearing. The Holy Spirit is at work in every Christian, bringing forth the fruit of holiness and righteousness. Christian character is being freed by Christ and brought to fruition by the Spirit. The works of the flesh will lead to unrighteousness and wickedness. The Spirit at work in the believer will bear fruit.

NOTES

CHAPTER FORTY: EPHESIANS

Assignment

READ ...

Ephesians, Chapters 1-6, or one chapter a day from Ephesians for a week.

MEMORIZE ...

Ephesians 2:8-10: "For it is by grace you have been saved, through faith – and this not from yourselves, it is the gift of God – not by works, so that no one can boast. For we are God's workmanship, created in Christ Jesus to do good works, which God prepared in advance for us to do."

and/or

Ephesians 4:3: "Make every effort to keep the unity of the Spirit through the bond of peace."

and/or

Ephesians 5:18: "Do not get drunk on wine, which leads to debauchery. Instead, be filled with the Spirit."

and/or

Ephesians 6:10, 11: "Finally, be strong in the Lord and in His mighty power. Put on the full armor of God so that you can take your stand against the devil's schemes."

PRAY ...

Thanking the Lord because He is sovereign in all things. He is in control of whatever comes to pass.

For the unity of the Church, so that our oneness in Christ can be obvious to all. Make every effort to love and forgive one another.

For every member of your family, thanking God for them and asking His blessings on them.

That the full armor of God might be yours, so that you stand against evil and temptation.

APPLY ...

In the light of Ephesians, what do you:

   BELIEVE about God?

   REPENT of as sin?

   OBEY as a command from God?

SHARE ...

According to what you have learned from Ephesians:

- Read Ephesians 5:22 – 6:4. Have a discussion about the commands with the different members of your family. Struggle with the nature of the commands and help other members of the family see the importance of obeying the Lord in the different roles within the family.

- Have a conversation with someone who is not in a congregation about what they think of the Church. Ask them if they think the Church is united or divided. Be ready to answer a common perception that the Church always is divided. Reflect on the unity of the Church in Ephesians 4 and how the unity of the Church is affirmed because of a oneness with Christ.

Ephesians:
Walk the Talk

INTRODUCTION

Paul wrote Ephesians while in prison. In Acts 28:30ff, there is a description of Paul in prison in Rome. A prison in Rome at that time was not like a barred jail or a dingy dungeon. It was house arrest, with the prisoner being chained to a Roman guard who was in charge of making sure there was no escape. While a Roman prisoner, the prisoner could receive visitors and send letters to the outside.

While in prison, Paul wrote several epistles:

- Ephesians.

- Philippians.

- Colossians.

- Philemon.

Ephesus was a commercial and religious center. It was the main market city of Asia Minor and, being an official Roman town, was able to do business with other cities in the empire. Ephesus was also a very religious city, with its magnificent temple of Diana (the Roman name) or Artemis (the Greek name). This temple of Diana was one of the seven wonders of the ancient world. Religion and the economy were associated with the temple.

The Ephesian Church had a special privilege: It was started by Aquila and Priscilla (Acts 18:18-21) and was pastored by Paul, Timothy and John. It might have been one of the strongest churches of that day. We know, however, that it did not stay that way, since its second generation was not as faithful. Addressed in Revelation 3 as one of the seven churches receiving letters, the Church of Ephesus was said to have "lost its first love."

THEME VERSE

I, therefore, the prisoner of the Lord, entreat you to walk
in a manner worthy of the calling with which you have been called.
Ephesians 4:1

I. THE BELIEVERS' HEAVENLY POSSESSIONS (1 – 3)

The prologue to this epistle identifies Paul as the author and the "saints" of Ephesus as the recipients. "Saints" is another word for Christian. We usually think of "saint" as a special holy person, but in the New Testament it is one of the common names for the believer. We are holy in Christ Jesus.

Then, in verses 3-14, there is one of the most powerful sentences in the whole of the New Testament – yes, one sentence. It is not that way in the English translations, but it is one sentence in the Greek. When Paul wrote it, he could not find a place to put a period, as his heart overflowed with praise for the God who redeems us. This sentence upholds the sovereignty of our God in our redemption. He is the One who chose us and predestined us. He is the One who has adopted and forgiven us. He is the One who is in control of all things in working out our salvation. We are to never think that we are so great or wise or praiseworthy because we became a Christian. It is all of God. He is the one to be praised for all eternity for our salvation. The sentence is: "In Him (Christ) we were also chosen, having been predestined according to the plan of Him who works out everything in conformity with the purpose of His will."

- The Father chose us (3-6).

- The Son redeems us (7-12).

- The Spirit seals us (13, 14).

- All is to the "praise of His glory" (6, 12-14).

Paul's Prayers

Paul often gives us a glimpse into his prayer life in his epistles. Verses 1:15-23 is one of the most perceptive passages that shows the depth of Paul's prayers for the Church. His prayer for the Ephesians is one of thanksgiving, for the Spirit to work in them so that they may be enlightened to know their hope and power in Jesus Christ. He gives another prayer in 3:14-21 that is absolutely remarkable. Read it. If you ever wonder about how to pray for the Church, here it is.

Alive in Christ

Chapter 2:1-10 gives an overview of what our redemption, our salvation, really is. We were dead in sin with no hope left to ourselves, but (4) "because of His great love for us, God, who is rich in mercy, made us alive with Christ. …" What might be the clearest statement of salvation is given in 2:8-10:

For it is by grace you have been saved, through faith – and this not from yourselves, it is the gift of God – not by works, so that no one can boast. For we are God's workmanship, created in Christ Jesus to do good works, which God prepared in advance for us to do.

One truth is crystal clear: "It is by grace you have been saved."

One in Christ

Paul makes it clear that salvation in Christ is not an individual or personal matter. It has a corporate dimension:

Consequently, you are no longer foreigners and aliens, but fellow citizens with God's people and members of God's household, built on the foundation of the apostles and prophets, with Christ Jesus Himself as the chief cornerstone.
2:19, 20

This corporate dimension was important for the Gentiles, who believed that they were just as much a part of the Body of Christ as the Jews. It is Christ who is their peace, and He has broken down the wall that separated the two. Paul wanted them to know that they were just as much a part of the people of God as anyone (2:22). "And in Christ you too are being built together to become a dwelling in which God lives by His Spirit."

The Mystery

Paul speaks of a "mystery" that he now proclaims. The word "mystery" is not used by Paul in the same way that it is used today. Today, a "mystery" is a riddle where the answer is not known or it is a "whodunnit" murder story where the murderer is not known until the last page or last scene.

"Mystery" for Paul, though, was what had not been known before, but now was known. The "mystery" was the Gospel of Jesus Christ. It was not clearly known in the Old Testament, but now it was clearly known in the death and resurrection of Jesus Christ. Paul put it this way (3:8, 9):

Although I am less than the least of all God's people, this grace was given me to preach to the Gentiles the unsearchable riches of Christ, and to make plain to everyone the administration of this mystery. ...

II. BELIEVERS' EARTHLY PRACTICE (4 – 6)

Ephesians 4:1 is a pivotal verse in Ephesians:

As a prisoner for the Lord, then, I urge you to live a life ("walk" in the King James Version) worthy of the calling you have received.

Paul wanted the Ephesians' position in Christ to become their life practice. The work of God was to become the walk of the Christian. The doctrine became the duty. The riches lead to responsibility.

Walk in Unity (4:2-16)

Our unity is to be expressed in how we live with one another in the fellowship. Such things as gentleness, humility, patience and love are to be lived out in the Church. Unity takes effort to maintain, and it is necessary because of the oneness we have in the faith – the seven-fold unity:

- One Body.

- One Spirit.

- One hope.

- One Lord.

- One faith.

- One baptism.

- One God and Father of all.

This unity is to be maintained through the diversity of the gifts of the members. One body, many members. Ephesians 4:12-14 presented the standard for ministry:

- God gives gifts to pastors and teachers.

- To prepare God's people.

- To do the works of ministry.

- So that the body can be built up.

The end result was that the Church matured (4:16):

From Christ the whole body, joined and held together by every supporting ligament, grows and builds itself up in love, as each part does its work.

Walk in Integrity (4:17-32)

The Christian was to be distinctive. He was not to be like he used to be. The old way of thinking and living was to be gone in one's new life in Christ. A constant struggle is to go on turning from our old self and seek the new creation of God within us.

Paul presented a series of commands that all touch on communication. This walk of integrity that we are to have was to affect everything that was spoken (4:25-32):

- Put off falsehood.

- Speak truthfully.

- Be angry, but do not sin.

- No unwholesome talk out of your mouth.

- Only say that which builds up.

- Get rid of bitterness.

- Be kind and compassionate to one another.

- Forgiving one another.

Walk in Holiness (5:1-21)

Paul exhorted the Christians in Ephesus to be imitators of God in their lives. The word for "imitator" is the Greek word that is transliterated "mimic." So, Paul confronted the sins of sexual immorality, impurity and greed. God's people are to be holy.

He then gave the way this life was to be lived (5:18): "Do not get drunk on wine, which leads to debauchery, instead, be filled with the Spirit." To be filled with the Spirit was a command that was continual. The filling of the Spirit was to be obvious in praise, in thanksgiving and in submission to one another.

Walk in Relationships (5:22 – 6:9)

Paul then got practical regarding the marriage, family and work relationships in the lives of Christians. There are instructions for wives, husbands, children, fathers, slaves (employees) and masters (employers).

For wives and husbands: "Wives, submit to your husbands as to the Lord. Husbands, love your wives as Christ loved the church."

The first thing that must be seen is how the husband-and-wife relationship is parallel to Christ and His church relationship. God has chosen marriage to be the earthly relationship to illustrate His relationship with His people. This makes the command to wives and husbands complementary, meaning that they are best understood and most beneficial when held together. In other words, the ideal is for a wife to submit to a loving husband, and a husband to love a submitting wife.

The command to the wives sounds old-fashioned to many ears today. It actually can be misused by some husbands to justify the abuse of their wives. A way to understand "submit," however, is to substitute the word "honor." To submit to someone is to honor them, respect them and value them. This is what a wife is to show to the husband – honor, respect and value.

The command to the husband sounds so elementary that it almost doesn't need to be said – of course he is to love his wife. The husband is to love the wife like Christ loved the Church and gave Himself up for her. Jesus died on the Cross for the Church. The husband is to have the same selfless and sacrificial love for his wife.

Walk in the Spirit (6:10-20)

Finally, be strong in the Lord and in His mighty power. Put on the full armor of God so that you can take your stand against the devil's schemes. (6:10)

The "full armor of God" was described here as the way that the Christian life was to be lived in the face of an enemy – the devil. The main command in the face of the enemy is to "stand." Paul says four times that we are to "stand" up against the attacks of the enemy using truth, righteousness, the Gospel, faith and salvation. The sword of the Spirit – the Word of God – is the only offensive weapon we have to advance the battle.

This walk in the Spirit was marked by prayer and the praying of all kinds of prayers. Paul requested that the Ephesian Church pray for him.

Lessons From Ephesians

1. God chose us in Christ before creation. The sovereign grace of God is held as high in Ephesians as in any book of the Bible. Before we even knew we had a choice, God exercised His gracious choice toward us. This means that our salvation is not based on anything we do, but only in His sovereign love.

2. Christ redeemed us by His blood. Even though we were dead in sin, we were made alive in Jesus Christ by His death and Resurrection. What we could not do for ourselves, Christ did for us. This means that our salvation is based on the price paid by Christ on our behalf.

3. The Holy Spirit fills us with His power. After the sovereign grace of God and the sacrificial love of Christ, the sanctifying power of the Holy Spirit comes to and abides with the believer. This means that, in our Christian lives, we are not left alone, but made victorious in the battle against the enemy.

NOTES

CHAPTER FORTY-ONE: PHILIPPIANS

Assignment

READ ...

Philippians, Chapters 1-4, or one chapter a day from Philippians during the week.

MEMORIZE ...

Philippians 1:21: "For to me, to live is Christ and to die is gain."

and/or

Philippians 3:13b, 14: "But one thing I do: Forgetting what is behind and straining toward what is ahead, I press on toward the goal to win the prize for which God has called me heavenward in Christ Jesus."

and/or

Philippians 4:6, 7: "Do not be anxious about anything, but in everything, by prayer and petition, with thanksgiving, present your requests to God. And the peace of God, which transcends all understanding, will guard your hearts and your minds in Christ Jesus."

PRAY ...

Thanking the Lord for your fellow church members. Ask that the love of God would grow in all of us.

Praising God for whom Jesus Christ is and why He came. Ask that the humility of Christ would be obvious in all our lives.

Thanking God for every circumstance you find yourself in now, whether it feels good or not. Be content in the Lord.

Using Philippians 4:6-7 to confront whatever is causing you to worry and be anxious.

APPLY ...

In the light of Philippians, what do you:

> BELIEVE about God?
>
> REPENT of as sin?
>
> OBEY as a command from God?

SHARE ...

According to what you have learned from Philippians:

- The Epistle to the Philippians is full of joy and rejoicing. Have a conversation with your family and talk about the times in which you have had the most fun and joy as a family. Never forget those good times. Then make some new plans for times in which the family will make new memories of having fun together.

- Share with a friend, whether in another congregation or not in any Church, about one truth from Philippians that meant a lot to you. Just share. Don't discuss. Don't try to impress. Please don't argue. Just share; then let it go. Pray for the person you share with and leave it to God.

Philippians:
A Letter About Joy

INTRODUCTION

The word "joy" in various forms occurs 16 times in Paul's Epistle to the Philippians. Paul was in prison, in trying circumstances, close to death. Paul, though, knew that his life in Christ was demonstrated the most when he rejoiced and had joy in the midst of terrible times.

Paul was a prisoner in Rome chained to a Roman guard when he wrote Philippians. He described himself as "being in chains," yet he could write of joy because:

• He was content in whatever circumstances he was in (4:11).

• He believed that to live is Christ and to die was gain (1:21).

• He could do all things through Christ who strengthened him (4:13).

THEME VERSE

Rejoice in the Lord always. I will say it again: Rejoice!
Philippians 4:4

Philippi was a military city, not a commercial center. It was named after King Philip, the father of Alexander the Great. The Romans captured it in 168 B.C. and it later became a Roman military outpost. There was no synagogue for the Jews in Philippi as in most other towns, so it makes sense that there are no Old Testament quotations in Philippians, which was rare for Paul. Paul knew the Philippian Church did not have a Jewish influence.

Acts 16:11ff tells the story of Paul's second missionary journey to Philippi where a lady by the name of Lydia was converted and then her whole household believed and all were baptized. Paul and Silas were in jail in Philippi, and after an earthquake, the Philippian jailer asked what he must do to be saved. Paul told him, "Believe on the Lord Jesus Christ and you will be saved. You and your whole household." Then another household baptism occurred.

The Philippian Church gave great support to Paul. They were sensitive to his financial needs (II Corinthians 8:11; Philippians 4:15-18). They sent a special messenger to Paul, Epaphroditus (2:25-30). Paul wrote this epistle, not because of any major crisis, but because he wanted to show his affection for the people of the Philippian Church. This possibly was his favorite Church. It reads almost like a missionary "thank you" letter.

I. SALUTATION (1:1, 2)

Paul began his letter to the Philippian Church in a way in which he didn't in any other epistle: He singles out the "elders and deacons." This was the only place in Paul's writings where the local officers are so addressed. All of the "saints" in the Philippian Church are mentioned, but the recognition of the officers demonstrated an intimate knowledge that Paul had of the Church.

II. REJOICING IN PRAYER (1:3-11)

Paul demonstrated his joy in prayer. He was thankful to God for the Philippians and he expressed his affection for them (1:7): "It is right for me to feel this way about all of you, since I have you in my heart."
He then prayed for their maturing in faith (1:9-11):

And this is my prayer: that your love may abound more and more in knowledge and depth of insight, so that you may be able to discern what is best and may be pure and blameless until the day of Christ, filled with the fruit of righteousness that comes through Jesus Christ – to the glory and praise of God.

III. REJOICING IN PROBLEMS (1:12-26)

Paul was in chains, but he could rejoice because it served to advance the Gospel. Paul had the opportunity to witness to the Roman guards, which encouraged other Christians to be bold.

Paul at the time was in a controversy with some other preachers who were preaching out of wrong motives, but Paul still could rejoice in them because Christ was being preached (1:18):

The important thing is that in every way, whether from false motives or true, Christ is preached. And because of this I rejoice.

Paul was confident about where he was in his relationship with God. He knew that death was as close as the nearest Roman soldier, but he also knew he still had a life to live for the Kingdom of God. He could rejoice in the nearness of death and in the opportunities that might be ahead. This confidence came from knowing that Christ would be exalted in his condition, whether by his life or by death (1:21):

For to me, to live is Christ and to die is gain.

IV. REJOICING IN HUMILITY (1:27 – 2:30)

Paul called for Christians to have humility. He exhorted them to worthy conduct and humility (2:3, 4):

Do nothing out of selfish ambition or vain conceit, but in humility consider others better than yourselves. Each of you should look not only to your own interests, but also to the interests of others.

He gave the best description of Christ's humility that was to become our own. This passage is one of the most profound Christological passages in the New Testament. Let the words sink in (2:6-11):

Who, being in very nature God, did not consider equality with God something to be grasped, but made Himself nothing, taking the very nature of a servant, being made in human likeness. And being found in appearance as a man, He humbled himself and became obedient to death – even death on a cross! Therefore God exalted Him to the highest place and gave Him the name that is above every name, that at the name of Jesus every knee should bow, in heaven and on earth and under the earth, and every tongue confess that Jesus Christ is Lord, to the glory of God the Father.

Paul then gave examples of humility in 2:12-30, when he talked about how Christians were to live, and the examples of Timothy (2:19-24) and Epaphroditus (2:25-30).

V. REJOICING IN RIGHTEOUSNESS (3:1 – 4:1)

Paul gave a warning about the Judaizers, the same false teaching that had bewitched the Galatian churches. Paul described them as "mutilators of the flesh," making reference to their demand that men had to be circumcised in order to become a Christian.

Paul's personal testimony in 3:4-14 described:

- His background ("circumcised on the eighth day of the people of Israel, of the tribe of Benjamin, a Hebrew of Hebrews; in regard to the law, a Pharisee").

- His outlook ("But whatever was to my profit I now consider loss for the sake of Christ. What is more, I consider everything a loss compared to the surpassing greatness of knowing Christ Jesus my Lord, for whose sake I have lost all things").

- His future ("Not that I have already obtained all this, or have already been made perfect, but I press on to take hold of that for which Christ Jesus took hold of me. … But one thing I do: Forgetting what is behind and straining toward what is ahead, I press on toward the goal to win the prize for which God has called me heavenward in Christ Jesus").

Paul exhorted the Philippians to follow the way of righteousness:

"Join with others in following my example, brothers, and take note of those who live according to the pattern we gave you … our citizenship is in heaven."

"Therefore, my brothers, you whom I love and long for, my joy and crown, that is how you should stand firm in the Lord, dear friends!" (4:1).

VI. REJOICING IN ATTITUDES (4:2-23)

Paul addressed a particular situation in the Philippian Church, exhorting two women to get along: "I plead with Euodia and I plead with Syntyiche to agree with each other in the Lord. "

Paul then presented one of the most beautiful and practical passages in all of Scripture (4:4-7):

Rejoice in the Lord always. I will say it again: Rejoice! Let your gentleness be evident to all. The Lord is near. Do not be anxious about anything, but in everything, by prayer and petition, with thanksgiving, present your requests to God. And the peace of God, which transcends all understanding, will guard your hearts and your minds in Christ Jesus.

The epistle ends with Paul giving personal thanks and appreciation for all the gifts that the Philippian Church had given him.

Lessons From Philippians

1. Rejoice … because to live is Christ and to die is gain. The Christian is in a "win-win" situation. We cannot lose if we are in Christ. We have importance and significance in living now, and we have confidence and hope if death comes.

2. Rejoice … because Christ has come. When Christ came, He came in all humility. He was obedient unto death and was raised to honor. His life and death are models for us, but they also accomplish life for us that is everlasting.

3. Rejoice … because the peace of God can be ours. No matter the circumstances, Christ can strengthen us through each and every one.

NOTES

CHAPTER FORTY-TWO: COLOSSIANS

Assignment

READ ...

Colossians, Chapters 1-4, or one chapter a day from Colossians during the week.

MEMORIZE ...

Colossians 1:18: "And Christ is the head of the body, the church; He is the beginning and the firstborn from among the dead, so that in everything He might have the supremacy."

and/or

Colossians 3:1, 2: "Since, then, you have been raised with Christ, set your hearts on things above, where Christ is seated at the right hand of God. Set your minds on things above, not on earthly things."

and/or

Colossians 3:5: "Put to death, therefore, whatever belongs to your earthly nature: sexual immorality, impurity, lust, evil desires and greed, which is idolatry."

PRAY ...

Rejoicing that Jesus Christ is superior to all things. He is the One in whom all things come into being and by whom all things remain in existence.

Thanking the Lord for the freedom Jesus Christ has brought to your life. No longer are you bound by human laws or religious regulations.

Asking for the kind of life that is focused on the things above, not on earthly things.

Confessing the sin in your life and asking for the power to die to sin and live for Christ.

APPLY ...

In the light of Colossians, what do you:

BELIEVE about God?

REPENT of as sin?

OBEY as a command from God?

SHARE ...

According to what you have learned from Colossians:

- Read Colossians 1:15-20 and have a discussion with your family about the nature of Jesus Christ. Who is Jesus Christ? Most of the time, we only think of Jesus in regard to what He has done for us (death and Resurrection). Think beyond the works of Christ to His person and nature.

- Talk with a friend you have known for a long time about the changes you see that have occurred in your own life over the years. Testify to the "dying to sin" in your own life and honestly ask your friend if he or she agrees with you or not. This can be a test of how you are progressing in your growth in grace.

Colossians:
The Supremacy of Christ

INTRODUCTION

There was a controversy in the Church in Colosse that had to do with a teaching known as Gnosticism. Gnosticism was a mixture of Jewish and Greek thought that said in order to be a Christian you had to have "secret knowledge" – a gnosis.

Some of the elements of Gnosticism were:

- Ceremonialism and legalism (2:16, 17).

- Asceticism (2:20-23).

- Angel worship (2:18).

- Reliance on human wisdom and tradition (2:8).

The hallmark trait of Gnosticism, though, was its low view of Christ. He was a created being and not the eternally begotten Son of God.

In the light of this controversy, Paul presented in his Epistle to the Colossians a case for the supremacy of Christ.

THEME VERSE

And He (Christ) is the head of the body, the church; He is the beginning and the firstborn
from among the dead, so that in everything He might have the supremacy.
Colossians 1:18

The Pauline authorship of Colossians has been disputed for some legitimate reasons:

- There are 55 Greek words in Colossians that are not used anywhere else in the New Testament.

- Its Christology sounds like John's Gospel, meaning that it could have been written in the latter part of the first century.

- It attacks Gnosticism, which was not fully developed as a heresy until the second century.

Even with these objections, however, the internal evidence (the epistle claims to have been written by Paul) and the external evidence (the Early Church accepted the Pauline authorship) all point to the truth that Paul wrote Colossians.

Colosse was a second-rate town. It had been a leading city in Asia Minor but, during the first century, it had diminished in its market value because of surrounding towns like Laodicea and Hierapolis. What made Colosse important to Paul apparently was one man – Epaphras. He had been converted while Paul was in Ephesus and had carried the Gospel to Colosse. When the young Church was attacked by heresy, Epaphras visited Paul in Rome, which led to the Epistle to the Colossians.

I. THE SUPREMACY OF CHRIST (1 – 2)

Colossians opened with Paul as the author, but he also included Timothy as part-author. He did this in II Corinthians, Philippians, I and II Thessalonians and Philemon. Timothy was a young pastor that Paul took under his wing in order to mentor him in the ministry. Notice that the first person plural pronoun – "we" –was often used in this epistle, expressing that Paul and Timothy were side-by-side in the sentiments of the letter.

Paul started with an extensive passage on thanksgiving in 1:3-8. Thanksgiving and thankfulness emerge as an underlying theme throughout Colossians. He expressed thanks in every section of the letter: 1:3-8; 1:12; 2:7; 3:15-17; 4:2. The key to thanksgiving and thankfulness is how it is expressed: It was expressed not toward the love and faith of men (remember, Paul might have had more of a reason to be thankful for the Philippian Church because they had done so much for him.), but it was expressed toward God. It was God who is thanked, because He is the source of all blessings.

Paul expressed his prayer for the Colossian Church. This was another insight into the prayer life of the apostle, who wanted the people to be filled with spiritual wisdom and understanding (1:10-12):

And we pray this in order that you may live a life worthy of the Lord and may please Him in every way: bearing fruit in every good work, growing in the knowledge of God, being strengthened with all power according to His glorious might so that you may have great endurance and patience, and joyfully giving thanks to the Father, who has qualified you to share in the inheritance of the saints in the kingdom of light.

The heart and soul of this letter is given in the magnificent passage on the supremacy of Christ in 1:15-20. Notice these truths about Christ:

- Image of the visible God – verse 15.

- First born of all creation – verse 15.

- He created all things – verse 16.

- All things were created for Him – verse 16.

- He is before all things – verse 17.

- In Him all things hold together – verse 17.

- He is the head of the Church – verse 18.

- He is the beginning and the first born among the dead – verse 18.

- All the fullness of God dwelt in Him – verse 19.

- He has reconciled all things to Himself – verse 20.

Paul stated it as plainly as he could, when he wrote (1:18): "… so that in everything Christ might have the supremacy."

Paul applied this deep theology about the person and work of Jesus Christ to all believers. The pronouns change from "Him" (Christ) to "you" (Christians). This application peaks in verse 27 where he wrote, "Christ in you, the hope of glory."

Paul demonstrated his love for and labor in the Church in 1:24 – 2:5, where the pronouns change again, but this time to "I" (Paul) and "we" (Paul and Timothy). He spoke of having suffered, being a servant, proclaiming the mystery of the Gospel, admonishing and teaching, struggling with the Church in their problems, and warning them about false teachers.

Paul boiled down his pastoral desire for the Christians in Colosse in 2:6, 7:

So then, just as you received Christ Jesus as Lord, continue to live in Him, rooted and built up in Him, strengthened in the faith as you were taught, and overflowing with thankfulness.

Paul closes the second chapter with a series of warnings about false teachers. Remember that it was the Gnostic heresy he was confronting, and the Gnostics upheld a very spiritual, as opposed to realistic, faith – a secret knowledge (gnosis) that only was for the "in crowd." Paul warned about false philosophy, legalistic rituals, improper worship and useless asceticism. At the heart of Paul's exhortation against false teaching was that if anything took one away from a real and faithful relationship with Jesus Christ, it was to be avoided.

II. SUBMISSION TO CHRIST (3 – 4)

Paul's pattern of first presenting theological content and then confronting an issue with practical exhortations was followed in Colossians. The last two chapters move to the normal Christian life lived day-by-day in the homes and in the marketplace, in the Church and in the world.

He began with a general exhortation about the Christian life that must be lived with union in Christ: "Set your minds on things above, not on earthly things." This must be done because we are one with Christ and our lives are hidden in Him.

Christians must consider themselves as dead to sin and alive to God. The heart of this call is found in 3:15-17 (Notice the interwoven call to "thankfulness"):

Let the peace of Christ rule in your hearts, since as members of one body you were called to peace. And be thankful. Let the word of Christ dwell in you richly as you teach and admonish one another with all wisdom, and as you sing psalms, hymns and spiritual songs with gratitude in your hearts to God. And whatever you do, whether in word or deed, do it all in the name of the Lord Jesus, giving thanks to God the Father through Him.

Paul never lets a Christian off with only living the solitary life. The Christian is to live in community, and that community was where the faith is expressed. In 3:18 – 4:1, he dealt with all the other communal relationships that must be affected by one's Christian commitment. He addressed wives, husbands, children, fathers, slaves (employees) and masters (employers). This passage is a good parallel to Ephesians 5.

The Christian life, then, is personal, communal and missional. In 4:2-6, Paul adds the aspect of the Christian life that never must be forgotten: the missional, the evangelistic, the outreach to others. He called for prayer, watchfulness, thankfulness, evangelism, loving actions toward outsiders, making the most of every opportunity, and graceful conversation. All of them are in the context of having an influence on others.

Paul closed Colossians with final greetings and an interesting list of people. Notice two of them. Tychicus was the messenger who carried this letter from Paul to the Colossian Church. With Tychicus was Onesimus. Onesimus becomes important later in the letter to Philemon, because Onesimus was the runaway slave who had been owned by Philemon, who lived in Colosse. More on that later in Paul's Epistle to Philemon.

Well, Colossians perhaps is the most Christ-centered book in the Bible, except possibly for the Gospel of John. In it, Paul stresses the supremacy of Christ and how our lives are never the same once we receive Jesus Christ as our Lord and Savior.

Lessons From Colossians

1. Christ has the supremacy. To be a Christian must mean that we have Christ at the heart and at the head of all we do and all we are. He gives meaning and message to our existence as Christians. It is all about Him.

2. Christians do not have supremacy The Christian life is not about us. We are to die to sin and live for Christ. He is to be the head of our lives, individually and corporately. We are not to live a religious life that depends on our law keeping and ritual observing. Christ in us is our only hope.

NOTES

CHAPTER FORTY-THREE: I AND II THESSALONIANS

Assignment

READ ...

I Thessalonians, Chapters 1-5, and II Thessalonians, Chapters 1-3, or one chapter a day from
I Thessalonians and II Thessalonians during the week.

MEMORIZE ...

I Thessalonians 2:13: "And we also thank God continually because, when you received the Word of God,
which you heard from us, you accepted it not as the word of men, but as it actually is, the Word
of God, which is at work in you who believe."

and/or

I Thessalonians 5:16-18: "Be joyful always; pray continually; give thanks in all circumstances; for this is
God's will for you in Christ Jesus."

and/or

II Thessalonians 2:13: "But we ought always to thank God for you, brothers loved by the Lord, because
from the beginning God chose you to be saved through the sanctifying work of the Spirit and through
belief in the truth."

and/or

II Thessalonians 3:3: "But the Lord is faithful, and He will strengthen and protect you from the evil one."

PRAY ...

Thanking the Lord that He is coming again. Meditate on the truth of the Second Coming and ask the Lord
to make you faithful to face these days.

Expressing thanksgiving for others in the Church because they have received the grace of God.

Giving thanks to God for all the things going on in your life, even if they do not feel good.

Read I Thessalonians 5:12-22 and pray about the matters that come to mind in the light of this Scripture.

APPLY ...

In the light of I and II Thessalonians, what do you:

> BELIEVE about God?
>
> REPENT of as sin?
>
> OBEY as a command from God?

SHARE ...

According to what you have learned from I and II Thessalonians:

- Have a discussion with your family about the importance of making every day count. Give the perspective that time is limited and the Lord may return at any time, and then talk about how that truth makes every day crucial and valuable.

- Talk with a friend, whether in another congregation or not in any Church, about the end of time. Simply ask them if they think the world will end one day and how that will happen. Listen, don't argue or criticize, but then share with him or her about the hope you have in the Second Coming of Christ. You may want to read I Thessalonians 4:13-18 with them.

I Thessalonians: The Second Coming

INTRODUCTION

The theme of I Thessalonians is the Second Coming of Jesus Christ. Every chapter of I Thessalonians ends with a reference to the Second Coming, and chapter 4 focuses on it.

The theme of II Thessalonians is also the Second Coming of Jesus Christ. I and II Thessalonians are known as the eschatological letters of Paul, meaning that they present teaching about the last times or the Second Coming.

The Book of Revelation is usually thought of as the only New Testament book focusing on the return of the Lord, but that is not the case. In the New Testament, the Second Coming is talked about most in a few places: Revelation, the Olivet Discourse in Matthew 24-25 and I and II Thessalonians.

The Second Coming is mentioned 318 times throughout the New Testament, which makes it more common in the New Testament than any other doctrine, other than salvation by grace through faith.

There is a lot of foolishness in the Church about the Second Coming. Either Christians are obsessed with it and read every headline into the Bible or Christians don't think about it at all.

THEME VERSE

For who is our hope or joy or crown of exultation?
Is it not even you, in the presence of our Lord Jesus at His coming?
I Thessalonians 2:19

Thessalonica was a prominent seaport and the capital of the Roman province of Macedonia. It was a prosperous city and had a population of 200,000 in the first century. It is still in existence today, but under the name of Salonika.

Thessalonica had a large Jewish population and many Gentiles, God-fearers, were attracted to the monotheism of Judaism. During Paul's second missionary journey (Acts 17:1-10) many "God-fearers" quickly responded to Paul's preaching, but it caused a stir among the Jewish population. Paul and Silas had to leave Thessalonica under pressure.

Paul accomplished five things in I Thessalonians.

I. EXPRESSION OF THANKSGIVING (1)

Paul was primarily thankful for the Thessalonians' change from heathenism to Christianity:

We always thank God for all of you, mentioning you in our prayers. We continually remember before our God and Father your work produced by faith, your labor prompted by love, and your endurance inspired by hope in our Lord Jesus Christ. (1:2, 3)

Notice the use of faith, love and hope – the triad of the Christian life.
Paul saw the faith of the Thessalonians as a genuine faith (4ff):

- Not words only.

- The conviction of the Holy Spirit.

- Imitated the apostles.

- In spite of suffering.

- Became model Christians.

- Their faith was known everywhere.

- True repentance.

- Faithful service.

- Waiting for the return (11): "… and to wait for His Son from heaven, whom He raised from the dead – Jesus, who rescues us from the coming wrath."

II. DEFENSE OF HIMSELF (2, 3)

Yet, Paul had to defend himself as he had in other churches, but the intensity is not as strong in Thessalonica as it was in Galatia or Corinth.

Paul reviewed his brief ministry (maybe one month) in Thessalonica. He defended his conduct and motives, apparently because there were some people who doubted those (2:3):

For the appeal we make does not spring from error or impure motives, nor are we trying to trick you.

He describes his devotion to them like that of a mother (2:7):

… but we were gentle among you, like a mother caring for her little children.

And like a father (2:11):

… for you know that we dealt with each of you as a father deals with his own children.

He was like a mother in his affection and like a father in his admonitions.

In chapters 2:17 – 3:10, Paul expressed his intense desire to see them again, but he was prohibited from doing so (2:18):

For we wanted to come to you – certainly I, Paul, did, again and again – but Satan stopped us.

Then Paul wrote (2:19):

For who is our hope or joy or crown of exultation? Is it not even you, in the presence of our Lord Jesus at His coming?

Though Paul would not be able to visit them, he was sending Timothy instead. Paul then prayed a prayer for them (3:11-13):

Now may our God and Father Himself and our Lord Jesus clear the way for us to come to you. May the Lord make your love increase and overflow for each other and for everyone else, just as ours does for you. May He strengthen your hearts so that you will be blameless and holy in the presence of our God and Father when our Lord Jesus comes with all His holy ones.

III. ENCOURAGEMENT TOWARD HOLINESS (4:1-12)

Paul expressed his desire for the Church in Thessalonica (4:1):

Finally, brothers, we instructed you how to live in order to please God.

Paul always got around to the practical Christian life and not just theological truth. He encouraged the Thessalonians in three areas:

- Sexual immorality: Paul got explicit again, as he often did in his letters about sexual immorality. In 4:3-5, he wrote one of the greatest passages about sexual purity:

  It is God's will that you should be sanctified: that you should avoid sexual immorality; that each of you should learn to control his own body in a way that is holy and honorable, not in passionate lust like the heathen, who do not know God.

- Loving one another: Paul wrote in 4:9, 10:

  Now about brotherly love we do not need to write to you, for you yourselves have been taught by God to love each other. And in fact, you do love all the brothers throughout Macedonia. Yet we urge you, brothers, to do so more and more.

- Slothfulness: There was a unique problem in the Church in Thessalonica that was not in any other Early Church. There were some people in the Church who understood the Second Coming of Christ to be so close that they thought they did not need to work. Paul said (4:11, 12):

  Make it your ambition to lead a quiet life, to mind your own business and to work with your hands, just as we told you, so that your daily life may win the respect of outsiders and so that you will not be dependent on anybody.

  Again, Paul said (5:14):

  And we urge you, brothers, warn those who are idle, encourage the timid, help the weak, be patient with everyone.

  And, in II Thessalonians 3:10, he said:

  For even when we were with you, we gave you this rule: "If a man will not work, he shall not eat."

IV. KNOWLEDGE ABOUT THE SECOND COMING (4:13 – 5:11)

If there ever was a prophetical Church, it was the Church at Thessalonica. The people had such a heightened expectation of the Second Coming that they went to extremes, like not working and asking about what would happen to those who died before the Second Coming.

In 4:13-18, Paul comforted them by teaching that those who die in the Lord will be resurrected at the parousia (coming, presence, advent). Verse 4:14 says: "We believe that Jesus died and rose again and so we believe that God will bring with Jesus those who have fallen asleep (died) in Him."

The only New Testament passage on the rapture is then given (read 4:16-18). This is no secret rapture, nor is it a divided event that happens and then there are years following it. No, it happens with a trumpet blast at the same time that the Lord returns.

In 5:1-11, Paul described "the day of the Lord," Old Testament language that was often used as the description of when the Lord comes, either in judgment or at the end of time. The Lord will come "as a thief in the night," but we are to be "alert and self-controlled." And twice, in 4:18 and 5:11, Paul tells the Church in Thessalonica to "encourage one another" with the expectation that Christ is coming again.

V. Instructions About Christian Conduct (5:12-28)

This section of I Thessalonians contains one of the most pithy and poignant passages that provide practical commands for the Christian life.

There are instructions toward others in 5:12-15:

- Respect those who labor among you.

- Live in peace with one another.

- Warn the idle.

- Encourage the timid.

- Help the weak.

- Be patient with everyone.

- Be kind to one another.

    There are instructions toward the believer in 5:16-22.
    There are instructions toward God in 5:23, 24.
    There are instruction toward Paul in 5:25-28:

- Pray for him.

- Greet one another.

II Thessalonians:
Waiting and Working

INTRODUCTION

II Thessalonians is a follow-up letter to I Thessalonians, because some of the people in the Church followed false teaching, especially about the Second Coming. Paul exhorted them to wait expectantly for the coming of Christ, but he also encouraged them to work in the meantime.

THEME VERSE

> *But we ought always to thank God for you, brothers loved by the Lord,*
> *because from the beginning God chose you to be saved through*
> *the sanctifying work of the Spirit and through belief in the truth.*
> *II Thessalonians 2:13*

I. DISCOURAGED BELIEVERS (1)

Paul began this letter like he did I Thessalonians, by acknowledging his pastoral team in Thessalonica: Paul, Silas and Timothy. He thanked God for the Church and acknowledged that the people probably suffered more persecution than those in Paul's other churches did.

Paul encouraged the people in their walk with Christ (1:5-10). He called for them to patiently endure, knowing that the Lord will judge their persecutors when he is "revealed from heaven with His mighty angels in flaming fire." In other words, the suffering they are going through now will be corrected one day, which was the encouragement of the Lord coming again one day in the future.

Paul's prayer for the Church in 1:11, 12 is remarkable (read it). The prayers of Paul for the Church in Thessalonica are highlighted in II Thessalonians:

- 1:11-12.

- 2:16-17.

- 3:5.

- 3:16.

II. Disturbed Believers (2)

There were many people in the Church disturbed about a rumor that the Second Coming already had occurred. In other words, there were some people in the Church who thought they had been left behind. The rumor was attributed to a letter from Paul. He warned them about such teaching, then tried to clarify some of the details about the Second Coming.

Paul taught that the Second Coming will not occur until the "man of lawlessness" appears. He wanted them to be sure that the day of the Lord was still in the future and that some things had to happen before the Lord returned.

This "man of lawlessness" is a mysterious reference. Paul referred to him four times in this one chapter (verses 3, 4, 8, 9). There is quite a debate about the identity of this "man of lawlessness," but generally it is recognized to be a description of who Christians commonly call the antichrist. Other passages that make references to the antichrist are Daniel 9:27; 12:11; Matthew 24:15; I John 2:18; Revelation 11:7; 13:19; and II Thessalonians 2.

Some general conclusions about the antichrist are:

- He is an individual, but not Satan.

- He is limited in his powers. In a minute, we will see Paul speaking of the one who restrains him.

- His coming is preliminary to the Second Coming of Christ.

- He has many predecessors. Paul, in verse 7, writes that, "The secret power of lawlessness is already at work." In I John, John writes that there are "many antichrists" and some of them are in the world now.

Paul, however, makes it clear that this "man of lawlessness" is confronted by "the one who holds him back" (New International Version) or the "restrainer" (King James Version). Evil, in general, and the antichrist, in particular, are never in control. God is in control, even when evil is most blatant and obvious. The identity of this "restrainer" is a mystery. The interpretations most often mentioned are:

- Government. Governments have been established by God for restraining evil, so they are God's agents to hold back the full impact of evil.

- The Church. The Church is called by God to be salt and light in the world, so its impact is to restrain evil.

- The Holy Spirit. This is God the Holy Spirit working in the world, sometimes through agencies and sometimes directly, to keep the worst from happening.

When the "restrainer" is taken out of the way, terrible things will go on in the world:

- The work of Satan displayed in counterfeit miracles, signs and wonders.

- Evil that is deceiving.

- A refusal to love the truth and be saved.

- They will believe lies.

- They will delight in wickedness.

Yet, in such a horrible description of the world, the Lord still is in the picture:

- The Lord Jesus will overthrow the man of lawlessness with the breath of His mouth.

- The Lord Jesus will destroy the man of lawlessness with the splendor of His coming.

- God "sends them a powerful delusion," which means that as people choose sin, God gives them up to that sin.

So, with such a terrible picture, Paul gave the Thessalonians the encouragement to "stand firm." Paul then prayed for them with a remarkable prayer in 2:16, 17:

May our Lord Jesus Christ Himself and God our Father, who loved us and by His grace gave us eternal encouragement and good hope, encourage your hearts and strengthen you in every good deed and word.

III. Disobedient Believers (3)

Paul requested prayer for himself and encouraged the Thessalonians again. Paul used a pattern – prayer and encouragement, prayer and encouragement. Go to God … help one another. Trust in God … love one another. Rely on the truths of God in prayer … teach the truths of God to one another.

Paul commanded the believers in the Church to be obedient in their walk. The apostle showed some tact as he encouraged, prayed, informed and then confronted.

There was apparently a problem with some people in the Church who thought that Jesus already had come or was so close to coming that they did not need to work. Paul used his own example as idleness being contradictory to expecting Jesus to come again.

Basically, Paul called them to have the balance of waiting for His coming and working until He comes.

Lessons From I And II Thessalonians

1. We need to be committed to one another in encouragement, prayer and love.

2. We need to take comfort in the truth that Jesus is coming again and will judge all things with righteousness.

3. We need to be busy in the Lord's work while we wait for His return.

NOTES

Chapter Forty-Four: I and II Timothy

Assignment

Read ...

I Timothy, Chapters 1-6, and II Timothy, Chapters 1-4, or one chapter a day from I Timothy and II Timothy during the week.

Memorize ...

I Timothy 2:1, 2: "I urge, then, first of all, that requests, prayers, intercession and thanksgiving be made for everyone – for kings and all those in authority, that we may live peaceful and quiet lives in all godliness and holiness."

and/or

I Timothy 6:10: "For the love of money is a root of all kinds of evil. Some people, eager for money, have wandered from the faith and pierced themselves with many griefs."

and/or

II Timothy 4:7, 8: "I have fought the good fight, I have finished the race, I have kept the faith. Now there is in store for me the crown of righteousness, which the Lord, the righteous Judge, will award to me on that day – and not only to me, but also to all who have longed for His appearing."

Pray ...

For the elders and deacons of the Church that the Lord's blessing would be upon them and that they would be faithful to their call.

Examining your life to see if you are "fighting the good fight, keeping the faith and finishing the course."

Thanking God for the truth that your salvation is based on what He has done for you and not on what you have done for yourself.

For any situation in your life where there is a need for reconciliation. Be reconciled to one another.

APPLY ...

In the light of I and II Timothy, what do you:

> BELIEVE about God?
>
> REPENT of as sin?
>
> OBEY as a command from God?

SHARE ...

According to what you have learned from I and II Timothy:

- Have a discussion with your family about the officers of the Church. Think about ways you can encourage them, support them and pray for them. Maybe contact an elder or deacon and let them know how much you appreciate them.

- Describe to someone you know Paul's description at the end of his life (4:7, 8). Get their reaction as to how they might see their lives at the end of their days.

I Timothy:
A Leadership Manual

INTRODUCTION

Leadership is crucial to the Church. The ministries of pastors, elders and deacons are essential to the stability, function and advance of the Gospel through the Church. Paul had established enough churches and confronted enough conflicts in them to know that leaders had to be taught, encouraged and disciplined. The maturity of the Church was at stake. In I Timothy, Paul informally presents a manual for challenging the leadership of the Church to be faithful and godly.

THEME VERSE

> *Although I hope to come to you soon, I am writing you these instructions so that,*
> *if I am delayed, you will know how people ought to conduct themselves in God's household,*
> *which is the church of the living God, the pillar and foundation of the truth.*
> *I Timothy 3:14, 15*

BACKGROUND FOR I AND II TIMOTHY

- I and II Timothy are the last epistles Paul wrote. Most scholarship will uphold that I Thessalonians was Paul's first epistle and II Timothy his last. So, as we come to I and II Timothy, we are hearing a mature apostle who, recognizing that he is at the end of his life and ministry, is concerned about those he will leave behind.

- I and II Timothy and Titus are the "Pastoral Epistles." The "Pastoral Epistles" are the letters of Paul that were written to individuals, rather than congregations. Notice that the names of these letters are to people, not churches. The Pastoral Epistles, though, have the distinctive purpose of preparing someone to lead the Church as a pastor when Paul is gone.

- Timothy was a unique man of God. Timothy appears 24 times in the New Testament and in 12 epistles. Paul would refer to him as "my child" and "my son" and "fellow servant." It is not certain, but Paul had probably discipled him in Christ. Timothy was a young man who had a godly heritage (II Timothy 1:5 and 3:14, 15).

I. REMINDERS (1)

Paul opened this first epistle to Timothy with the salutation, "my true son in the faith." Paul immediately gave a warning about the false teachings of the Judaizers, as well as myths and genealogies (1:3-11).

Paul shared his testimony (1:12-17), clearly speaking of his conversion and his call to ministry. Paul was not afraid to share something personal. He gave his testimony before government officials, out in the market square and in the Church. He gave it in situations to evangelize out in the world, as well as in situations to edify the Church, like he did here with Timothy.

The primary emphasis in Paul's testimony was the grace of God. Paul never got over the grace of God, which covered his great sin (remember that Paul was a persecutor of Christians):

> Even though I was once a blasphemer and a persecutor and a violent man, I was shown
> mercy because I acted in ignorance and unbelief. The grace of our Lord was poured out on me
> abundantly, along with the faith and love that are in Christ Jesus. Here is a trustworthy saying
> that deserves full acceptance: Christ Jesus came into the world to save sinners – of whom I am
> the worst. (1:13-15)

Paul gave God all the glory, and encouraged Timothy to "fight the good fight."

II. REGULATIONS (2:1 – 3:13)

Paul instructed Timothy about some of the central matters of being a pastor.

Instructions for Worship (2)

Paul began his instruction with prayer:

> I urge, then first of all, that requests, prayers, intercessions and thanksgiving be made for
> everyone – for kings and all those in authority, that we may live peaceful and quiet lives in all
> godliness and holiness.

Paul then dove into a topic that was a controversy in his time and is explosive today – women in the Church. The debate over women teaching and having authority over men centers on verse 2:12:

> "I do not permit a woman to teach or to have authority over a man; she must be silent."

There have been two ways in which the Church has taken this teaching:

- Paul was confronting a specific problem in Ephesus regarding domineering women who were teaching false doctrine and exercising authority that wasn't theirs.

- Paul was prohibiting women for all time and in every Church from teaching men or having authority in the Church.

Instructions for Officers (3:1-14)

The qualifications and responsibilities of elders and deacons are given in great detail here and in Titus 1:6-9. One of the significant debates from this passage is over two words – *episcopos* and *presbuteros*. They are two words that are interchangeable in the description of the "overseer" or the "elder." The debate, though, is over the nature of the office. Is a person being described who stands alone in his authority in the Church or is it a person standing with others in having authority?

For elders and deacons and their character and call, I Timothy 3:1-14 is important.

III. RESPONSIBILITIES (3:14 – 6:21)

Paul stated the purpose of this letter in I Timothy 3:14, 15:

> Although I hope to come to you soon, I am writing you these instructions so that, if I am

*delayed, you will know how people ought to conduct themselves in God's household, which is
the church of the living God, the pillar and foundation of the truth.*

He looked at three areas of responsibilities that are important for all spiritual leaders to understand:

- Preserve pure doctrine (3:16 – 4:16). Sound doctrine is foundational to ministry. Paul expressed it plainly in 4:11-13:

  *Command and teach these things. Don't let anyone look down on you because you are young,
  but set an example for the believers in speech, in life, in love, in faith and in purity. Until I
  come, devote yourself to the public reading of Scripture, to preaching and to teaching.*

- Pastor all the people (5:1 – 6:2). The Church is made up of many members and many segments. Paul showed pastoral sensitivity as he gave customized advice to pastors and various groups in the Church:

  1 Older men.

  2. Younger men.

  3. Older women.

  4. Younger women.

  5. Widows (verses 3-16).

  6. Elders.

  7. Slaves.

  8. Masters.

- Personally practice the faith (6:3-19).

  Timothy was exhorted by Paul to be sure that he practiced what he preached. He told him to be careful about his doctrine, to avoid quarrels and strife, to be content with what you have, and to watch out for the "love of money" (10).

  Timothy was given a charge by Paul (6:11-19) to flee from sin, fight the good fight, take hold of eternal life, to be like Christ and command the rich to see that wealth is more than money.

II Timothy:
Paul's Last Will and Testament

INTRODUCTION

This is Paul's last epistle. He knew death was not far away (4:6-8). He was pouring out his heart to a younger man (Timothy probably is about 40 years old), and he was very personal (Paul refers to more than 20 individuals, some who are not mentioned anywhere else in the New Testament).

This was Paul's last will and testament – the words of a dying man who is ready to die.

THEME VERSE

> *I have fought the good fight, I have finished the race, I have kept the faith.*
> *Now there is in store for me the crown of righteousness, which the Lord, the righteous Judge,*
> *will award to me on that day – and not only to me, but also to all who have longed for His appearing.*
> *II Timothy 4:6-8*

I. THE POWER OF THE GOSPEL (1)

Paul expressed thanksgiving for Timothy and told him that he was praying for him. There was great emotion in these opening words as Paul was passing on the mantle of leadership to Timothy (1:6, 7):

> *For this reason I remind you to fan into flame the gift of God, which is in you through the laying on of my hands. For God did not give us a spirit of timidity, but a spirit of power, of love and of self-discipline.*

Paul encouraged Timothy not to be ashamed of the Lord, to be ready for suffering and to remain faithful (1:14):

> *Guard the good deposit that was entrusted to you – guard it with the help of the Holy Spirit who lives in us.*

II. PERSEVERANCE OF THE GOSPEL MINISTER (2)

Paul gave six metaphors for the pastor:

- A good soldier who should be ready for hardship (3).

- An athlete who should be ready for honor (5).

- A farmer who is hardworking (6).

- A workman rightly handling the Word of truth (21).

- An instrument who is holy (21).

- A servant who always is hopeful (24).

III. PROTECTION OF THE GOSPEL MESSAGE (3)

Paul proclaimed a warning about godlessness. His warning was about morality more than theology. Paul gave another one of his famous lists of sins, but put them in the context of the last days. People will do terrible things in the last days. In some sense, things will get worse in the world and in the Church as the Second Coming approaches. Paul confronted Timothy with this exhortation: "Have nothing to do with them."

Paul told Timothy to follow his example. Paul had nothing to cover. He was not ashamed of anything he had done, so he boldly told Timothy to do what he had done.

Paul highlighted the place of the Scriptures in Timothy's ministry: (3:16, 17):

All Scripture is God-breathed and is useful for teaching, rebuking, correcting and training in righteousness, so that the man of God may be thoroughly equipped for every good work.

IV. PROCLAMATION OF THE GOSPEL (4)

Paul presented another charge to Timothy in the light of the teaching on Scripture (4:1, 2):

In the presence of God and of Christ Jesus, who will judge the living and the dead, and in view of His appearing and His kingdom, I give you this charge: Preach the Word; be prepared in season and out of season; correct, rebuke and encourage – with great patience and careful instruction.

Paul then spoke of confidence about his future (4:6-8):

I have fought the good fight, I have finished the race, I have kept the faith. Now there is in store for me the crown of righteousness, which the Lord, the righteous Judge, will award to me on that day – and not only to me, but also to all who have longed for His appearing.

Lessons From I and II Timothy

1. The call of God is that we be faithful with the Gospel. At the very heart of the ministry of the Church is the proclamation of the truth that there is one God and one mediator between God and men, the man Christ Jesus.

2. The call of God is that we be faithful in leadership. Pastors, elders and deacons are called by God for the benefit of the Church. The leadership must be true in their walk with God and their belief in God.

3. The call of God is that we be faithful until the end. To fight the good fight and to keep the faith is a call for our whole lives as Christians. Through good times and bad, the call is to be faithful to our Lord.

NOTES

CHAPTER FORTY-FIVE: TITUS AND PHILEMON

Assignment

READ ...

Titus, Chapters 1-3, and Philemon or one chapter a day from Titus and Philemon during the week.

MEMORIZE ...

Titus 1:9: "He must hold firmly to the trustworthy message as it has been taught, so that he can encourage others by sound doctrine and refute those who oppose it."

and/or

Titus 3:4, 5: "But when the kindness and love of God our Savior appeared, He saved us, not because of righteous things we had done, but because of His mercy."

PRAY ...

For the leaders of the Church, that they might be trustworthy in holding the Gospel in truth.

Acknowledging that your good works do not save you and that your salvation is yours in spite of yourself.

Thanking God for the truth that your salvation is based on what He has done for you and not on what you have done for yourself.

Seeking reconciliation in any situation in your life where you might be at odds with a brother or sister in the faith.

APPLY ...

In the light of Titus and Philemon, what do you:

BELIEVE about God?

REPENT of as sin?

OBEY as a command from God?

SHARE ...

According to what you have learned from Titus and Philemon:

- Have a family time when you talk about doing good works. Keep a balance in that discussion so that it is clear that salvation does not come by our good works, but that our salvation does produce good works in us.

- Tell the story of Philemon to a friend. Let your friend know that the desire of Paul was the reconciliation of two men who were in a relationship with one another, but that relationship had been broken. Ask the friend if he or she has any broken relationships in his or her life and if he or she would like them to be reconciled.

Titus:
Sound Doctrine

INTRODUCTION

Paul's letter to Titus is very similar to I Timothy. Once again, Paul is giving leadership training to an individual, this time to Titus. Yet, when the two epistles are read together, Titus is less personal than I Timothy. Paul obviously was closer to Timothy.

Titus, though, was a close companion to Paul. Titus is not mentioned in Acts, but there are 13 references to him in the Pauline epistles. He probably was a convert of Paul's and Paul referred to him as "brother" (II Corinthians 2:13), "partner and fellow worker" (II Corinthians 8:23), and "child" (Titus 1:4).

There was an emphasis on "sound" doctrine in Titus. The word "sound" occurs five times (1:9, 13; 2:1, 2, 8). It is a word that connects to "integrity" and "wholeness." Paul's exhortation to "sound doctrine" was to a continuity of what is taught and what is done with the integrity of the truth.

THEME VERSE

But when the kindness and love of God our Savior appeared, He saved us,
not because of righteous things we had done, but because of His mercy.
Titus 3:5

I. PROTECTION OF SOUND DOCTRINE (1)

Paul opened Titus in a very doctrinal (theological) way. He jumped right into talking about faith, the elect, truth, hope, eternal life, the nature of God, the promises of God, His Word and preaching.

He then got personal by referring to Titus as "my true son in our common faith."

Sound doctrine was to be protected by the leadership of elders (1:5-9). Paul commanded that elders be appointed and that they have a godly character.

Sound doctrine also was to be protected by the warning about false teachers. Titus should not be surprised by the presence of false teachers, but he must not follow them. Titus was to confront false teachers "… so that they will be sound in the faith" (1:13).

II. PREACHING OF SOUND DOCTRINE (2)

Sound doctrine must not only be taught to everyone in the Church, but it must be preached so that the Gospel would be believed.

Paul put the emphasis on the grace of God in our salvation and in our sanctification.

III. Practice of Sound Doctrine (3)

Sound doctrine will lead to sound practice. What one believes should impact what is done. Belief and behavior go together. It is called integrity.

In chapter 3, Paul calls for this soundness of doctrine to be seen in the good works of people's lives. Paul spoke plainly when he said that Christians are "to be ready to do whatever is good."

Based on what God has done, good works are to be done. Salvation does not come by good works (3:5); but that did not keep Paul from stressing the doing of good works (1:16; 2:7; 2:14; 3:1; 3:8; 3:14):

- Be ready to do whatever is good (3:1).

- Devote themselves to doing what is good (3:8).

- Our people must learn to devote themselves to doing what is good (3:14).

There will always be diversions from godliness, but Christians are not to be diverted from being like Christ.

Philemon:
From Bondage to Brotherhood

INTRODUCTION

Philemon is a little postcard compared to the other letters by Paul. It is small and apparently insignificant, but it has a message of hope, grace and forgiveness – and that message never is small and insignificant.

In Philemon, some unfamiliar names are given: Onesemus, Philemon, Aristarcus, Aphia, Archipas and Demas. A very familiar story, though, is told – forgive and accept one another.

The setting of Philemon is distinctive from today. Today is a time of freedom, but Philemon lived in the time of slavery, and it was a normal part of their communal life.

The particular story of Philemon has to do with one master, one slave and one family. Philemon is a slave owner. He experienced the unspeakable, a runaway slave. His slave, Onesimus chose to flee from Philemon's home. He went to Rome to blend into the crowd of other runaway slaves. Many of them had an "F" on their forehead, for the Latin *fugitivus* or fugitive, which always marked a runaway slave.

Somehow, Onesimus met Paul, who was in chains as a prisoner, and Paul led him to Christ – a prisoner led a slave to Christ. This makes for a very interesting situation. A runaway slave with a debt to pay to his master, and now he is converted. What would Christ have him do?

Paul is placed right in the middle of this situation, since he was a friend of Philemon's, a member of the Church at Colossus. Now in Rome, the Lord used Paul to convert Philemon's runaway slave.

In the body of the letter, Paul makes a request. He tells of his prayers and the good reputation of Philemon. Paul does not come to his point at first. He gives hearty greetings of encouragement and says good things to Philemon. This is a good lesson to us all. We are to be affirmers, encouragers, the givers of good words. It should not be empty flattery or manipulative sweet talk, but it should be edifying.

Paul then appeals to Philemon, saying twice (9-10), "I appeal to you." He could have commanded, but didn't. There is no heavy fist, but an arm around the shoulder. Paul calls Onesimus his "child," a reference to his spiritual fatherhood over him.

Paul gets to the heart of the matter: Philemon and Onesimus need to be reconciled to one another, just like we are to be reconciled to God.

In verse 11, Paul writes that Onesimus is useful to him and to Philemon. Paul is sending Onesimus back to Philemon, even though Paul wanted to keep Onesimus with him. Paul was convinced that it was best for everyone for him to go back.

There was a Roman law of advocacy, where a friend could step in to help with a dispute between a master and a slave. Paul was doing this. There were some cases when the slave was adopted into the family – like Ben Hur.

"Charge this to my account," Paul writes. Paul does not ask Philemon to ignore the debt or consequences.

This is important. There must be an accounting. Paul is putting his credit on the line.

The bottom line is this: Paul was calling on both Philemon the master, and Onesimus the slave, to be Christians in their conditions. There were no demands except to be Christ-like in their treatment of one another.

Fifty years after Philemon was written, Ignatius, an Early Church father, was arrested and was to be executed, but he was allowed to write letters of encouragement to churches. He wrote one in Smyran to the Church at Ephesus. In the first chapter, he speaks of the pastor of that congregation, whose name was Onesimus. Maybe coincidental, but Ignatius used the identical phrase as Paul – "who formerly was useless, but now is useful." That is what grace can do: Take a slave and make him a pastor.

Lessons From Titus and Philemon

1.   We are to be people of good works, based on the Gospel (Titus).

2.   We are to be people of reconciliation, based on the Gospel (Philemon).

NOTES

Assignment

READ ...

Hebrews, Chapters 1-13, or selected chapters from Hebrews (one a day for a week) as follows:

Hebrews 1 – The superiority of the Son.

Hebrews 5 – Jesus the great high priest.

Hebrews 6 – The danger of falling away.

Hebrews 10 – Christ's sacrifice.

Hebrews 11 – The hall of fame of faith.

Hebrews 12 – Living as the children of God.

MEMORIZE ...

Hebrews 4:12: "For the word of God is living and active. Sharper than any double-edged sword, it penetrates even to dividing soul and spirit, joints and marrow; it judges the thoughts and attitudes of the heart."

and/or

Hebrews 4:14, 15: "Therefore, since we have a great high priest who has gone through the heavens, Jesus the Son of God, let us hold firmly to the faith we profess. For we do not have a high priest who is unable to sympathize with our weaknesses, but we have one who has been tempted in every way, just as we are – yet without sin."

and/or

Hebrews 12:2: "Let us fix our eyes on Jesus, the author and perfecter of our faith, who for the joy set before Him endured the cross, scorning its shame, and sat down at the right hand of the throne of God."

PRAY ...

For an understanding to see Jesus as He really is. Know that there is no one and nothing that can compare with Jesus. Praise Him.

According to Hebrews 4:16: "Let us then approach the throne of grace with confidence, so that we may receive mercy and find grace to help us in our time of need."

Asking God to give you a true faith in Him that will stand through anything.

Confessing the sin that is besetting you and keeping you from a closer walk with your God.

APPLY ...

In the light of Hebrews, what do you:

>   BELIEVE about God?

>   REPENT of as sin?

>   OBEY as a command from God?

SHARE ...

According to what you have learned from Hebrews:

- Read Hebrews 11 with your family. Have a discussion about what faith is and how faith was shown in the lives of these saints. Ask one another how faith has been shown in your lives or the lives of others.

- Hebrews is a book with many warnings in it. Think of someone you know who used to walk with the Lord, but is not doing so now. This is a serious matter, but with all the love and prayer you can, talk to that person about the dangers they are in for once walking with God, but now being away from Him.

Hebrews:
Better and More Mature

INTRODUCTION

Hebrews is one of the most intimidating books of the Bible. It can be put it in the same category of other intimidating books like Leviticus, Ezekiel, Romans and Revelation. This means that it has a depth, conviction and mystery that sets it apart from other books of the Bible. Hebrews is not milk. It is red meat.

THEME VERSE

Therefore leaving the elementary teaching about Christ, let us press on to maturity.
Hebrews 6:1a

BACKGROUND

The recipients of this letter were not in one church or one city, neither were they one individual. Hebrews was written to people who needed special instruction and encouragement. They were Jewish believers, wherever they might be, who were suffering because of their faith in Jesus and were being tempted to go back to their old faith. Hebrews 10:32-34 gives insight into their particular experience in the faith:

Remember those earlier days after you had received the light, when you stood your ground
in a great contest in the face of suffering. Sometimes you were publicly exposed to insult
and persecution; at other times you stood side by side with those who were so treated. You
sympathized with those in prison and joyfully accepted the confiscation of your property,
because you knew that you yourselves had better and lasting possessions.

The author of Hebrews is a mystery. It is the only book in the New Testament whose authorship has remained a question mark. Those who received the letter knew its author because of Hebrews 13:18, 19:

Pray for us. We are sure that we have a clear conscience and desire to live honorably in every
way. I particularly urge you to pray so that I may be restored to you soon.

The letter, though, does not claim an author and Church history has been mixed on who it has identified as the author. Some who have been considered as the author of Hebrews have been Paul, Barnabas, Luke, Apollos, Philip and Priscilla. The most common opinion is Paul, who is credited as the author in the King James Version. Pauline authorship, however, is doubted for the following reasons:

- Paul does not refer to himself in the epistle as he normally did.

- The Greek style of Hebrews is more polished than Paul's epistles.

- The references to Christ are simpler in Hebrews than in Paul's epistles.

To say who did not write Hebrews, however, is a far cry from declaring who did. We might be wise to agree with third-century theologian Origen, who wrote, "Who it was that really wrote the Epistle to the Hebrews, God only knows."

I. A SUPERIOR PERSON (1:1 – 4:13)

There is no salutation like in most epistles. The author does not introduce himself, but jumps right into the message, and the letter opens with a very majestic passage (read 1:1-4).

The thrust of these first chapters is to show that Jesus, the Son of God, is superior to the angels (1:4 – 2:18) and Moses (3:1-6). To the Jew, angels were the most exalted beings and Moses was the most exalted human being. They were not to be compared with Jesus Christ.

Warnings

In this first section, there are two warnings. Warnings are sprinkled throughout Hebrews because the recipients were apparently considering going back to the old covenant faith of the Old Testament. It was thought that if they were being persecuted for being Christians, and if they made some adjustments in their faith, the persecutions would cease or at least lessen.

The writer to the Hebrews, however, would have none of this kind of logic. First of all, to stop following Jesus would be to stop following God Himself. Second, to stop following Jesus had dire consequences, thus the need of warnings.

There are five solemn warnings in Hebrews:

- 2:1-4.

- 3:7 – 4:13.

- 5:11 – 6:20.

- 10:19-39.

- 12:25-29.

These warnings are given with encouragements so that in the heat of persecution, Christians would stick together.

II. A SUPERIOR PREISTHOOD (4:14 – 10:18)

The Superiority of Christ's Priesthood (4:14 – 7:28)

Jesus as the great high priest is upheld. He is great and mighty because He is the One "who has passed into the heavens." He is close and intimate, though, because He can "sympathize with our weaknesses." There is no ordinary priest who can compare with Jesus.

In this section, one of the most mysterious characters in the Bible is mentioned. Melchizedek the priest is focused on in chapter 7. Melchizedek is an obscure Old Testament character we read about in Genesis 14:18-20. Melchizedek did not have a lineage and was both a king and a priest, and he was so revered that Abraham gave him a tithe of all he had. What chapter 7 does is present the case that Christ was a priest "after the order of Melchizedek," which meant that He was not like the Levi or Aaronic priest. Christ was totally unique and special in His priesthood, like Melchizedek.

The Superiority of Christ's Covenant (8)

Jesus is the priest of a superior covenant. The new covenant is better than the old covenant because it is based on the promise of God, "I will put my laws in their minds and write them on their hearts. I will be their God, and they will be my people," and there is no reason to go back to the old covenant.

The Superiority of Christ's Sacrifice (9:1 – 10:18)

The heart of Christ's superiority comes from His sacrifice. It was unlike any sacrifice of the old covenant. Here are some the unique features of Christ's sacrifice:

- He was a tabernacle (temple) not made with hands.

- He did not need the blood of bulls and goats.

- He was a priest who offered Himself as the sacrifice.

- His sacrifice was once and for all.

- He offered Himself voluntarily.

- His blood cleansed the consciences of those who believed.

- His sacrifice set men free.

- His blood ushered in the new covenant.

III. A SUPERIOR POWER (10:19 – 13)

Hebrews ends with the most basic of messages for Christians going through hard times – it's all worth it!

The Danger of Leaving the Faith (10:19 – 39)

This final section begins with another warning (10:28-29, 31):

Anyone who rejected the law of Moses died without mercy on the testimony of two or three witnesses. How much more severely do you think a man deserves to be punished who has trampled the Son of God under foot, who has treated as an unholy thing the blood of the covenant that sanctified him, and who has insulted the Spirit of grace? ... It is a dreadful thing to fall into the hands of the living God.

This warning, though, is not without encouragement. In the light of such a warning, a call to persevere is given (10:22-25):

... let us draw near to God with a sincere heart in full assurance of faith. ... Let us hold unswervingly to the hope we profess, for He who promised is faithful. And let us consider how we may spur one another on toward love and good deeds. Let us not give up meeting together, as some are in the habit of doing, but let us encourage one another – and all the more as you see the Day approaching.

Demonstration of Living Faith (11)

The author of Hebrews gives a perspective of the people of God. The recipients of this letter might be going through hard times and even persecution, but they were not the first and they will not be the last.

What can be called the hall of fame of faith gives the perspective of the people of God who have lived through tough times and have always been marked by faith – trusting God before, during and after those tough times.

Abel, Enoch, Noah, Abraham, Isaac, Jacob, Joseph, Moses – are covered in some detail. Gideon, Barak, Samson, Jephthah, David, Samuel and the prophets are mentioned in passing. Then others are mentioned, not by name, but by their fate: Some faced jeers and flogging, while still others were chained and put in prison. They were stoned; they were sawed in two; they were put to death by the sword.

What marked every one of them was that they were willing to go through what they had to go through "by faith."

The definition of faith is found here (11:1):

Faith is being sure of what we hope for and certain of what we do not see.

In other words, faith is a confidence (being sure of) of things in the future that we know not, and a certainty of things in the present that we see not, and it all has to do with God. Because God exists and has promised, we can be confident and certain in faith.

A deeper look at faith is given in verse 6:

And without faith it is impossible to please God, because anyone who comes to Him must believe that He exists and that He rewards those who earnestly seek Him.

Discipline of a Loving Father (12)

Chapter 12 begins with an inspiring image: an athletic event with the stands filled with "witnesses" and we, as Christians, are the athletes about to compete (1b, 2):

… let us throw off everything that hinders and the sin that so easily entangles, and let us run with perseverance the race marked out for us. Let us fix our eyes on Jesus, the author and perfecter of our faith, who for the joy set before Him endured the cross, scorning its shame, and sat down at the right hand of the throne of God.

Another perspective is given regarding hard times. It might be the discipline of a loving heavenly Father. That is hard to accept because we usually think of hard times and difficulty as being only evil and of no benefit. But listen to these words (7, 8):

Endure hardship as discipline; God is treating you as sons. For what son is not disciplined by his father? If you are not disciplined (and everyone undergoes discipline), then you are illegitimate children [bastards] and not true sons.

And the thought continues (11):

No discipline seems pleasant at the time, but painful. Later on, however, it produces a harvest of righteousness and peace for those who have been trained by it.

The final warning of Hebrews is in 12:25-29. We must be careful not to refuse the Lord. Instead, we must revere Him (28, 29):

Therefore, since we are receiving a kingdom that cannot be shaken, let us be thankful, and so worship God acceptably with reverence and awe, for our "God is a consuming fire."

Dedication of an Alive Faith (13)

Hebrews concludes with general exhortations that will be evidence of a faith that is alive:

- Love one another.

- Honor marriage.

- Do not love money.

- Be content with what you have.

- Remember that God will never forsake you.

- Remember your leaders.

- Do not be carried away by strange teachings.

- Be strengthened by grace.

- Offer God a sacrifice of praise.

- Submit to authority.

- Keep watch over yourselves.

- Pray.

   In the midst of all these exhortations is the eternal truth (8):

   Jesus Christ is the same yesterday and today and forever.

   Hebrews ends with one of the great benedictions of the Bible (13:20, 21):

   May the God of peace, who through the blood of the eternal covenant brought back from the dead our Lord Jesus, that great Shepherd of the sheep, equip you with everything good for doing His will, and may He work in us what is pleasing to Him, through Jesus Christ, to whom be glory for ever and ever. Amen.

Lessons From Hebrews

1. Christ is better. This means that Christ is superior to the old covenant way of doing things that depended on sacrifices, priests and laws. He is superior to everyone else, no matter if they are angels or a great man like Moses. The word for "better" or "superior" occurs 12 times in Hebrews and it is always used to compare Christ with something or someone else. Every time, Christ ends up standing head and shoulders above them.

2. Christians are to be better. This means that those who follow Christ need to be more mature in their faith. We must not stay in one place. We must not settle for "elementary teaching." We must not settle for the status quo. We need to learn the truth and grow up in the faith. For this to take place, encouragement is of prime importance. "Let us …" is a constant refrain in Hebrews when Christians are encouraged to be all that God has called us to be in Christ.

NOTES

Chapter Forty-Seven: James

Assignment

READ ...

James, Chapters 1-5, or selected chapters from James throughout the week.

MEMORIZE ...

James 1:13: "When tempted, no one should say, 'God is tempting me.' For God cannot be tempted by evil, nor does He tempt anyone."

and/or

James 1:22: "Do not merely listen to the Word, and so deceive yourselves. Do what it says."

and/or

James 2:19: "You believe that there is one God. Good! Even the demons believe that – and shudder."

and/or

James 4:6: "God opposes the proud but gives grace to the humble."

and/or

James 5:16: "The prayer of a righteous man is powerful and effective."

PRAY ...

Asking the Lord to give you joy in the midst of your troubles and problems. Ask for the grace to persevere through your tough times and to mature in the faith.

About the sermons you have recently heard and think of what you need to do about what you heard. Be responsive to hearing the Word by doing what you have learned.

Confessing and repenting of the sins you have committed by saying something that hurt someone else. Ask for the Lord to help you with your tongue.

Humbling yourself before the Lord. Do away with the pride in your life and seek to be God's man or woman.

APPLY ...

In the light of James, what do you:

> BELIEVE about God?

> REPENT of as sin?

> OBEY as a command from God?

SHARE ...

According to what you have learned from James:

- Talk to your family about the tough times you have had together. Get each family member to reflect on when they hurt and needed relief. Get them to share about the lessons learned by going through those tough times. Then talk about tough times that might happen and how you should respond to them. Read James 1:2-8.

- Share with a friend about the tension in your Christian life from hearing a lot of sermons and lessons, but not always putting them into practice. Be humble as you share this and give an example of where you might be struggling right now in your faith. Simply share, and don't make a demand of your friend to do anything else but listen.

James:
Practical Christianity

INTRODUCTION

The Bible deals with two main themes: the way to God and the walk with God:

- One is written to unbelievers. The other is written to believers.

- One is to bring us to God. The other is to keep us with God.

- One is evangelistic. The other is educational.

- One leads to justification. The other leads to sanctification.

- One prepares us for eternity. The other prepares us for now.

James is about the walk with God, to force us to be authentic, genuine, real and practical.

James moves us from the profession of faith to the performance of faith, from assent to action, from words to works.

James is the Proverbs of the New Testament and is intensely practical.

THEME VERSE

> *... so faith without deeds is dead.*
> *James 2:17*

RECIPIENTS

James is a general epistle, which means that it was sent to a general audience. It was a circular letter passed on from church to church – Christian to Christian. A general epistle bears the name of the author, rather than the recipient. Paul's epistles were different. They were to a particular church or person and the titles told the recipients this.

The recipients of the Letter of James were Jews who had been dispersed abroad (1:1), "to the twelve tribes scattered among the nations." The diaspora was the dispersion of Jews throughout the Roman Empire and James was writing to them to pastorally help them to live the Christian life while separated from others.

AUTHOR

Four men are named James in the New Testament:

- James, the father of Judas (not Iscariot), one of the disciples, mentioned in Luke 6:16 and Acts 1:13. Not mentioned elsewhere.

- James, the son of Alphaeus, one of the disciples, mentioned in Matthew 10:3; Mark 3:18; Luke 6:15; and Acts 1:13. He is referred to only when he is included in a list with the other disciples. He does not appear again in the rest of the New Testament.

- James, the son of Zebedee, the brother of John, mentioned in Matthew 4:21; 10:2; 17:1; Mark 3:17; 10:35; 13:3; Luke 9:54; and Acts 1:13. He was one of Jesus' intimate disciples and was martyred (Acts 12:2).

- James, the Lord's brother, mentioned in Matthew 13:55; Mark 6:3; and Galatians 1:19. He was considered one of the "pillars" in the Church in Jerusalem (Acts 12:17; 15:13-21; 21:18; and Galatians 2:9, 12).

Traditionally, James, the Lord's half-brother, is understood to be the author of the Letter of James, and his mother was Mary.

Imagine the impact on James of being in Jesus' family. He put off faith in Christ until after the Resurrection. He was not an early disciple. It took some time. He was skeptical. He finally did believe and became a leader of the Church.

The way James wrote his epistle is as a skeptic. He didn't believe just because it is true. It must make a difference. It must be seen in changed lives. James looks deeper than what is said. He went to the level of life.

I. CHARACTER OF FAITH (1 – 2)

Stands Up Under Trials (1:1-12)

James was realistic in recognizing that trials and troubles are normal in the Christian life. They were not necessarily signs of sin or Satan over one's life. These trials served to strengthen faith. That was the reason he could write: "Consider it pure joy, my brothers, whenever you face trials of many kinds."

Faith shows its true colors in the middle of hard times. Anybody can believe when everything is going great. Only real faith will stand when things aren't so great.

Stands Up Before Temptations (1:13-18)

James also was realistic in recognizing that temptations are normal in the Christian life. Trials come from the outside. Temptations come from the inside (1:13-15):

When tempted, no one should say, "God is tempting me." For God cannot be tempted by evil, nor does He tempt anyone, but each one is tempted when, by his own evil desire, he is dragged away and enticed. Then, after desire has conceived, it gives birth to sin; and sin, when it is full-grown, gives birth to death.

Faith knows the truth about God and mankind, and the truth about mankind was not a pretty picture. It was very possible to believe what the Bible taught about who God was, but not to believe what the Bible taught about mankind.

Stands Up for the Word (1:19-27)

Just sitting in a pew and listening to a sermon does not make one a Christian. Hearing the truth is always the prelude to doing the truth. Hearing the truth and never doing the truth, however, is damaging to one's spiritual life.

James put it this way in 1:22:

Do not merely listen to the Word, and so deceive yourselves. Do what it says.

This was where James' practical religion is at its best. The faith never was meant to be only something preached, talked about or shared. The faith ultimately has its import only when it is lived out and obeyed.

James, in 1:27, spoke of "pure religion" as something that was recognizable in deeds:

Religion that God our Father accepts as pure and faultless is this: to look after orphans and widows in their distress and to keep oneself from being polluted by the world.

True religion (true faith) was not just listening, but doing.

Stands Up Against Favoritism (2:1-13)

True faith will show itself in how it tangibly loves others. He spoke of a situation in the Church when a rich man was favored over a poor man. James said real faith will not do that (2:5, 6):

Listen, my dear brothers: Has not God chosen those who are poor in the eyes of the world to be rich in faith and to inherit the kingdom He promised those who love Him? But you have insulted the poor.

Be merciful; not judgmental (2:13).

Stands Out by Works (2:14-26)

Martin Luther called James an "epistle of straw," mainly because of Luther's emphasis on grace and faith apart from works. James' contribution is to stress the place of works in our faith. James emphasized a faith that works, deeds that demonstrate faith, belief that behaves.

In Romans 4, Paul used the example of Abraham to show that justification is by faith, not by works. James, though, said Abraham was justified by works (2:21). In spite of the apparent contradiction, Romans 4 and James 2 really are two sides of the same coin. In context, Paul was writing about justification before God while James was writing of the evidence of justification before men. While God knows the heart, men need an external manifestation of the heart's attitude to know the difference between profession and reality. A faith that produces no change is not saving faith.

II. CONTROL OF FAITH (3)

The Tongue (3:1-12)

Talk about practical faith! What about the words we speak? Gossip? Criticism? Blame? Slander? Judgment? Lies? Bragging? Complaints? Rumors? Disapproval? Condemnation?

A genuine faith controls the tongue. The tongue is small, like a bit, a rudder or a spark, but it can control larger objects and cause enormous damage. In 3:9, 10, James wrote:

With the tongue we praise our Lord and Father, and with it we curse men, who have been made in God's likeness. Out of the same mouth come praise and cursing. My brother, this should not be.

Wisdom (3:13-18)

James, as the Proverbs of the New Testament, supremely is shown in his teaching about wisdom. There are two kinds of wisdom: One that does not come from heaven (3:14-16) and one that comes from heaven (3:17, 18).

● Earthly wisdom is marked by "envy and selfish ambition."

● Heavenly wisdom is "… pure, peace loving, considerate, submissive, full of mercy and good fruit, impartial and sincere" (3:17).

III. CONFLICTS OF FAITH (4:1 – 5:6)

Worldiness (4:1-12)

The pursuit of pleasure and selfishness produces fighting, envy and enmity with God. This is made clear when James wrote: "God opposes the proud but gives grace to the humble" (4:6) and "Humble yourselves before the Lord, and He will lift you up" (4:10).

The world will always be self-centered, and this leads to strife, fights and war. The call of real faith is to submit to God, humility before God and living for God.

Wealth (4:13 – 5:6)

James confronted the wealthy with two evils inherent in their riches:

- The wealthy can think they are in control. Just doing business can lead to a life lived as if God did not exist or He is irrelevant.

- The wealthy can oppress others. Some of the strongest words against the wealthy are given in this passage, but it is because the wealthy have gotten their wealth off the backs of others and have been unfair to them.

Basically, the warning is that wealth can lead to pride and injustice.

IV. CONSUMMATION OF FAITH (5:7-20)

Patience (5:7-12)

One of the most practical parts of the Christian life is patience. When things are going well, there is a temptation not to trust God. It is in the face of suffering, however, that real faith will show itself as patience.

In this section, James refers to Job. Job is remembered as an example of patience. He suffered and he persevered through that suffering to the blessings of God. That time of persevering through suffering was patience. Patience leads to the blessing of God.

Prayer (5:13-20)

Just as patience is an evidence of faith, so is prayer.

James wrote about the "prayer offered in faith," which is a way to describe all godly prayer. Prayer was offered to God and there is a dependence upon God for the outcome. That is faith. It is trusting God with the situations of life.

James referred to several situations of life in this passage: being in trouble, happy, sick and guilty of sin. In each situation, prayer is appropriate. A special kind of prayer in calling for the elders is referred to here.

The main thrust of this passage, however, is to teach about the power of prayer (16):

The prayer of a righteous man is powerful and effective.

So, James called for the practical Christian life where faith is obvious and lives and lips show it.

Lessons From James

1. The Christian life stands up under all pressure.

2. The Christian life grows up with good deeds.

NOTES

CHAPTER FORTY-EIGHT: I PETER

Assignment

READ ...

I Peter, Chapters 1-5, or selected chapters from I Peter throughout the week.

MEMORIZE ...

I Peter 1:8: "Though you have not seen Him, you love Him; and even though you do not see Him now, you believe in Him and are filled with an inexpressible and glorious joy."

and/or

I Peter 2:2: "Like newborn babies, crave pure spiritual milk, so that by it you may grow up in your salvation."

and/or

I Peter 4:12, 13: "Dear friends, do not be surprised at the painful trial you are suffering, as though something strange were happening to you. But rejoice that you participate in the sufferings of Christ, so that you may be overjoyed when His glory is revealed."

PRAY ...

Being honest with the Lord about where you hurt right now. Realize the closeness of the Lord in your pain.

Asking the Lord to give you joy in all the circumstances of your life, even when the pain is real and the hurt is lingering.

Desiring to grow and mature in the faith.

APPLY ...

In the light of I Peter, what do you:

> BELIEVE about God?
>
> REPENT of as sin?
>
> OBEY as a command from God?

SHARE ...

According to what you have learned from I Peter:

- Have a conversation with someone in the Church about the hurt they might have had in their lives. Maybe it is a hurt you know about or maybe it is just knowing that everyone is hurting in one way or another. Be transparent about your own hurt and struggles, and share about how the Lord has been faithful to you in your hurt. Then pray with your Christian friend for grace to go through difficult times.

- Go visit someone not in the Church who you know has had a difficult time in their lives. Maybe take a meal or a gift, but go spend time with them simply because you care. Don't preach, don't judge; simply love, listen, share and pray.

I Peter:
The Job of the New Testament

INTRODUCTION

If the Epistle of James is the Proverbs of the New Testament, Peter's First Epistle is the Job of the New Testament.

I Peter is a book on pain, persecution and suffering, and it provides hope in such extreme situations.

Years ago, Scott Peck wrote a book that received wide acceptance, including many Christians, even though Peck was not a Christian. The book was *The Road Less Traveled*. Its thesis is that "the road less traveled" is the road we naturally do not choose to travel – it is the road of pain, suffering and trial. Instead, we choose the roads of pleasure, comfort and acceptance.

The truth, however, is that the road of pain, suffering and trial teaches us the greatest lessons of life – although we never would choose it for ourselves.

Like the Book of Job, I Peter presents a dual perspective that is confusing:

- Pain is often undeserved suffering, and we agonize over the question "Why?"

- Power in submission to the sovereignty of God in the midst of suffering, and we realize "Why."

THEME VERSE

To this you were called, because Christ suffered for you,
leaving you an example, that you should follow in His steps.
I Peter 2:21

I Peter was written to Christians throughout Asia Minor who were suffering persecution, probably under Nero. Nero fostered many lies about Christians that caused the Roman Empire to be suspicious of them. Some of the lies propounded by Nero about Christians were:

- Cannibalism: Christians were called cannibals because they had a ceremony where they ate flesh and drank blood. That ceremony, of course, is The Lord's Supper.

- The burning of Rome: Even though there is evidence that Nero started the fire that burned Rome because he wanted to rebuild parts of the city to his own glory, Christians were blamed for it because they would preach about a judgment of fire.

- The destruction of the family: Christians were accused of destroying family relationships because they taught a higher allegiance to Jesus over the family. This was terribly foreign to the Romans, where the father of the family had supreme power – even the power to kill his own children.

Author

There is no doubt. The author of I Peter was Peter the Apostle. He did not have a close relationship with these churches, as Paul had with his churches, but Peter had a great interest in spreading the Gospel to the Gentiles, and he wrote a general epistle to help with as many churches as he could.

One evidence of Peter's authorship is the high level of authoritativeness in the epistle. There are 34 imperatives – commands. Peter was leading and stepping out in front, as he always did.

I. Salvation (1:1 – 2:10)

I Peter begins with a strong salutation identifying Peter as the writer, and the Triune God as the author of salvation. God the Father chose us. God the Holy Spirit sanctified us. God the Son is the One we follow and obey.

Our Salvation Is Secure (1:3-12)

Because salvation is based in the actions of the Triune God, Peter can speak of salvation being secure (1:3-12).

Our salvation is secure in the future because of our "living hope." Hope is not "wishful thinking" – it is a certainty. Our hope is sure. This future hope includes an inheritance that will not fade – heaven that is kept for God's people and the Second Coming when everything will become clear to everyone.

Our salvation also is secure in the present. Now, this didn't make sense to the readers of this letter because, for them, the present was not pleasant. They were suffering:

> … for a little while you may have had to suffer grief in all kinds of trials.

Peter then pointed out to them that their faith, love and joy were evidence that they were distinctive in their faith, even though they were going through difficult times.

Our salvation has been secure from the past. Peter spoke of the prophets of old who told about this salvation that is experienced and enjoyed now. In other words, Peter wanted his readers to know that they were standing on the shoulders of faithful men from the past, who longed to see and hear what they were seeing and hearing.

Our Salvation Leads to Sanctification (1:13 – 2:10)

Peter gives command after command to those who are saved. Salvation not only is to be secure in heaven one day, but is to produce holiness right now. The children of God are to live like the children of God. We are to be holy because God is holy – like Father, like children:

- God the Father is our judge, so we must live in "reverent fear."

- The precious blood of Christ has redeemed us, so we are to live by faith in Him.

- We have been born again, so we must show it in our lives.

> Therefore, rid yourselves of all malice and all deceit, hypocrisy, envy and slander of every kind. Like newborn babies, crave pure spiritual milk, so that by it you may grow up in your salvation, now that you have tasted that the Lord is good. (2:1-3)

The motivation of being holy is knowing who we are as Christians (2:9, 10):

> But you are a chosen people, a royal priesthood, a holy nation, a people belonging to God, that you may declare the praises of Him who called you out of darkness into His wonderful light. Once you were not a people, but now you are the people of God; once you had not received mercy, but now you have received mercy.

II. Submission (2:11 – 3:12)

Peter focused on all God has done in salvation and on the greatness of salvation. He then instructed about the believers' relationships in the world. Peter called for two things that are liked the least: submission and suffering.

We are to be submissive for the Lord's sake in the government (2:13-17), in society (2:18-21) and in the family (3:1-7). This submission is to be Christlike in that we do not seek our own will. We are to recognize that where we are in our relationships is a working of God's providence, and the government, our place in society and our family are not for our selfish desires. In a real sense, they are there to curb our selfish ways.

We also are to be ready to suffer, as seen in our theme verse (2:21):

To this you were called, because Christ suffered for you, leaving you an example that you should follow in His steps.

III. Suffering (3:13 – 5:14)

Suffering by believers must be for righteousness sake, not as a result of sinful behavior. As a matter of fact, Peter says this three times (3:17, 4:15, 4:16) to make it clear that we are to suffer like Christ, who was innocent on every count, but suffered immensely.

Peter presented three simple steps to follow when suffering:

- Avoid sin and live for God (4:1-6). We are to be so focused on God that it puts our suffering in the context of God's fatherly care.

- Avoid sin and love one another (4:7-11). Even when we hurt, we are not to be self-consumed. Our call to love one another still stands in the midst of pain.

- Avoid sin and don't be surprised by suffering (4:12-19): "Dear friends, do not be surprised at the painful trial you are suffering, as though something strange were happening to you." Suffering is part of the normal Christian life.

Right in the middle of all this teaching about suffering, Peter gives one of the strangest passages in all of Scripture – 3:18-22. Some people even call this the most difficult text to interpret in the whole New Testament. Many people think that Jesus' preaching to the spirits in prison is what is meant by "he descended into hell" in the Apostles' Creed, but this is too obscure a passage on which to make a major doctrine.

I Peter ended with instructions to believers (5:1-13) that are very practical and personal. Words are directed to elders (5:1-4) and to young men (5:5-9). Peter then provided final greetings.

Lessons From I Peter

1. In the midst of suffering, know that you always have hope. This hope is found not in the terrible conditions of the current situation, but in the gracious acts of Jesus Christ in the middle of the pain. Suffering offers a closeness to Christ that no other experience in the Christian's life offers.

2. In the midst of suffering, live the life of faith. Hard times are never excuses for unrighteousness. They become opportunities to obey and believe when there is no other place to turn. We must never be surprised by suffering, but we also must never turn to sin in suffering.

NOTES

CHAPTER FORTY-NINE: II PETER AND JUDE

Assignment

READ ...

II Peter, Chapters 1-3, and Jude, or selected chapters from II Peter and Jude throughout the week.

MEMORIZE ...

II Peter 3:8, 9: "But do not forget this one thing, dear friends: With the Lord a day is like a thousand years, and a thousand years are like a day. The Lord is not slow in keeping His promise, as some understand slowness. He is patient with you, not wanting anyone to perish, but everyone to come to repentance."

and/or

II Peter 1:20, 21: "Above all, you must understand that no prophecy of Scripture came about by the prophet's own interpretation. For prophecy never had its origin in the will of man, but men spoke from God as they were carried along by the Holy Spirit."

and/or

Jude 3: "I felt I had to write and urge you to contend for the faith that was once for all entrusted to the saints."

PRAY ...

Thanking the Lord for His Word. Scripture has been given so that we might know the will of God and be able to follow the truth.

For the Lord's strength to stand for the truth. Ask for the wisdom to know the faith and then ask for the strength to be faithful to that faith.

For the Church universal, where there might be false teachings. Ask for the Lord's mercy and grace when the Church is in danger of false teachers.

APPLY ...

In the light of II Peter and Jude, what do you:

>   BELIEVE about God?

>   REPENT of as sin?

>   OBEY as a command from God?

SHARE ...

According to what you have learned from II Peter and Jude:

- Get the family together and read through the Apostles' Creed. This simple summary of the faith can help to pinpoint the most essential truths from Scripture about the Triune God. Discuss how one can stand for the truth of the faith in the light of opposition or unbelief from someone else, either in the Church or in the culture.

- Have a conversation with a friend about heresy. Ask your friend if he has ever heard a "false teaching" and discuss why something in the Church can be called "false" or "heretical."

II Peter and Jude:
Apostates and Apologetics

INTRODUCTION

There are some books of the Bible that have similar messages:

- The four Gospels – the life of Christ.

- The prison epistles – Ephesians, Philippians and Colossians.

- The pastoral epistles – I and II Timothy and Titus.

II Peter and Jude share the same message. As a matter of fact, there is a scholarly debate about whether Jude had II Peter in front of him when he wrote, or whether Peter had Jude in front of him when he wrote. They are that similar. These two books have a dual purpose:

1. To be aware of apostates – those who had left the true faith and were teaching false doctrine and were still in the Church (II Peter 2:1 and Jude 4).

2. To call to apologetics – this is not "apologizing" for the faith, but defending the faith (Jude 3).

THEME VERSES

But there were also false prophets among the people, just as there will be false teachers among you.
II Peter 2:1

... appealing that you contend earnestly for the faith which was once for all delivered to the saints.
Jude 3

Since both II Peter and Jude confront the issue of false teachers in the Church, the walk through these epistles will be done by pointing out the truths highlighted about false teachers. The characteristics of false teachers will be listed, along with the antidote to be applied to confront false teachers.

CHARACTERISTICS OF FALSE TEACHERS

With each one of these observations about false teachers, I want to give the antidote, which is a medicine for counteracting the effects of poison or disease. False teachings in the Church never leave us defenseless. The reality of false teachings calls us to Biblical responses.

- *False teachers are more interested in personal gain than telling the truth* (II Peter 2:1-3).

  Antidote: The way to fight false teachers is with the truth of Scripture (II Peter 1:20, 21). Jude puts the same truth this way: "Contend for the faith once for all delivered to the saints" (Jude 3). The "faith" Jude refers to is not the verb "to believe," but the noun referring to a body of truth or, specifically, the Biblical apostolic faith.

  The first line of attack against false teachings in the Church is for us to be Biblical. Preach the Word. Teach the Word. Proclaim the truth.

- *False teachers are interested in getting more than in giving.*

  Jude 12: "they feed only themselves;" and Jude 16: "for their own advantage."

  Antidote: II Peter 1:5-7: "For this very reason, make every effort to add to your faith goodness; and to goodness, knowledge; and to knowledge, self-control; and to self-control, perseverance; and to perseverance, godliness; and to godliness, brotherly kindness; and to brotherly kindness, love."

  We are to give ourselves to God. The most important thing to do in the light of false teachers getting money, power, influence and attention in the Church is for us to give ourselves to God.

- *False teachers' personal lives are marked by immorality.*

  II Peter 2:13, 14: "Their idea of pleasure is to carouse in broad daylight. They are blots and blemishes, reveling in their pleasures while they feast with you. With eyes full of adultery, they never stop sinning; they seduce the unstable; they are experts in greed – an accursed brood."

  Jude 4b: "… who change the grace of our God into a license for immorality. …"

  Antidote: II Peter 3:18: "… but grow in the grace and knowledge of our Lord and Savior Jesus Christ."

  Jude 20a: "… build yourselves up in your most holy faith."

  Let them follow their sinful desires. Let us be sure we do not. We are called to holiness and righteousness.

- *False teachers lead people away from God, rather than closer to God. They are blasphemous – anti-God.*

  II Peter 2:10b-12a: "Bold and arrogant, these men are not afraid to slander celestial beings; yet even angels, although they are stronger and more powerful, do not bring slanderous accusations against such beings in the presence of the Lord. But these men blaspheme in matters they do not understand."

  Antidote: Jude 21: "Keep yourselves in God's love. …"

  II Peter 1:10, 11: "Therefore, my brothers, be all the more eager to make your calling and election sure. For if you do these things, you will never fall, and you will receive a rich welcome into the eternal kingdom of our Lord and Savior Jesus Christ."

So, what is to be done as believers in the light of false teachers? Generally, it is a call to be faithful and persevere (II Peter 1:3, 4). Specifically, Jude gives three commands in Jude 17-23:

- Remember (17-19).

  Remember the truth of Scripture.

  Remember the prophecies of Scripture that recall the truth that false teachers always have been with God's people and always will be with God's people. It even will intensify in the last days.

  Remember the unity of the Church. Do not let them divide the Church.

  Remember who have the Spirit of God.

- Remain (20, 21).

  Build yourselves up in your most holy faith; grow and mature.

  Pray in the Holy Spirit, which is a reference to true prayer. Do not just utter words toward the ceiling. Really communicate with God as the Spirit leads in one's prayer life.

  Keep yourselves in God's love. God's love should be the truth one clings to no matter what else happens.

Waiting for God to take us to heaven and to judge the false teachers (Jude 14, 15 and II Peter 3:4-9).

- Reach out (22, 23).

Have mercy on some. Have pity on some who may not be false teachers, but victims of false teachers. They are doubters.

Be careful of blanket judgments. It is very easy to be so upset with un-Biblical behavior and teaching that one loses sight of showing mercy in some cases.

Save others – evangelism within the Church. Hate the sin, but love the sinner. This is dangerous business: "… show mercy, mixed with fear – hating even the clothing stained by corrupt flesh."

Lessons From II Peter and Jude

1. There will be opposition to the truth. The existence of false teachers has been a constant in the history of the Church. It never should come as a surprise that there are men who twist and tear the truth of God for their own advantage and pleasure.

2. There always is a need to stand for the truth. The godly call in the face of false teachings is to stand and be faithful. The temptation is to overlook the false teachings or to run from them. Contending for the faith is a call for the Christian.

NOTES

CHAPTER FIFTY: I, II AND III JOHN

Assignment

READ ...

I John, Chapters 1-5, II John and III John, or selected chapters from I, II and III John throughout the week.

MEMORIZE ...

I John 1:9, 10: "If we confess our sins, He is faithful and just and will forgive us our sins and purify us from all our righteousness. If we claim we have not sinned, we make Him out to be a liar and His word has no place in our lives."

and/or

I John 2:1, 2: "But if anybody does sin, we have one who speaks to the Father in our defense – Jesus Christ, the Righteous One. He is the atoning sacrifice for our sins, and not only for ours but also for the sins of the whole world."

and/or

I John 3:16: "This is how we know what love is: Jesus Christ laid down His life for us. And we ought to lay down our lives for our brothers."

and/or

I John 4:16: "And so we know and rely on the love God has for us. God is love. Whoever lives in love lives in God, and God in him.

PRAY ...

Confessing your sin to the Lord. Know that He always is ready to forgive and to give us a new beginning.

Asking for the love of God to be shown through your life. I John is clear in teaching that, if we have experienced the love of God for us in Jesus Christ, that will be clear in our love for one another.

For the Lord to increase your love and faith.

For 10 members of your congregation. Pray by name for members you have not thought of in a while.

APPLY ...

In the light of I, II and III John, what do you:

> BELIEVE about God?
>
> REPENT of as sin?
>
> OBEY as a command from God?

SHARE ...

According to what you have learned from I, II and III John:

- Think about how faithful you are in loving others. Evaluate every area of your life (i.e., your congregation, family, neighborhood, school, work, etc.) and ask yourself if you have loved others like Christ has loved you. Have a conversation with your family about how as a family, you can more faithfully show a love for others.

- Have a conversation with someone you know, whether a member of a congregation or not, and ask them about a situation they know of where real love was shown toward someone in great need. Then continue to talk about how love is so needed in our lives and how central it is to anyone who claims to follow Christ.

I John:
Fellowship With God

INTRODUCTION

I John was written to believers in several congregations as a general epistle and it appears that these congregations were well-established in the faith. John writes to them as being mature in the faith. He writes several times that they have been faithful from "the beginning," and he was not writing anything new; he simply wanted to encourage them in the faith.

There is no persecution mentioned in the epistle, but false teachings and the antichrist are mentioned. The main heresy at the time of John was Gnosticism, which was the belief that "secret knowledge" was necessary to know in order to be saved. This "secret knowledge" did not believe in the Incarnation, because Gnostics believed that matter was evil, so it was impossible for God to become flesh. Since they held to a "secret knowledge" above all other matters of the faith, they formed a kind of spiritual elite who thought they could put aside the normal distinctions of right and wrong and thereby disregard Christian ethics.

THEME VERSE

What we have seen and heard we proclaim to you also, that you also may have fellowship with us; and indeed our fellowship is with the Father, and with His Son Jesus Christ.
I John 1:3

AUTHOR

John, the beloved disciple, the brother of James, the author of the Gospel of John and the Book of Revelation, was the author of these epistles.

John probably wrote them while in Ephesus, after the writing of the Gospel and before the writing of Revelation.

John, true to his nature as the "beloved disciple," showed great affection for the recipients of the letter, as he frequently used the terms "beloved" and "my little children."

John was elderly when he wrote the epistles and at that time may have been the only living member of the twelve.

I. THE MEANING OF FELLOWSHIP (1:1 – 2:27)

The prologue of I John (1:1-4) jumps immediately into the theme of "fellowship." John states that the beginning of fellowship was with the apostles' experience, that the fellowship can be shared by all who believe, and that the nature of the fellowship is with Christ Himself. John emphasizes the audio (hearing) and video (seeing) aspects of this fellowship, which stresses the concrete nature of Christian fellowship – it is with one another, which is the common understanding of "fellowship" but, supremely, it is with Jesus Christ, which is the uncommon understanding of "fellowship."

Prerequisites of Fellowship (1:5 – 2:2)

Fellowship with Jesus Christ, though, does not happen in a void. There are conditions or prerequisites for it. John provides two "if" statements to give those conditions:

If we claim to have fellowship with Him yet walk in the darkness, we lie and do not live by the truth (1:6).

If we claim we have not sinned, we make Him out to be a liar, and His Word has no place in our lives (1:10).

The two prerequisites of fellowship are:

1. Obedience: This is "walking in the light" as opposed to "walking in the darkness."

2. Confession: This is admitting that we are not perfect in our obedience.

These two balanced truths are crucial to our Christian walk and fellowship. We are to strive to obey the Lord – it is the passion of our lives; but, at the same time, we are to admit that we still sin – it is the pathos of our lives.

This must be seen as opposing the Gnostic understanding that Christian morality was not important. The Gnostics believed that if you had the "secret knowledge," then everything else didn't matter. If you knew the secret, you could do whatever you wanted. John confronts that head-on by declaring that we must "walk in the light," but when we sin, we have an advocate in Jesus Christ.

Products of Fellowship (2:3-11)

Fellowship is not just a relationship with someone or something we do, it also produces something in our lives. Fellowship is a "means of grace" that leads to more virtues in our lives.

John highlights two products of fellowship in our lives:

*   Obedience: Notice that obedience is a prerequisite and a product of fellowship (6): "Whoever claims to live in Him must walk as Jesus did."

*   Love: We are not to hate, but to love. John will develop the product of love in our lives in greater detail in the rest of the epistle.

Perils of Fellowship (2:12-27)

There are some perils, however, that must be recognized for those in the fellowship. John names two:

*   The world (2:15-17). This is a peril that is external to the Church. The Church must understand itself as being in enemy territory in order to survive. John could not be plainer when he wrote, "Do not love the world or anything in the world" (2:15).

*   False teaching (2:18-27). This is a peril that is internal to the Church. Not only is the Church in enemy territory, but there are spies in the land. There are some people in the Church who are against the Church.

John mentions the "antichrist" in this section, making two important distinctions:

1. "The antichrist is coming." John upholds the other accounts in Scripture that teach about a particularly evil individual at the end of time.

2.   "Many antichrists have come." John, though, makes an important observation, which Paul also made in II Thessalonians, that even though the antichrist will come at the end of time, we must beware of those who are "anti-Christ" – that is, against Christ – who are in the Church and in the world today. In particular, John was speaking about the false teachers in the Church.

II. THE MANIFESTATIONS OF FELLOWSHIP (2:28 – 4:21)

Fellowship with Jesus Christ will show itself in several obvious and powerful ways:

- Who we are as children of God will be clear. We will not live for sin any longer (2:28 – 3:10a).

- What we do in loving one another will be constant. The doing of good deeds will be shown principally in loving one another. Verses 3:10b-23 is one of the most powerful passages in Scripture on loving one another. We know what love is because of Jesus' love when He laid down His life for us. We are to love in the same way:

  Dear children, let us not love with words or tongue but with actions and in truth (18).

- How we live by the Holy Spirit will be correct (4:1-6). There are many spiritual dynamics in the world, but we must be wise in testing the spirits to know what is true. The primary test has to do with Jesus Christ and this is the main evidence of the Holy Spirit – Jesus Christ will be believed as coming in the flesh. The presence of the Spirit also is powerful in the Christian: "because the one who is in you is greater than the one who is in the world" (4:4).

- Why we love is crucial (4:7-21). "This is love: not that we loved God, but that He loved us and sent His Son as an atoning sacrifice for our sins. Dear friends, since God so loved us, we also ought to love one another No one has ever seen God; but if we love one another, God lives in us and His love is made complete in us" (10-12). The great equation is given: "God is love" (4:16).

- When we live for God, faith is central (5:1-12). John – whether in his Gospel, Epistles or the Book of Revelation – profusely spoke about love, faith and obedience. All three come together in this last chapter (1-3):

  Everyone who believes that Jesus is the Christ is born of God, and everyone who loves the father loves his child as well. This is how we know that we love the children of God: by loving God and carrying out His commands. This is love for God: to obey His commands.

  The value of faith is stated clearly when he writes (5:4):

  This is the victory that has overcome the world, even our faith.

  The object of our faith obviously is Jesus Christ and it is through Jesus Christ that we have life (5:12):

  He who has the Son has life; he who does not have the Son of God does not have life.

III. EPILOGUE (5:18-21)

John's concluding remarks are not as personal as Paul's. He mentions no names, gives no greetings, expresses no thanks. He simply continues to encourage and give guidance. John really is like a grandfather talking to his grandchildren.

One of the most encouraging things he gives at the end of his epistle (5:14, 15) is about prayer:

This is the confidence we have in approaching God: that if we ask anything according to His will, He hears us. And if we know that He hears us – whatever we ask – we know that we have what we asked of Him.

John then ends his first epistle with a powerful, yet strange exhortation (5:21):

Dear children, keep yourselves from idols.

This might be the most basic admonition for us as Christians. We are to follow the one true God, not any other god.

II John and III John:
The Balance of
Love and Truth

THEME VERSES

Anyone who runs ahead and does not continue in the teaching of Christ does not have God;
whoever continues in the teaching has both the Father and the Son.
II John 9

I have no greater joy than to hear that my children are walking in the truth.
III John 4

RELATIONSHIP TO EACH OTHER

All three epistles deal with fellowship:

- I John – fellowship with God.

- II John – fellowship with the enemies of the truth.

- III John – fellowship with the proclaimers of the truth.

There are some central themes common with II John and III John:

- The word "love" appears four times in II John; two times (four times "beloved") in III John.

- The word "truth" appears five times in II John and six times in III John.

- The words "walking in the truth" appears four times in II John and four times in III John.

BACKGROUND

The situation with itinerant preachers, both true and false teachers, is the background for II and III John. The Church was in a state of flux. Persecution was hitting it hard and it often lacked leadership. The Church depended on men traveling from one congregation to another to help with the ministry. This was the kind of ministry that Paul had, and it continued for many years after him. The Church during this time depended on an itinerant ministry.

II John basically warns against hospitality to false teachers, while III John commends hospitality to true teachers.

A balance of love and truth is called for in both II John and III John. One writer puts it this way: "Truth without love produces autocratic severity, but love without truth leads to blind sentimentality."

The people were encouraged to show loving hospitality to those who taught the truth, but not to those who did not teach the truth.

II John

Abide (1-6)

Abiding in the truth is encouraged. "Truth" is mentioned four times in the first three verses. John addresses "the chosen lady and her children," which probably refers to a local house church that was meeting in the home of a lady John knew.

This walking in the truth involves obedience to God's commandments and loving one another, a very common combination for John.

Avoid (7-13)

There are two things to hold in balance: basic Christian behavior (love) and basic Christian belief (truth, specifically the truth about Christ).

John warns the people about false teachers who deceive, "who do not acknowledge Jesus Christ as coming in the flesh." In other words, these false teachers were Gnostics who held to salvation by some "secret knowledge" and not through Christ alone.

John tells the people not to give the slightest assistance or encouragement to such teachers (10, 11).

III John

Commendation of Gaius (1-8)

In III John, John names names. None of this "chosen lady" and "children" stuff, no generics here, only specifics. He commends a behavior that gave him "great joy."

The source of this joy came from a man named Gaius, who held onto the truth. Gaius' traits were faithfulness, love and generosity (3). John encourages Gaius to continue supporting traveling preachers and missionaries who go out "for the sake of the Name" (5-8).

Condemnation of Diotrephes (9-14)

The positive tone of the letter then suddenly turns negative. John describes a man, Diotrephes, who is just the opposite of Gaius. Remember, they both are in the Church. Imagine the dynamics.

Diotrephes rejected John's apostolic authority and refused to receive the faithful itinerant teachers. He had the attitude where he "loved to be first;" the word used here refers to the place of preeminence reserved only for Christ in the rest of the New Testament (Colossians 1:18). Diotrephes was not condemned for his orthodoxy (believing the right thing), but for his orthopraxy (doing the right thing).

John also gives a full recommendation to a third man, Demetrius, who probably is the one who delivered the letter.

Lessons From I, II and III John

1. Our Christian walk never is alone. We have been called into a fellowship with God through Jesus Christ and with other believers. This sharing of a spiritual life together is the source of maturity and love.

2. Our Christian walk never is aloof. We are not called to be distant or in discord with one another. Love is to be the dominant characteristic of our lives as we follow the example of Jesus Christ.

NOTES

CHAPTER FIFTY-ONE: REVELATION

Assignment

READ ...

Revelation, Chapters 1-22, or selected chapters from Revelations, one each day throughout the week as follows:

Revelation 1   –   The setting for Revelation.

Revelation 2   –   Letters to four churches.

Revelation 3   –   Letters to three churches.

Revelation 4   –   The throne in heaven.

Revelation 7   –   The great multitude.

Revelation 19 –   Praise for the victory.

Revelation 22 –   Jesus is coming.

MEMORIZE ...

Revelation 1:17b, 18: "Do not be afraid. I am the First and the Last. I am the Living One; I was dead, and behold I am alive for ever and ever! And I hold the keys of death and Hades."

and/or

Revelation 3:20: "Here I am! I stand at the door and knock. If anyone hears my voice and opens the door, I will come in and eat with him, and he with me."

and/or

Revelation 4:11: "You are worthy, our Lord and God, to receive glory and honor and power, for you created all things, and by your will they were created and have their being."

PRAY ...

Praising Jesus Christ for who He is. Praise Him as the one who is the Alpha and the Omega, the beginning and the end.

For your local congregation. The seven letters to the seven churches demonstrates the Lord's personal relationship with each congregation. Ask Him to work directly and personally with us.

For the wisdom to see good and evil for what they really are.

Asking for the patience and power to live between now and the time that the Lord will return.

APPLY ...

In the light of Revelation, what do you:

> BELIEVE about God?
>
> REPENT of as sin?
>
> OBEY as a command from God?

SHARE ...

According to what you have learned from Revelation:

- Have a conversation with your family about loved ones who have passed on to glory. Remember and honor them by sharing their unique contributions to you and your family, but then talk about the glory that is theirs by their hope of heaven. Jesus' coming again should give us all hope to go through the trials of our lives.

- Talk with someone about your reading of the Book of Revelation and simply wait for their response. Let their response lead you to share some truths that you learned from Revelation, and encourage them to know that the future is in the Lord's hands.

Revelation: Jesus Christ Without Costume

THEME VERSE

Blessed is the one who reads the words of this prophecy,
and blessed are those who hear it and take to heart
what is written in it, because the time is near.
Revelation 1:3

AUTHOR

The author is John – the apostle, the beloved disciple, the brother of James, the author of the Gospel of John and the Epistles of John. He identifies himself four times in Revelation as the author (1:1, 4, 9; 22:8).

John is writing at a time of persecution for Christians. There were two major periods of the persecution of Christians in the latter half of the first century: Under Nero (A.D. 54-68) and under Domitian (A.D. 81-96). Most scholars place the date of Revelation as under Domitian around A.D. 95.

John was the last living apostle. In A.D. 94, he was pastoring the Church in Ephesus. This was 60 years after the Crucifixion and Resurrection of Jesus, and John was probably more than 90 years old. There still, however, was some fire in his bones. He preached against the emperor, was arrested and, probably because of his age, was exiled to the island of Patmos, rather than executed.

PURPOSE

Revelation was written to give encouragement to churches that were going through persecution. In order to do that, John writes in a unique style, apocalyptic, which is highly symbolic. It is a style that takes the reader into realms of truth that are inexpressible by normal, prepositional statements. The apocalyptic style was never meant to be mysterious or speculative. It was meant to emphasize truths beyond the current situation. Apocalyptic writing was designed to give hope for the future, when the present was painful. It raises one above the realities of the present toward the realities of the future.

The way this purpose is presented by John, though, is to give a clear view of Jesus Christ. Revelation is not a book that primarily reveals the future. It is a book that primarily reveals Jesus Christ. It is all about His power, grace, presence and His churches. It is all about His worship, work and victory. It is all about His enemies, His coming again, His judgment and His eternal reign.

Make no mistake about it, Revelation is a revelation of Jesus Christ.

In this book, we will see Jesus Christ "without costume." Revelation 1:1:

"The revelation of Jesus Christ. ..."

The very first words give us the purpose of this last book of the Bible. "The revelation of Jesus Christ" means that the revelation (apocalypse) comes from Jesus and is about Jesus. He is the author and the subject and it is all about Him. This is the key lost in most approaches to Revelation.

If the reading of Revelation does not help you see beyond the Jesus of the Gospels (that is Jesus "in costume," in the flesh) so that you see Jesus without costume, then you have not studied the book correctly. It is not primarily about John or the Church or the antichrist or the tribulation or the millennium or Judgment Day or the end of the world or heaven. It is about Jesus, who is in control of all of those things, and they all will bring glory to Him.

Revelation is written to enhance our worship of God focused on Jesus Christ.

DIFFERENT INTERPRETATIONS

Because apocalyptic literature uses symbols and visions, the key is the interpretations of them. What do they mean? There are more than 300 symbols in Revelation so, if you don't know what they mean, the meaning of Revelation will remain a mystery.

There are four different perspectives in how to interpret Revelation. Whatever perspective you take will affect how you interpret the book:

- Preterist: Everything in Revelation happened during the time of John or soon after John.

- Historist: Everything in Revelation gives an overview of the history of the Church from the Resurrection to the Second Coming.

- Futurist: Most of Revelation, except chapters 2-3, depicts events still in the future.

- Poetic: Everything in Revelation is not about the past, present or future, but is about moralistic teaching regarding lessons for life, such as good and evil always will be at war, but the good will win out in the end.

I hold a mild futurist view. What I mean is that I believe Revelation was written in a historical context in the first century and held great relevance for them. I also believe that there are many lessons from Revelation for us today, and many of them have nothing to do with the future. Revelation, though, gives us an insight into the future that no other book in the Bible does. It is not totally about the future, but it principally is.

OUTLINE

I. VISION OF CHRIST (1 – 3)

Christ Without Costume (1)

John is in exile and has a visitation by an angel. Angels are important and central to Revelation. There are 109 occurrences of angels in the New Testament and 50 of them are in Revelation.

John, who was in the Spirit on the Lord's Day, had a vision (and Revelation is filled with "visions"), and this first vision is of Jesus Christ (read 1:12-16). I call this "Christ without costume" because of this vision.

John sees Christ, then hears Him (1:17, 18).

Christ Within the Churches (2 – 3)

Christ gives John seven letters to seven churches in Asia Minor to reveal Himself, commend them, confront them, correct them and challenge them to be faithful churches. Each church is given individual treatment, as Christ demonstrates that He knows them and loves them.

II. VISION OF THE THRONE IN HEAVEN (4 – 5)

The One Who Sits on the Throne (4)

John has another vision. The first one was on earth (the churches) and this one is in heaven. This vision really runs from chapter 4 through chapter 16. So, most of Revelation gives the perspective of heaven regarding the problems on earth.

This vision starts with a look at God, the one who sits on the throne, who receives all the glory: "Holy, holy, holy is the Lord God Almighty, who was, and is, and is to come" (lyrics from Isaiah 6, which are the basis for the hymn *Holy, Holy, Holy*.)

The Lamb and the Scroll (5)

A drama develops in this vision about who is worthy to open the scroll. The Lamb of God is revealed as being the only one who is worthy:

You are worthy to take the scroll and to open its seals, because you were slain, and with your blood you purchased men for God from every tribe and language and people and nation.

III. THE SEVEN SEALS (6:1 – 8:5)

Note: The pattern of the seals (6:1 – 8:5); the trumpets (8:6 – 11:19); and the bowls (16:1-21) is the same:

- Six.

- Interlude.

- Seventh.

The First Four Seals (6:1-8)

The first four seals are commonly known as "the four horsemen of the Apocalypse:"

- The first horse is white and goes out to conquer.

- The second horse is red and is violent.

- The third horse is black and brings famine.

- The fourth horse is pale and brings death.

The Next Two Seals (6:9-17)

The fifth and sixth seals speak of the struggle of God's people in difficult times and the beginning of judgment for the whole earth.

The Interlude (7:1-17)

This interlude continues the heavenly vision of the 144,000, along with the great multitude praising God: "Amen! Praise and glory and wisdom and thanks and honor and power and strength be to our God for ever and ever. Amen!"

The 144,000 and the "great multitude" reveal that it is the people of God who will be able to stand in the face of judgment because their robes have been made white in the blood of the Lamb.

The Seventh Seal (8:1-5)

The seventh seal causes a period of reverent silence in heaven, as well as the beginning of the seven trumpets.

The seventh seal opens to the seven trumpets and the seventh trumpet opens to the seven bowls.

IV. The Seven Trumpets (8:6 – 11:19)

Judgment on Nature (8:6-12)

Trumpets 1-4 are judgments on nature. Notice that the judgment is partial – one-third of everything. The curse of sin was upon all of creation, not just the souls of men and women.

Judgment on Mankind (9:1-21)

Trumpets 5-6 are judgments on mankind. A "fallen star," probably symbolic of Satan, is loose and exercises his limited authority, with terrible things happening to humankind. The occurrence of evil things should lead to repentance, a desire to get right with God. The hardness of men's hearts, however, is shown when they refuse to repent of their sins – even when the truth of judgment is made clear to them.

Interlude (10:1 – 11:14)

The Angel and the Little Scroll (10)

This interlude begins with the appearance of an angel with a little scroll. This angel is accompanied by great sounds and graphic sights, and they all had to do with the "mystery of God." This mystery is commonly understood to be the Gospel. John takes the scroll and eats it, which is very similar to the call of Ezekiel in the Old Testament. This is a confirmation of the call of John.

The Two Witnesses (11:1-14)

The particular call of John is to measure the Temple; then the "two witnesses" appear. Who are these guys? Some people say they represent Israel and the Old Testament (Elijah and Moses – the Law and the prophets); some say the Church with Elijah as John the Baptist and Moses as Jesus, a prophet like Moses; and some say it refers to two actual men in the future. Whatever the interpretation, the picture is clear: There is an apparent defeat that is turned into a victory.

The Seventh Trumpet (11:15-19)

The seventh trumpet then is sounded, and there is rejoicing about the Kingdom of God being established. This is not the final Kingdom, but it is a time of praise to God for the victories of the Kingdom in a world that is deserving judgment.

V. Interlude After Seventh Trumpet (12 – 14)

In this Interlude, there are seven mystical figures:

- A woman.

- A child.

- A dragon.

- The angel Michael.

- A beast of the sea.

- A beast of the earth.

- A lamb on Mount Zion.

The Woman and the Dragon (12)

A woman appears as a sign, and then a dragon, strong and powerful, endangers the woman as she is about to deliver a child. The woman and child are protected, but the dragon pursues her with evil intent. The interpretation of who the woman is has been split between Israel and the Church.

The Two Beasts (13)

Chapter 13 is as full of evil as any book of the Bible. The "beast out of the sea" and the "beast out of the earth" are vicious manifestations of evil at the end of time, usually associated with the antichrist. One of the most puzzling numbers from Revelation is in verse 18 – the number 666. The only thing clear by this number is that it symbolizes evil and wickedness.

The Lamb and the 144,000 (14:1-5)

After such evil as that shown in chapters 12-13 with the dragon and the two beasts, chapter 14 offers a welcome perspective – that of the Lamb, one of the favorite pictures of Christ in Revelation that is used 26 times. Notice that the Lamb in Revelation always is a victorious Lamb, not a sacrificial Lamb.

The Lamb and the Church (144,000 being symbolic of the Church) are producing a "new song" and living holy lives.

Three Angels (14:6-20)

Then, in a vision of three angels, the Gospel goes forth, evil (Babylon) falls, evil is cast into hell; and our hope in Christ is expressed (I often use this verse at a graveside service):

'"Blessed are the dead who die in the Lord from now on.' 'Yes,' says the Spirit, 'they will rest from their labor, for their deeds will follow them.'"

VI. THE SEVEN BOWLS (15, 16)

Two Visions (15)

Before the seven bowls, two visions are seen by John. These two positive visions come just before the bowls of wrath are to be poured out.

Seven Bowls (16)

Seven angels pour out seven bowls in succession, which all are manifestations of the judgment of God.

With the sixth bowl, Armageddon is referred to as the place of the final victory of God over His enemies.

VII. BABYLON (17, 18)

The Mystery of Babylon (17)

Babylon is described as a harlot that leads the world into adultery, which more than likely is a reference to spiritual adultery. The identity of Babylon is multiple in the various interpretations, but the sure thing is that it will be against the things of God and it will fall.

The Fall of Babylon (18)

The fall of Babylon is given in great detail in chapter 18, with the statement of "Woe" upon the evil city clear and certain.

VIII. THE TWO SUPPERS (19)

Praise for the Fall of Babylon (19:1-5)

With the fall of Babylon, there is great rejoicing in heaven. Hallelujahs abound. God is given the glory and the enemies of God are defeated.

The Wedding Supper of the Lamb (19:6-10)

The wedding supper (feast) occurs, and it is a picture of the victory of the Lamb and the beginning of a new era. The Lord's Supper is a foreshadowing of this meal.

The Great Supper of God (19:11-21)

As the Rider on the White Horse is described – there is no doubt that it is Jesus who is "King of kings and Lord of lords" – a great supper of God is held. It is a grim contrast to the wedding supper of the Lamb, since the enemies of the Lord are consumed.

IX. The Millennium (20)

The Thousand Years (20:1-6)

This might be one of the most controversial chapters in the whole Bible. Christians call themselves Premil, Amil or Postmil relating to the millennium – the 1,000 years – of this chapter. There are the Premil holding to the Coming of Christ before the millennium; the Amil believing that there is no literal millennium; and the Postmil maintaining that the Coming of Christ would come after the millennium.

Whatever view of the millennium is held, one thing is for sure – the millennium is a time of victory and rule by the Lord.

Satan's Doom (20:7-10)

Satan's doom is made definite and eternal. There is no more time for seals, trumpets or bowls. No more limited or partial judgments. The time of final judgment has come (10):

The devil, who deceived them, was thrown into the lake of burning sulfur, where the beast and the false prophet had been thrown. They will be tormented day and night for ever and ever.

The Great White Throne Judgment (20:11-15)

This final judgment will not only be for Satan, but for all the dead who will be judged. This is the Judgment Day.

This is the end of all the "bad stuff" – "judgment stuff" – in Revelation. Only glory and heaven are left.

X. New Heaven and New Earth (21, 22)

New Jerusalem (21)

The new heaven and the new earth are described as the new Jerusalem. This heavenly vision takes all the facts and images of the Old Testament and brings them together into their full meaning and significance in heaven (3, 4):

Now the dwelling of God is with men, and He will live with them. They will be His people, and God Himself will be with them and be their God. He will wipe every tear from their eyes. There will be no more death or mourning or crying or pain, for the old order of things has passed away.

The River of Life (22:1-7)

John then sees the river of life, and the description of heaven continues (3-5):

No longer will there be any curse. The throne of God and of the Lamb will be in the city, and His servants will serve Him. They will see His face, and His name will be on their foreheads. There will be no more night. They will not need the light of a lamp or the light of the sun, for the Lord God will give them light. And they will reign for ever and ever.

Jesus Is Coming (22:8-21)

Revelation and the Bible end with the promise of Christ:

Behold, I am coming soon! Blessed is he who keeps the words of the prophecy of this book.

And, with our desire:

Amen. Come Lord Jesus.

Lessons From Revelation

1.   Christ is coming again.

2.   We are privileged to worship Him now.

NOTES

About the Author

The Rev. Dr. Don Elliott has been the pastor at First Presbyterian Church in Corinth, Mississippi, since 1985. He received a doctor of ministry degree from Fuller Theological Seminary in Pasadena, California; a master of divinity degree from Reformed Theological Seminary in Jackson, Mississippi; and a bachelor of arts degree from Belhaven College, also in Jackson.

He served previous pastorates in Monroeville, Alabama, and in Menlo, Georgia. He became a member of the board of directors of Presbyterians Pro-Life in 1984 and served as the organization's president from 1995-2007. He also was on the Board of the Presbyterian Coalition and served as its secretary and treasurer.

Don has served in the Presbyterian Church (USA) most of his ministry, but in 2008 joined the Evangelical Presbyterian Church along with his congregation.

He and his wife, Lynn, have three married sons: Andy and Erin Elliott live in Norfolk, Virginia, and have a daughter, Caitlyn. Marc and Taylore Elliott live in Houston, Texas. Chris and Batina Elliott live in Corinth, Mississippi, and have a son, Cooper.

States
/4/P

9 781934 453032